Terrorism in an unstable world

Other books by the same author:

Across the River (as Richard Jocelyn) (1957) London: Constable.
The Long, Long War (1966) London: Cassell, and New York: Praeger.
Protest and the Urban Guerrilla (1973) London: Cassell, and New York: Abelard Schuman.
Riot and Revolution in Singapore and Malaya, 1948–63 (1973) London: Faber and Faber.
Living with Terrorism (1975) London: Faber and Faber, and New York: Arlington House.
Guerrillas and Terrorists, (1977) London: Faber and Faber, and (1980) Athens Ohio: Athens University Press.
Kidnap and Ransom (1977) London and Boston: Faber and Faber.
Britain in Agony (1978) London: Faber and Faber, and (1980) Harmondsworth: Penguin.
The Media and Political Violence (1981 and 1983) London: Macmillan, and New Jersey: Humanities Press.
Industrial Conflict and Democracy (1984) London: Macmillan.
Conflict and Violence in Singapore and Malaysia 1948–83 (1984) Boulder, Colorado: Westview Press, and (1985) Singapore: Graham Brash.
The Future of Political Violence (1986) London: Macmillan, and New York: St Martins Press.
Kidnap, Hijack and Extortion (1987) London: Macmillan, and New York: St Martin's Press.
Terrorism and Guerrilla Warfare (1990) London and New York: Routledge
Terrorism, Drugs and Crime in Europe after 1992 (1990) London and New York: Routledge.
International Crisis and Conflict (1993) London: Macmillan, and New York: St Martins Press.

Terrorism in an unstable world

Richard Clutterbuck

London and New York

First published 1994
by Routledge
11 New Fetter Lane, London EC4P 4EE

Simultaneously published in the USA and Canada
by Routledge
29 West 35th Street, New York, NY 10001

© 1994 Richard Clutterbuck

Typeset in Times by
Ponting–Green Publishing Services, Chesham, Bucks

Printed and bound in Great Britain by
T.J. Press (Padstow) Ltd, Padstow, Cornwall

Printed on acid free paper

British Library Cataloguing in Publication Data
A catalogue record for this book is available from the
British Library.

Library of Congress Cataloging in Publication Data
has been applied for.

ISBN 0–415–10340–1

Contents

Figures and tables

Preface

This book looks at how emerging technology can help us to cope with the explosion of regional conflict and terrorism – especially in the form of ethnic cleansing – and of drug trafficking and other international crime, which has followed the end of the Cold War, and at how we can best organize the concerted military strength of east and west which is now available to keep the peace.

The revolutions of 1989–92 changed the world more fundamentally than any others since 1789. During the Cold War, regional conflicts were restrained by the superpowers because of their mutual fear of nuclear war. No longer – and there are even more people now suffering from terror and disruption of their lives, due to religious, nationalist, tribal and ethnic conflicts. Tactics and techniques have changed and these conflicts have become more cruel and vicious than ever.

In analysing the likeliest trouble spots for the future, I have described how their problems arose (e.g. in Bosnia, Cambodia, Somalia, Sudan, Northern and Southern Africa, the Middle East, Afghanistan, Central Asia, India, the Philippines, Colombia and Peru), and I have projected forward from their current situations. The worst troubles in the future may be in eastern Europe and the former Soviet states, and the consequent flood of refugees could also shake the stability of western Europe.

There are some very interesting technological developments coming on stream. I began studying the effects of technology on terrorism in 1981, when the British SAS Regiment asked me to introduce a study period on their likely tasks in the coming five or ten years. Since then I have written seven more books. Routledge have now asked me to apply what I have learned to the new and radically different range of conflicts.

Weapons have not changed all that much. The hand-held missiles now available to terrorists took shape in 1984. In automatic weapons, the developments have been in miniaturization and sights, including night vision and laser, rather than in range or rates of fire. Most of the current sophisticated bomb fuses were in use in 1984.

The encouraging thing is that advances in security technology have been far greater, especially in explosive detection by enhanced X-ray and vapour detectors. Detecting the vapour of Semtex is equivalent to detecting a glass of whisky in Loch Ness. Computer science offers growing scope for acquiring and processing intelligence and for identification and prevention of impersonation. These could help significantly in catching and convicting criminals, drug traffickers and terrorists, and in making airport check-in faster and more secure. I have described some pioneering experiments in progress at Amsterdam and Frankfurt airports. One problem will be to prevent abuse of this technology from eroding civil liberties.

This book is not science fiction. I am a layman writing for lay people. Since no one can be an expert in all these fields, I have tried to make each chapter self-contained and comprehensible to the non-professional. Electronics experts can skip my child's guide to computer development, but I hope that my basic explanations of the technologies of weapons, of detecting explosives and for preventing impersonation will be useful to them, and vice versa.

Saddam Hussein, among others, has reminded us that we cannot yet dismantle our armed forces: the Serbs have shown us the urgency of restructuring these forces for peacekeeping and peacemaking on a far wider scale than before. The UN Security Council can usually now take positive decisions without a veto, as it did in the Gulf and Cambodia, though less successfully over Bosnia. The UN, however, has a poor record of executive action, and its most successful peacemaking operations have been those delegated to a member country to organize on its behalf, as in Korea in 1950, Kuwait in 1990 and Somalia in 1992. Perhaps NATO should now act regularly as the UN's executive agency.

We shall need all that science and technology can give us to protect people from the arrogance of the warlords, the terrorists or the religious fanatics who wish to impose their ideology or develop their power; from the drug traffickers or criminals who will callously ruin the lives of others to get rich; or from the ethnic cleansers who terrorize the families of other communities into abandoning their homes; in other words, to stop people killing each other.

Richard Clutterbuck
Exeter

Abbreviations

For foreign acronyms and in other cases where it is judged to be more helpful to the reader, an English description (in parentheses) is given instead of spelling out the words.

ACR	Advanced Combat Rifle
AD M19	(political party of M19 – qv) (Colombia)
AFR	Automatic Fingerprint Recognition
AGV	Autonomous Guided Vehicle
AI	Artificial Intelligence
AIIB	Anti-Imperialist International Brigade
AISSF	All India Sikh Students Federation
ALF	Animal Liberation Front
ANC	African National Congress
ARENA	(Republican National Alliance) (El Salvador)
ASU	Active Service Unit
ATF	Alcohol, Tobacco and Firearms Bureau (USA)
BBC	British Broadcasting Corporation
BCP	Burmese Communist Party
BGS	(Federal Border Guard) (Germany)
BJP	Bharatiya Janata Party (India)
BSIA	British Security Industry Association
CAT	computer aided tomography
CAWS	Close Assault Weapon System
CCCD	(Constituent Assembly) (Peru)
CCTV	closed circuit television
CGSB	(Simón Bolívar Guerrilla Co-ordination) (Colombia)
CIA	Central Intelligence Agency (USA)
CIS	Commonwealth of Independent States

CPNX	Combined Pulse Neutron X-ray Interrogator
CPP	Cambodian People's Party
CS	(anti-riot gas) (UK)
DEA	Drug Enforcement Administration (USA)
DNA	(genetic molecule in body fluids)
DP	detection probability
EC	European Community
ECM	electronic counter-measures
ECOWAS	Economic Community of West African States
EDP	electronic data processing
EFTA	European Free Trade Association
El Al	(Israeli Airlines)
ELN	(National Liberation Army) (Colombia)
EPL	(People's Liberation Army) (Colombia)
ETA	(Basque terrorist independence movement) (Spain)
FAA	Federal Aviation Authority (USA)
FACES	Facial Analysis Comparison and Elimination System
FAR	false alarm rate
FARC	(Armed Revolutionary Forces of Colombia)
FBI	Federal Bureau of Investigation (USA)
FIS	(Islamic Salvation Front) (Algeria)
FMLN	(National Liberation Front) (El Salvador)
FN	(Belgian arms manufacturer)
FRELIMO	(Mozambique Liberation Movement) (now Government)
FRG	Federal Republic of Germany
FUNCINPEC	(Royalist political party) (Cambodia)
G7	Group of Seven countries (USA, Japan, Germany, France, UK, Italy and Canada)
GIGN	(French anti-terrorist commando)
GNP	gross national product
GPHMG	general purpose heavy machine-gun
GSG9	(German anti-terrorist commando)
HB	(political party supporting ETA) (Spain)
HMG	heavy machine-gun
HOLMES	Home Office Large and Major Enquiry System
ICAO	International Civil Aviation Organization (UN)

ID card	identification card
IED	improvised explosive device
IFF	Identification Friend or Foe
II	image intensification
INF	Islamic National Front (Sudan)
INLA	Irish National Liberation Army
IPKF	Indian Peacekeeping Force (Sri Lanka)
IR	infra-red
IRA	Irish Republican Army
ISO	International Standardization Organization (UN)
IW	individual weapon
IZL	Irgun Zvai Leumi (Israel)
JAL	Japanese Airlines
JVP	(People's Liberation Front) (Sri Lanka)
KGB	(Soviet Intelligence Organization)
kph	kilometres per hour
KR	Khmers Rouges (Cambodia)
LAW	light anti-tank weapon
LIPS	logical inferences per second
LSW	light support weapon
LTTE	Liberation Tigers of Tamil Elam (Sri Lanka)
M19	(19 April Movement) (Colombia)
MI 5	(colloquial name for Security Service) (UK)
MI 6	(colloquial name for Secret Intelligence Service) (UK)
MCLOS	manual command to line of sight
MILAN	(NATO hand-held anti-tank missile)
MNF	(multinational peacekeeping force) (Lebanon)
MNLF	Moro National Liberation Front (Philippines)
mph	miles per hour
MPLA	(Angolan Liberation Movement) (now Government)
mps	metres per second
MR	machine readable
MRI	machine-readable identity card
MRP	machine-readable passport
MRTA	(Tupac Amaro Revolutionary Movement) (Colombia)
MRV	machine-readable visa
NACC	North Atlantic Co-operation Council

NATO	North Atlantic Treaty Organization
NDF	National Democratic Front (Myanmar/Philippines)
NGO	non-government organization
NPA	New People's Army (Philippines)
NPC	national police computer
OAU	Organization for African Unity
OCR	optical character reading
OTA	Office of Technology Assessment (US Congress)
PCIED	Projectile Controlled Improvised Explosive Device
PETN	(an explosive ingredient of Semtex)
PFLP	Popular Front for the Liberation of Palestine
PFLP(GC)	PFLP (General Command)
PIN	personal identification number
PJ	(New town – squatter settlement) (Peru)
PLF	Palestine Liberation Front
PLO	Palestine Liberation Organization
PROD	Photo Retrieval from Optical Disc
RAF	Red Army Faction (Germany)
RDX	(an explosive ingredient of Semtex)
RENAMO	(Rebel guerrilla movement) (Mozambique)
Risc	reduced instruction set computers
RISCT	Research Institute for the Study of Conflict and Terrorism
RUC	Royal Ulster Constabulary
SACLOS	semi-automatic command to line of sight
SAM	surface-to-air missile
SAS	Special Air Service Regiment (UK)
SEP	Surrendered Enemy Personnel
SL	*Sendero Luminoso* (Shining Path) (Peru)
SLAP	Saboted Light Armour Penetration
SLFP	Sri Lanka Freedom Party
SNC	Supreme National Council (Cambodia)
SPAS	Special Purpose Automatic Shotgun
SPLA	Sudanese People's Liberation Army
SSM	surface-to-surface missile
STOL	short take-off and landing
STP	Schiphol Travel Pass (Netherlands)
TI	thermal imagery

TMP	Tactical Machine Pistol
TNA	Thermal Neutron Analysis
UN	United Nations
UNFDAC	UN Fund for Drug Abuse Control
UNITA	(rebel movement) (Angola)
UNO	(centre political party) (Nicaragua)
UNTAC	UN Transitional Authority for Cambodia
UP	(Patriotic Front) (Colombia)
USC	United Somali Congress
VDU	visual display unit
VIP	very important person
VTOL	vertical take-off and landing

Part I
Introduction

1 Conflict in the post-Communist world

Despite the end of the Cold War. . .

The world has never been so unstable since the 1950s. Between 1989 and 1993, twenty-seven new independent democratic governments came into being following the collapse of the USSR and Soviet Communism in eastern Europe, each with complex ethnic mixtures, and it was in the states of the former Yugoslavia that the modern reincarnation of Hitler's 'ethnic cleansing' began.

The terrorism sponsored by the USSR, Cuba and China, and the Marxist terrorism in Europe, have largely subsided, but communal violence continues in India, nationalist violence in Sri Lanka, Spain and Northern Ireland and between rival warlords in Africa. Drug-related terrorism plagues both Latin America and South and East Asia. Islamic fundamentalism has overtaken Marxism as the prime ideological generator of international terrorism.

During the Cold War, the USA and the USSR and most of their client states were always anxious lest a regional conflict might lead to a superpower confrontation (as it threatened to do on the Suez Canal in 1973), and this fear imposed a restraining influence which is now noticeably lacking. So, despite the end of the Cold War, tens of thousands of people die every year from various kinds of terrorism. Though weapons change, and politics change, the technique of terrorizing innocent people continues, as it has for thousands of years. Sadly, it shows no sign of abating.

Ten thousand years of terrorism

The essential aims and techniques of terrorism have not changed. They were best distilled by Sun Tzu 2,500 years ago: 'Kill one – frighten ten thousand'. This technique of intimidation has been used by governments to discipline their people and by dissidents and religious sects to weaken and overturn the established authority since the dawn of civilization, and certainly since humans discovered agriculture and settled to form villages on the best soil around sources of water. Nomads and hunter-gatherers will have envied the well-fed and prosperous villagers and coveted their land, so the villagers had to organize to defend their property and their community. They also needed law and order within.

These two early imperatives – security and the rule of law – required village chiefs with hierarchies of guards and officers to organize village defence, and to prevent dishonest villagers from stealing their neighbours' crops or animals – or daughters. Some chiefs ruled by popular consent and others by seizing the power and exercising it through hierarchies whose loyalty was ensured by the grant of privileges (they were the forerunners of the Soviet *nomenklatura*) and then by their fear of what retribution might come from the people if their chief were overthrown. These hierarchies used terror to discipline dissidents and the dissidents used terror to demoralize the chief's henchmen or to replace him with their own candidate. They still do.

Villages sometimes used their strength to compete with other villages for the best land, but perhaps more often they co-operated against their common enemy – the predatory nomads around them. The earliest agricultural settlements in what was to become Europe and West Asia probably formed beside the Tigris and Euphrates; some of these were isolated villages in places where the rainwater gathered beside the barren upper reaches, in what are now the Kurdish mountains; others further downstream in more fertile areas soon coalesced into agricultural communities in the rich valleys of Babylon.

Next came walled city-states and, much later, nation-states. Village and city defence forces merged into armies which fought wars (like those between Athens and Sparta). They formed alliances and bigger wars developed. In conjunction with the armies, guerrilla groups raided and harassed the opposing populations using the already familiar techniques of terrorism. And terrorism continued to be used in the internal competition for power, through the next 2,000 years.

In more modern times, some governments encouraged, armed and financed dissident groups to weaken or destabilize their neighbours, from within, that is as a tool of foreign policy. This technique became widespread only in the twentieth century when the Communist powers – the USSR, China, Cuba, North Vietnam and North Korea – used it in attempts to destabilize their capitalist rivals.

Intimidation and terror

Terrorism is simply a lethal kind of intimidation. Intimidation, as a means of exerting social and political pressure, can take many forms. At its lowest and in some ways most distasteful form, parents encourage their children to harass and bully the children of other ethnic or religious communities to induce their families to move away. Before they started killing, the Nazi Stormtroopers harassed German Jews by arousing their neighbours against them, by smashing their homes and their shops, and later by personal violence. Journalists, teachers and other opinion formers are sometimes selected as targets for intimidation. In countries where there are liberal forms of law, witnesses, juries, lawyers, magistrates and judges are terrorized out of giving evidence or finding prisoners guilty, with the express intention of making those liberal forms of law unworkable, because the terrorists know that more arbitrary legal processes breed dissent in a democracy.

'One man's terrorist is another man's freedom fighter' is a cliché which betrays a lack of understanding of what terrorism is. Terrorism is a technique – 'killing one to frighten ten thousand' – used by *all* sides: by guerrillas, by freedom fighters, by dissidents, by political activists of the left or right, by nationalists, by ethnic and religious groups, by Mafia-style criminal gangs, by drug-trafficking organizations, and – perhaps most of all – by authoritarian governments (whether they style themselves left or right), and by their 'death squads' to which they turn a blind eye or which they discreetly sponsor. Even where it is used in a justifiable cause (e.g. by freedom fighters resisting invasion or occupation by a foreign army) terrorism against unarmed victims – killing without due process of law in order to terrorize the rest of the population into complying with the wishes of the killer – is never justifiable and should always be treated as a criminal (not a political) offence.

The aftermath of Marxism

Even if the old Communist bureaucrats – the (*nomenklatura*) were to regain power and influence in Russia, they would not be able to rebuild the Warsaw Pact or to recreate the now largely defunct Marxist terrorist organizations in Germany, Italy or France. Europe has new (and in some ways worse) problems, as will be described in the next section. Most of the eastern European countries, particularly those with a long history of cultured civilization such as Poland, the Czech and Slovak republics and Hungary, are managing their recovery from Communism well. Others, such as the former Yugoslav republics, are wracked by

horrific conflict as bad as in the worst days of Hitler and Stalin. In some
of these too, the old Communist *nomenklatura* still hang on to power,
calling themselves nationalists rather than Communists. No matter what
name they use, they are in fact mainly concerned with power and
privileges for themselves.

There are, however, still a few vicious Marxist revolutionary movements trying to seize power in Latin America and in Cambodia. China
and Cuba still have nominally Communist governments, but China is
now fully committed to attracting international investment and developing a market economy under a strictly authoritarian nationalist
government, with her eyes on becoming the world's biggest economy in
the first few decades of the twenty-first century. China may then become
more internationally aggressive, but is unlikely to alienate investors by
dabbling in the export of its philosophies until it has built up its
strength. Castro still avows Communism in Cuba, but acts increasingly
like a chicken with its head cut off, and when he dies (if not before)
Cuba is likely to try to re-enter the mainstream of Latin American
politics, which has become increasingly democratic and market-
oriented. Cuba is in no state to sponsor or support overseas Marxist
revolutionaries, now that its Soviet subsidies have gone.

North Korea still has a dictator professing Communism, and is still
prepared to try to export it, but is unlikely to master the economic
strength to carry this very far. Vietnam, under another broken-backed
Marxist regime, is trying hard to re-enter the world of international
development and trade.

The most dangerous instability in the world, as often before in
history, is in the Balkans, and especially in what was Yugoslavia, where
Serbs, Croats and Muslims are carrying out the most ruthless form of
terrorism – ethnic cleansing – which will be examined more fully later.
There is a very real threat that other countries, notably Albania, Turkey
and Greece, may get involved in the conflicts, especially if they spread
to Kosovo and Macedonia. There is also serious concern that the
resulting flood of refugees into western Europe (438,000 sought asylum
in Germany alone in 1992) is arousing a neo-facist backlash.

The Middle East and Islamic fundamentalism

In 1991, the initiation of peace talks caused the Arab-Israeli conflict to
subside, since both the Israeli government and the PLO leadership had
a genuine interest in reaching a settlement, though progress was slow
because each side had sticking points unacceptable to the other. There
were, however, other more militant Palestinian movements and Islamic

fundamentalists who were determined to derail the peace process by initiating terrorist actions and armed conflict and particularly by provoking Israeli overreaction. The talks were on the brink of breaking down several times in 1993.

In December 1992, a number of Israeli soldiers and others were murdered in the occupied Gaza Strip. The Israelis responded by deporting 415 Palestinians who included leading members of the fundamentalist Hamas organization. Lebanon refused to accept the deportees, who remained encamped in the Israeli 'security zone' on the Lebanese side of the northern Israeli frontier throughout the winter until the end of 1993. One of the aims of provoking this Israeli reaction was clearly to arouse Palestinian passions so that support would swing away from the PLO to Hamas, who were adamantly opposed to any settlement which recognized the continued existence of Israel. To many people's surprise, however, the peace talks continued.

On 22 July 1993, the Iranian-sponsored Lebanese fundamentalist 'Army of God' (Hezbollah) attacked two military posts in the 'security zone'; in the ensuing fighting two Israeli soldiers were killed. Next day, both sides continued artillery and mortar exchanges and Hezbollah fired Katyusha rockets on to villages in Galilee in Northern Israel. The Israeli government, dependent on a coalition with some of the most extreme religious political parties, and urged on by outraged public opinion, replied with airstrikes on villages in which Hezbollah were located, both in South Lebanon and in the main Syrian army base in the Beka'a Valley. Despite US pressure for restraint, the Israeli air attacks spread and Hezbollah fired 50 more rockets into Galilee. A cease-fire was signed on 31 July, by which time 150 people had been killed and 500 injured. More than 200,000 refugees fled from 70 villages in South Lebanon. As with Hamas, Hezbollah's aim was clearly to arouse such passions that the PLO would be unable to continue the peace talks.

On 19 August the world drew its breath when Hezbollah killed nine more Israeli soldiers on land mines but the Israelis did not retaliate. Ten days later the reason became apparent. Israeli and PLO representatives had been conducting highly confidential talks in Norway, without notifying Syria, Jordan or any other Arab countries. On 29 August it was announced that, subject to approval of their respective governing bodies or Parliaments, Israel and the PLO would recognize each other; the PLO would renounce terrorism and would establish limited self-rule in the Gaza strip and Jericho as a first step towards further developments over the coming years. The agreement was duly implemented and received the approval (after some initial umbrage over not being consulted) by Syria, Jordan and the Arab states of the Gulf Co-operation Council. This was certainly the biggest break-through yet achieved in the peace process and it remains to be seen whether Hamas, Hezbollah or Israeli extremists will succeed in disrupting it.

Both sides had intended that Israel would hand over security control of the Gaza Strip and Jericho to Palestinian police on 13 December 1993, with Israeli security forces operating only in the Israeli settlements. Arab and Jewish extremists succeeded in delaying this deadline by violence and counterviolence and there was some wrangling over who should control the crossing points in and out of Egypt and Jordan. The dawn of 1994, however, saw the Israeli Prime Minister and Yassir Arafat still negotiating and there was little doubt that they, at least, intended to rein back their extremists and make the agreement work.

Islamic fundamentalism for the time being poses a bigger threat to peace in the Middle East than the Arab–Israeli dispute, though the two are linked. It is spreading fast from Iran and the Sudan and the Iranians in 1993 intensified their efforts in other African countries, most of which have large Muslim populations. If the fundamentalists manage to oust the secular governments of Algeria and Egypt, these too may become bases for a further expansion of militant Islam.

The Arab world has more than its share of dictators. Gadafi grew up as a boy in Mussolini's prize colony of Libya, and clearly found a role model for himself. His echoes of Mussolini – populism, posturing and farce – are very striking. Saddam Hussein is made of harder stuff, but his reckless ambition has probably hobbled him for the time being. Hafez Assad in Syria seems to be modifying both his international and internal terrorist activities to attract trade and investment from the west, now that he no longer has Soviet support.

Some of the conservative Gulf states, notably Saudi Arabia and Kuwait, are very vulnerable to internal revolution, but their ruling families go out of their way to maintain a privileged status for their Bedouin population, in some cases with negative taxation, while employing large numbers of immigrants from the Indian subcontinent and elsewhere, with no prospect of citizenship, and subject to summary cancellation of their work permits and deportation. The Bedouin will probably be content to retain their status, and the challenge, if it came, would be led by the rising Arab middle class, expecially in Kuwait. But the governments will probably be able to use their wealth and resources to head this off. They have very effective intelligence and security services.

Central, South and East Asia

Among the many instabilities left by the collapse of the Soviet Union is that of its former southern republics, mainly (but not entirely) Muslim – Turkmenistan, Uzbekistan, Kazakhstan, Tajikistan, Kirghizstan. Some have very large Russian minorities – Kazakhstan 41 per cent – and all have ethnic minorities from neighbouring states, for example there are 23 per cent Uzbeks in Tajikistan, 12 per cent in Kirghizstan and 9 per cent in Turkmenistan. Afghanistan, already torn apart by rival *mujahideen* groups, also has large Uzbek and Tajik minorities on which some of these groups are based, challenging the traditional dominance of the Pathans. But the competition for their alignment outside is also potentially very destabilizing. The Khazakhstanis are Oriental (Mongolian) in their origins. Many of the other peoples in these countries are ethnically Turkic. Some of the Shia sect of Islam look to Iran for support, the Sunni fundamentalists to Saudi Arabia, and many of the Pathans to Pakistan. Some of the governments and minorities still rely on the support of the Russian army. There is an alarming potential for conflict here, and in many places (e.g. in Tajikistan and Afghanistan, and in the European Muslim state of Azerbaijan) it is already rife. Their prospects are examined more fully in Chapter 13.

Another generator of conflict is the cultivation of opium and the traffic in heroin from the countries of the Golden Crescent – Iran, Pakistan and Afghanistan. If the conflict continues in Afghanistan, the competing *mujahideen* groups will be desperate for money to buy arms, and those in opium-growing areas will increase their production and export of heroin.

Sikh–Hindu–Muslim conflict shows no sign of abating in India; nor does Tamil–Sinhalese conflict in Sri Lanka.

Further east, opium and heroin again have a malignant influence in the Golden Triangle – Myanmar, Laos and Thailand – with the heroin traffic passing mainly through Bangkok and Hong Kong. As elsewhere, it generates international crime and terrorism.

Whether or not Cambodia, with the aid of its very large UN Transitional Authority (UNTAC), succeeds in establishing an enduring government, the Khmers Rouges (KR) are likely to continue to use terrorism to destroy it, and to capitalize on the historical hostility of Cambodians (Khmers) for Vietnamese (Tongkingese). And the Philippines still faces two powerful and persistent internal terrorist movements.

Africa

Most of the African states, and especially the twenty-four states partly or wholly south of the Sahara, suffer from two deeply rooted problems:

their tribal structure does not coincide with their frontiers, which are based on the boundaries thrashed out between their former colonial masters; and, in many of them, advances in medicine and hygiene are resulting in their populations growing faster than their gross national products (GNPs), and faster than they can provide and distribute enough food for them. On top of that, some of them will for a long time suffer the after-effects of twenty or thirty years under 'Marxist' governments which were even more inefficient than those in Europe, Asia or Latin America, since they lacked the depth of education, administrative experience and infrastructures to run their theoretically centralized command economies.

Some states may disintegrate into anarchy, with rival warlords holding sway over their fiefdoms, as in Somalia. Some may face sporadic bursts of civil war, with thousands of casualties in a week, as Angola has. Some, in desperation, may rally to authoritarian governments. Others, with a façade of democracy, may sink more and more deeply into corruption and organized crime. Black Africa's stability and prosperity depends a great deal on the success of South Africa's attempt to evolve into a multiracial democracy. As in Palestine, De Klerk and Mandela are challenged by their own extremists who will continue to provoke violence to poison their co-operation. If the new black dominated government can secure the continued contribution of white capital, commercial and technical knowhow and the inflow of foreign investment as Kenya and Zimbabwe did, South African prosperity will bring an enormous boost to the continent as a whole. Otherwise, the rich world may turn its back on Africa as an unattractive field for longterm investment and the prospect will be bleak.

Latin America

The 1980s were a tortured decade for Latin America, with some of the bloodiest rural guerrilla conflicts in her history. The two bloodiest were 75,000 killed out of a population of 6 million in El Salvador and 70,000 out of 4 million in Nicaragua; these were 25 times bloodier in numbers killed per year as a proportion of the population than Northern Ireland, which has been by far the bloodiest in western Europe.

These conflicts have exhausted the countries of Central America and, with Cuba no longer supporting attempts at revolution, they are likely to become more stable and prosperous with US aid.

Colombia and Peru have for years been poisoned by a cynical alliance between Mafia-style drug barons and Marxist revolutionaries. As will be described in later chapters, the cocaine trade brings into the region billions of dollars which are used in the corrupt exercise of power over politicians and the judiciaries: they also finance terrorist movements whose role is to keep government forces from interfering with the cultivation and processing of coca, and to prepare and protect the hundreds of airstrips from which the coca paste is flown out. In Peru, the conflict between the Shining Path (SL) guerrillas and the government resulted in over 25,000 dead in 12 years (1980–92). In Colombia it was estimated that terrorism and crime, including drug-related crime, caused an average of 30,000 deaths every year.

There were some major government successes in 1991–3. In Colombia, a number of leading drug barons were captured or surrendered, culminating in the killing of Pablo Escobar, once the most powerful of them all, on 2 December 1993. In Peru, the founder and leader of SL, Dr Abimael Guzman, was captured in a brilliant intelligence operation in September 1992. Nevertheless, the drug Mafias and SL have shown that they have the organization to survive. Shamefully, the suffering of the Colombian and Peruvian people is ultimately financed by drug addicts on the prosperous streets of North America and Europe. For this, some drastic remedies are suggested later in the book.

Terrorism against the rich world

Though Marxist terrorism had largely disappeared in western Europe by 1993, ethnic or communal terrorism persisted in the UK (Northern Ireland) and in Spain, but in both countries it had ceased to be of political significance. In Northern Ireland, out of a population of 1.5 million, 467 had been killed in 1972, but in the decade 1983 to 1992 the average was 76 each year, the highest being 94. The majority of these were sectarian murders by Protestant and Catholic terrorists of citizens of the other community. In 1992 only three regular British soldiers and three part-time Irish soldiers were killed. In Spain, the homicide rate per thousand was only about half that in Northern Ireland; the end of Basque terrorism seemed to be in sight. In Northern Ireland, terrorism by the Irish Republican Army (IRA) and by Protestant terrorists seemed likely to continue, but even the IRA found it wise to express regret about a group of its terrorists who exploded two bombs in a busy shopping area in Warrington, England, in March 1993, on the day before Mother's Day, when large numbers of children were predictably buying presents and cards. They killed two children aged 3 and 12. They were even more vehemently disowned by the people of the Republic of Ireland whom they claimed to represent. It could be that such disapproval from this quarter might lead the IRA to follow the Basques in questioning the effectiveness of the armed struggle. The IRA is discussed more fully in Chapter 15.

Like its European counterparts, the Japanese Red Army, once one of the most vicious of puritanical Marxist movements, has scarcely appeared since 1988. Japanese business people overseas are, however, a popular target as 'international capitalists' for revolutionary movements in Latin American, especially in Peru.

Citizens of the USA have also, for some years, been more at risk when overseas, as with the mass bombings in Lebanon in 1983 and the killing of 270, mainly Americans, in the bombing of a Pan American airliner in December 1988. Terrorism hit mainland USA on 26 February 1993, however, when a huge truck bomb exploded in the car park under the World Trade Center in New York, killing 5 and injuring over 1,000 people. A number of people with extremist Islamic links were later arrested; this is now probably the likeliest source of terrorism against the USA.

All of these manifestations of terrorism will be discussed more fully in subsequent chapters: the organization of drug trafficking in Chapters 9–11; the techniques, development and prospects of rural guerrilla war in Chapters 12–14 and of urban terrorism in Chapters 15–18.

2 A New kind of peacekeeping

Hardly an occupation for a gentleman

To meet this increasing threat of destabilization of the international order and of legitimate national governments, and the growing menace of communal strife as illustrated in the Balkans, Africa and India, the world will need something tougher than the rather gentlemanly UN peacekeeping operations of the 1970s and 1980s. The UN had some modest successes in the Middle East in 1956, when it terminated the war in Sinai – only to fail to keep the peace in 1967 – and it resolved an even more dangerous situation at Suez in 1973. Though it was unable to prevent the Greek Cypriot coup which provoked a Turkish invasion in 1974, it has otherwise generally contained the conflict in Cyprus for twenty years. But these operations worked only when both parties to the conflict were content for the UN to restrain the conflict.

In 1992 the explosion of violence in Croatia, Bosnia, Cambodia and Somalia demanded something on quite a different scale. The UN sent 22,000 peacekeeping troops to Croatia and Bosnia in 1992, and were ready to increase it to 75,000 in 1993, including both US and Russian contingents, as soon as there was a peace to keep. In Cambodia the UN deployed 16,000 plus 6,000 police and civilians to supervise elections. The 500 sent to Somalia, limited by an agreement with the warlord in control of the airport, achieved nothing, so the UN approved the dispatch of 28,000 US troops under US command in December 1982, which was replaced by a similar UN force in May 1993. These operations were, however, very different from their predecessors. Nearly all the parties to the conflict wished simply to exploit the UN for their own purposes – to have their rivals restrained while they pursued their own aims. In many cases they did not hesitate to shoot at the UN troops, especially the Serbs in Bosnia. The UN membership now accepts that UN troops must be authorized to use their weapons if prevented by armed troops from carrying out their tasks (peacemaking in place of peacekeeping).

The end of the Cold War has strengthened the ability of the UN to act decisively, as all the five permanent members of the Security Council are prepared to accept this without use of the veto – though China, and Russia if she reverts to Communist-style government under another name, may become more difficult. The Gulf Crisis and War of 1990–1 showed what a difference this can make. The UN is also more ready to authorize others to act on its behalf, like the US-led allied forces in the Gulf War and in Somalia. NATO – probably reinforced by troops from Russian and some of the newly democratized eastern European countries – is likely in the future to act more often as an executive agency for the UN. The continued existence of ambitious and unscrupulous leaders ready to use force, like those of Iraq and the Bosnian Serbs, means that the rest of the world will still need armed forces sufficient to crush them and, while not so employed, they should be made available for peacemaking or peacekeeping operations. This will be discussed more fully in Chapter 19.

The rule of law

So, since there is no machinery for enforcing international law as such, the UN has to develop better means of enforcing either existing international law or, where that is inadequate, of enforcing its own resolutions enacted in accordance with its Charter. There is no other practical means of maintaining international stability.

The internal stability of democratic countries is also under threat from terrorism, subversion and crime, the defeat of which depends on the rule of law. This phrase could only raise a hollow laugh in Bosnia or Somalia, but it does still apply in North America, western Europe and similar democracies further east. In a democracy with an independent judiciary, the rule of law is enforced by the security forces (the army, police and intelligence services), and then only if they can obtain good intelligence about the threat. The first essential for the rule of law is that these security forces should themselves act within the law. If the laws designed for a normally tranquil society are inadequate for dealing with a terrorist or criminal threat – especially if the terrorists calculatedly aim to make the law unworkable by intimidating witnesses, juries and judges – it is better to introduce emergency laws than for the security forces to act outside their own laws. Britain, France, Germany, the Republic of Ireland and Spain have all, since the late 1960s, had to introduce such emergency laws, for example for non-jury trial, powers of detention, powers of search and for dealing with lawyers who deliberately disrupt the processes of law. Emergency laws are further discussed in Chapter 20.

A disturbing trend in the 1990s has been the growth (or perhaps just the unmasking) of corruption, abuse of power, falsification or concealment of evidence, and links between politicians and international criminal gangs, including the Mafia in Italy and the drug barons in Colombia. All of these things can be mortal diseases for a democracy and need to be dealt with ruthlessly.

Security and intelligence

It is very easy to place bombs to kill the citizens of a free society going about their business, provided that the perpetrators have no conscience about killing indiscriminately, like those who placed a bomb under the New York World Trade Center in February 1993, or bombed a busy shopping centre in England in March 1993. In an increasingly tolerant society it is easy for young criminals to steal, rob and rape. The law enforcement agencies can provide only a very slender barrier against these people. Only two things can reinforce this barrier: a very real fear among the criminals and terrorists of being caught, and of the consequences if they are; and active co-operation and vigilance by citizens prepared to face the risks of giving information and evidence to convict.

Intelligence comes from technical and human sources. Valuable though technical intelligence can be, human intelligence is decisive. Creating an intelligence system and then building up the flow of intelligence through it are, however, long and arduous processes. To prosper, they must grow in parallel with the development of a climate of public confidence at two levels: confidence that the government will, in the end, prevail, and confidence that individuals who co-operate with the government will have their identities protected, and therefore that they and their families will not suffer. Once these basic levels of confidence have been established, it should be possible to turn the uncommitted public against crime and the idea of change being brought about by violence. These are the bulk of ordinary people who are more concerned about family safety than about political conflict, and normally comprise more than 80 per cent of the population, even in the most strife-torn communities.

The intelligence system couples the hardware to acquire technical intelligence (e.g. by interception and electronic surveillance) with a network of handlers, safe houses, and so on for acquiring human intelligence. To collate, analyse and evaluate this can be greatly facilitated by electronic data storage and processing, and some of the possible developments of this are examined later in the book. Computers, however, can as yet only assist and extend the capacity of human brains, not replace them, and ultimately the quality of intelligence will depend on people – the staffs, agents and informers who comprise an intelligence organization.

Intelligence can be divided into background information and contact information. Background information comes from a mass of largely overt sources – studying facts and statistics and the *modus operandi* of criminals and terrorists, monitoring publications and broadcasts, briefing police officers and soldiers on what to look for and report in the course of normal duties, and providing a safe channel for casual information from the public. Contact information is what enables the security forces to find their enemies by knowing their intentions or likely actions in advance, and is more delicate. It normally comes either from technical sources (e.g. intercepts) or from covert informers in contact with or living in the environment of the criminals, guerrillas or terrorist cells, or of those who support them.

While spies have sometimes been infiltrated into criminal or terrorist cells, it is far more common to achieve success by 'turning' someone who is already in the organization or is an auxiliary who has contact with them (e.g. the couriers, cut-outs or suppliers, who are the links between clandestine cells and their accomplices among the public). 'Turning' is the intelligence jargon for persuading such a person to become an informer. This may be best achieved by spotting a participant whose heart is not in it or who, for personal or family reasons, wants to 'get off the hook'. Pressure to turn may be exercised by arousing fear of prosecution or by offering rewards, perhaps large enough to enable informers to go far away, with their families, to start a new life with a new identity. An essential feature is that informers are made confident that they and their families will be protected against retribution. Examples of successful recruitment and subsequent handling of such informers are given in Parts IV and V of this book, including the sometimes spectacular cases of the 'super SEPs' (p. 126) in Malaya, the 'supergrasses' in Northern Ireland and the *'pentiti'* in Italy.

There is nothing more demoralizing to hard-core criminals or terrorists than the fear that people inside their movement or trusted supporters among the public are giving information. They will try to stifle it by ruthless exemplary punishments, but this increases the desire of the waverers to get off the hook: to avoid being caught between the Scylla of government surveillance and the Charybdis of terrorist reprisal. As sympathizers are detected and terrorists arrested, they are increasingly ready to be turned if this offers the best hope of escape from intolerable insecurity.

As this leads to further arrests, and to more districts being freed from the scourge of violence, this same urge spreads to other districts still afflicted, where the people look with envy at neighbourhoods no longer subject to the cross-fire of terrorists and soldiers and, as it becomes clearer that the terrorists are not going to win, there is a growing incentive to get rid of them. Demoralization of the terrorists and their supporters yields more defectors, the flow of information becomes a flood, and the whole organization begins to crumble. Even though a residue of violence and defiance may persist, if there is no hope of victory or popular support it declines into a fringe of violent criminals; the threat of destabilization, insurgency and civil war has been removed.

Technology

Criminals and terrorists tend to use basic weapons whose essentials have not very much changed since the 1940s – hand guns and bombs. Sub-machine-guns have been miniaturized, explosives are harder to detect and there are sophisticated bomb fuses which can be set for a precise time, like the setting of a video recorder. Terrorists can also use hand-held guided missiles, small enough to conceal in the boot of a car, to fire accurately on armoured vehicles, aircraft and helicopters.

These developments are reviewed in Chapters 3–8, and are applied to the particular problems of aviation security in Chapter 18. Finally, in the light of both political and technological developments, Chapters 19 and 20 assess the dilemma of protecting the public against terrorism and violent crime without unacceptably putting their civil liberties at risk.

Part II

Technological development

3 A vulnerable society

The microelectronics revolution

The microelectronics boom, the fifth industrial revolution, will continue to be the fastest industrial revolution of all time, especially in the fields of robotics and information technology. In 1970, 40 per cent of the working population in industrial countries were employed in productive industries, that is manufacturing or extractive (e.g. mining, agriculture, etc). By the early 1990s this had fallen to 30 per cent, with 60 per cent in service industries, and 10 per cent unemployed. By the year 2000 we may well see only about 20 per cent in productive industries and 80 per cent in service industries, the biggest growth being in the leisure industries. Moreover, the proper harnessing of robotics and information technology should not only eliminate the drudgery of the assembly line and paper-pushing, but also enable us to reduce the standard working week to about thirty hours if we wish. Many more people will be able to work at home.

With so much more time and energy saved by shorter hours and freedom from rush-hour travel, there will be a growth not only in DIY (do it yourself) but also in moonlighting: mainly by bartering useful services within the neighbourhood, for example, 'I'll repair your computer if you baby-sit for us'. This will raise the standard of living but leave still more money to be spent on travel and leisure. However, this can all be poisoned through the malign influences of drugs, violence and lust for money and power, which are the interlocking themes running through this book.

The flood of information already pouring into every household will further explode with access to some fifty television channels, by cable and satellite, mostly in pictorial form which gives greater ability to manipulate the emotions. Authoritarian governments will take control of these sources to exercise a tighter grip on the minds of their people. Pluralist societies, maintaining the principle of freedom of speech and communication, will allow all sources to use this access to people's minds with only the loosest restraints on flagrant pornography and incitement to violence and crime. These restrictions will be easily overcome, and there will be a bonanza for mind-benders, including foreign mind-benders through the satellite aerials, all of whom will dress up their messages in appetizing and entertaining programmes. The opportunities for propaganda by official sources, commercial interests, determined minorities and foreign governments will be immense. Unlike the authoritarian societies, the pluralist societies will be much more vulnerable to destabilization; though if this overreaches itself to the extent of alarming the mainstream of the public, it may lead pluralist governments to ride on a tide of populism to become more authoritarian themselves.

The sinews of the new society

The sinews of the post-industrial society are already taking shape – the network of electronic data-processing and communications – and these sinews are already becoming more vulnerable to disruption and terrorism. The service industries, in particular, are increasingly inter-independent, and ripe for attack by fraudsters, hackers, eavesdroppers, disrupters and extortionists.

Economies of scale have now concentrated vast amounts of data-processing into huge main computer centres, sometimes at the heart of a giant multinational corporation, and sometimes in a communal centre run by the big computer firms, with a mass of hardware serving corporations all over a large city. The data come in, are automatically processed and go out, untouched by human operators and totally secure – except against the hacker and the electronic eavesdropper. The computer centre itself is vulnerable to sabotage, and to extortion by the threat to damage or disrupt it. Software is especially vulnerable to malicious disruption or espionage, and the volume of business is now so great that many cannot afford the expense of software duplication. Cable communications can be tapped and radio communications intercepted – subject to a constant battle between defence (e.g. by encryption and burst transmission) and interception (by code-breaking or unscrambling). Fibre-optics currently offer the best security against interception but here too the technological battle between attack and defence will continue.

Cash, electronic transfer and extortion

Cash is needed less and less. As well as credit cards, there are debit cards which can transfer money direct from a buyer's to a seller's bank account, with no more than the tapping of numbers on the keyboard. The principle of the green phone-card, bought anywhere (with a credit card instead of cash), where residual value is electronically recorded on the card for each time unit on the telephone, could be extended to almost every day-to-day transaction, from paying a bus fare to buying a cup of coffee. The tills of the supermarket checkout will steadily be replaced by electronic diodes and debit cards. The last surviving Edwardian pay-days in cash through a window will surely be phased out by the end of the 1990s. Electronic transfer will dominate the marketplace so there will be less and less cash in the pocket, in the tills, in the safes, in the bank vaults and (most vulnerable of all) in the bags of money in the security vans plying the streets of the city centres and suburban shopping areas. Opportunities for theft and robbery will decline and they will largely be replaced by fraud and extortion.

Fraud involves criminal abuse of this electronic system. Extortion involves applying pressure to induce a person who has a legitimate key to it to transfer or release the money. This pressure may be exerted by kidnap, or the threat of murder, maiming, product contamination, bombing, arson, sabotage or disruption (e.g. of the computer system).

A new and developing art form is the disposal and laundering of this money. One way is through conversion into drugs, which have become an international currency with a huge circulation and, after a few transactions, almost impossible to trace. Another way is through multiple transfers between international banks.

An extortionist may make the acceptance of a ransom or blackmail payment conditional on its being electronically transferred to a named bank in a foreign country, or perhaps split between many different banks in different countries. This can now be done within a few seconds. In most civilized industrial countries (including Switzerland, despite a myth to the contrary) bank accounts can be made available, if ordered by the courts, to government or police inspection if a case can be made out that money in the account was acquired by criminal means. This, however, takes time, and a sophisticated international criminal or terrorist group will have installed accomplices with legal access to these accounts to transfer it quickly to others in other countries. Moreover, there are many 'tax haven' banks which do not permit official inspection of suspect accounts, and certainly not at the request of the authorities outside the country. The criminal or terrorist has only to process the money through one, or better still two, of these banks to ensure that it cannot be traced; $12 million acquired by the Colombian M19 movement in the early 1980s and transferred in this way has never been traced and probably never will be. It can be (and some no doubt has been) transferred piecemeal by these means back to a perfectly respectable bank in Colombia, held by an apparently respectable pillar of the establishment who collaborated with M19, for use as required. Where drugs are involved, the amounts of money available are ample for the rewarding of such collaborators world-wide. These problems, and possible answers to them, are discussed further in Part III and Chapter 19.

As will be illustrated in some case studies in later chapters, there is a great overlap in these fields, and between both of them and corrupt officials, politicians and business people, not only in Third World countries but also in some of the advanced countries.

Bombs in city centres

A new trend developed in 1991–3, mainly in Britain and the USA. The IRA began it in London in February 1991 with a bomb in Victoria railway station during the morning rush-hour which killed one passenger and injured thirty-eight others. This had been preceded by a warning to 'close all fourteen London termini'. Similar incidents followed and there were sporadic closures of parts of the London railway system throughout the year. British Rail became adept at switching traffic to suburban stations like Ealing and Finsbury Park, and at deciding whether to close any lines. There were over thousand warning calls during the year, most of them hoaxes, and they closed lines only ten times, seven of them necessarily (i.e. bombs exploded or were disarmed). The travelling public generally took the disruption in their stride.

In April 1992 the IRA exploded a huge truck bomb containing several thousand pounds of improvised explosives in the heart of the City of London, killing three people and damaging office buildings over a wide area. In April 1993 they exploded a similar device, again in the City, killing one more person. The estimated damage from each of these was £300 million ($500 million). In the following month, bombs with 1,000 lb of explosive or more were detonated in the main shopping centres of Belfast and other cities in Northern Ireland.

On 26 February 1993 a similar gigantic bomb was exploded in a vehicle in the underground car park below the World Trade Center in New York City. Six people were killed and over a thousand injured. A number of arrests were made, all with Islamic connections.

The purpose of these bombs was to disrupt the financial centres of London and New York and to do extensive economic damage, usually at weekends to avoid the counter-productive mass slaughter which would otherwise have resulted. The people of London and Belfast had become accustomed to living with bombs. The World Trade Center bomb did, however, shatter the confidence of the US public so that, although abroad American and US aircraft were frequent targets, their homeland was largely immune.

There were many arrests arising from these incidents and from other attempts which failed. Arrests and convictions are the best deterrent, but the bombs did do a lot of damage and attracted a lot of publicity, so more attacks of this kind must be expected.

Human targets

People, however, remain the most effective targets for terrorists. Though the damage done by bombing and arson in Germany is enormous, its impact on the decision-makers in the military industrial complex targets is relatively small, because it is generally covered by insurance or government compensation. The prospect of death, injury, or kidnap (including kidnap of families), however, causes them far greater concern.

This applies also to the public at large because, if the price of giving information to the police may be death or loss of a member of the family, many people will keep their mouths shut. This, as described elsewhere in the book, is particularly effective in making the law unworkable by intimidating witnesses and juries, and also in deterring 'opinion formers' from speaking out – journalists, teachers, civil servants and politicians.

As in many quite lawful human activities, the aim of the political terrorist and criminal is power, measured in terms of exercising influence or control over other people, and the acquisition of money which provides this power and influence.

4 Personal weapons

A mature market

Personal weapons fired at short ranges are the primary weapons of the guerrilla and terrorist and of the police offier and soldier fighting them, and the first impression gained from comparing personal weapons is that they have changed a lot less since the 1940s than other weapons (such as missiles, artillery and aircraft). They have been little affected by the great technological revolutions in nuclear, electronic and aerodynamic guidance and control systems. The weapons are smaller and lighter with more advanced sights but the ranges and rates of fire have changed little. The Maxim gun (1884) fired thirteen rounds per second. So do the Armalite and AK74 (see Table 1).

The most significant change in personal weapons is probably the controlled burst: this comprises a setting between single shot and sustained automatic fire whereby the gun fires a short controlled burst of three rounds (or other choices). In some cases, e.g. the Heckler & Koch 4.7 G11 assault rifle, the three rounds leave the barrel before the gun has time to kick and this can give a very tight grouping. Even without the G11's facility, three-round bursts conserve ammunition and give more effective fire for normal use. Another development, which may well go further, is the use of caseless ammunition, obviating the need to eject a cartridge. Plastic ammunition has thus far been designed primarily for training but could be effective at short ranges where the use of metal rounds could be undesirable, e.g. in executing or countering a hijack. An attempt has been made to develop a gun in which everything, including bullets, screws, springs and firing mechanisms, is non-metallic. If developed and proved, these will not only be lighter but also be more likely to evade detection at airport hand-baggage checks (as will be discussed in Chapter 7). Most experts, however, are sceptical about it being a working proposition.

Closely linked with weapons are the sights: the laser sight, in particular, may enable terrorists to fire accurately from a briefcase without appearing to be carrying a gun or taking aim, as described later. The development of night vision equipment – infra-red (IR), image intensification (II) and thermal imagery (TI) – will also have an increasing effect on the options available for the use of weapons in attack and defence, but sophisticated night vision sights can cost ten times as much as the weapon itself.

This chapter looks at developments in ammunition, then at the most revolutionary of weapons under trial, the German G11 assult rifle, then briefly at other rifles and sights and finally at sub-machines-guns, machine pistols and shotguns.

Ammunition

There are three main areas of contemporary debate about small arms ammunition: calibre, stopping power and the use of caseless ammunition.

The great majority of sub-machine-guns, pistols and machine pistols fire 9 mm short, blunt bullets, with low muzzle velocity, designed for use at ranges of 100 metres at most (usually much less) but with good stopping power. Some use 7.62 and even 5.45 mm ammunition, for example the very small Russian PSM police pistol, designed for concealed carrying, whose bullet is probably designed to be unstable so that it tumbles as it hits the target and stops rather than penetrates.

Calibres around 7.62 remain the commonest ammunition for machine-guns, combining long range with stability and good ballistic qualities. For infantry personal weapons, however, most armies have now switched over to smaller calibres to save weight, with higher muzzle velocities, such as the 5.56 Armalite or M16. These have a shorter effective range (450 rather 600 metres) but infantry weapons (other than sniper's rifles) are very seldom fired at more than 300 metres in any case. The revolutionary Heckler & Koch G11 fires 4.7 mm caseless ammunition at a very high cyclic rate (see pp. 31–3).

The weight of 4.7 mm ammunition is about half that of 5.56 mm, and the weight of 5.56 mm is about half that of 7.62 mm, but many experienced combat soldiers have doubts about the stopping power of the 5.56 bullet in close-quarter combat. With its high muzzle velocity and stable flight, it is likely to penetrate a soft target at short range and tumbles only when it hits at longer range. A Royal Marine in the Falklands campaign complained that he fired his Armalite four times at an oncoming enemy soldier at 20 metres and he still kept on coming.

Table 1 Examples of small arms development

Period	Weapon	Origin	Weight (loaded) (kg)	Length (mm)	Muzzle velocity (mps)	Cyclic* rate of fire (rds/min)	Remarks
			Rifles (including assault rifles)				
1930s (WW2)	.303 Lee Enfield No 4 Rifle	UK	4.10	1,130	751	20	manual
1950s (current)	7.62 L1A1	UK	4.30	1,143	838	40	semi-automatic single shot
Late 1960s (current)	5.56 Armalite M16 A2	USA	3.58	940	1,000	800	fully automatic three-round burst
Late 1970s (current	5.45 AK74/AKS/74	Russia	4.70(?)	930 (690 AKS)	900	650	bullet nose distorts to cause tumble
Late 1980s	5.56 L85 A1 (IW)	UK	4.98	785	940	600–850	optical or II sight with grenade launcher
Late 1980s (user trials)	4.7 G11 Heckler & Koch	FRG	4.30	750	930	600 2,000	automatic three-round burst
			Light machine-guns				
1930s (WW2)	.303 Bren MK III	UK	8.76	1,080	744	480	
Late 1980s	5.56 L86 A1 (LSW)	UK	6.88	900	970	700 (to 850)	same system as 5.56 L85A1 rifle

Period	Weapon	Origin	Weight loaded (kg)	Length with stock (mm)	Length without stock (mm)	Muzzle velocity (mps)	Cyclic* rate of fire (rds/min)	Remarks
Sub-machine-guns								
1920s	Thompson .45	USA	5.37	810	NA	282	700	
1941 (WW2)	9 mm Sten, Mark II	UK	3.44	762	NA	366	550	
1950s	9 mm Ingram Model 11	USA	2.10	460	222	293	1,200	
1960s	9 mm MP5 Heckler & Koch	FRG	2.73	660	490	400	800	
1970s	9 mm MP5 KA1 Heckler & Koch	FRG	2.52	NA	325	375	900	with three-round burst
1983	9 mm Spectre	Italy	3.10	580	350	400	900	double action
1993	5.7 mm FN P90	Belg	3.20	NA	500	350	900	
1993	9 mm Steyr TMP	Austria	1.3 (empty)	NA	282	380	900	

Sources: Jane's Infantry Weapons 1987–88, London, Jane's 1987, and manufacturers' specifications

Note: *Manufacturers' specifications and textbooks usually quote the 'cyclic rate', i.e. the number of rounds the gun would fire in a sustained burst of one minute. This, of course, is purely theoretical, and it is easier for the non-expert to visualize the performance of the gun in rounds per second by dividing by 60, e.g. a gun with a cyclic rate of 600 fires 10 rounds per second.

The Russian 5.45 bullet fired by the AK74 Kalashnikov rifle is tapered at the base (boat-tailed – see Figure 1). Inside the streamlined jacket it has a steel core with a small lead plug in front; in front of this again is a 3 mm air gap inside the nose of the bullet. This not only brings the centre of gravity back but also causes the nose to bend over on hitting even soft targets at short range so that it has quite good stopping power. The 5.7 × 28 mm round fired by the FN P90 sub-machine-gun (see p. 40) tumbles on entering a soft target, so it also has good stopping power.

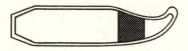

Figure 1 The Russian 5.45 bullet

Caseless ammunition is also a recent innovation which is likely to develop in one or more of several current designs. The principal idea is to dispense with the cartridge in order to save weight and avoid the propensity for jamming involved in its ejection. In the German G11 ammunition (4.7 mm) the propellant is a hard block in which the bullet is embedded and which burns up completely in the breech, so there is nothing to eject. Among other things, this allows a very high cyclic rate of fire for the three-round controlled burst and will be described more fully in the next section dealing with the G11.

Plastic ammunition is useful not only for training but also for use in operations at very short ranges in circumstances where there is a desire to limit the area in which casualties or damage may be inflicted, for example in an area crowded with bystanders or in an aircraft during a hijack. Heckler & Koch make a 9 mm plastic round for use in their MP5PT training sub-machine-gun and P7PT8 training pistol. The maximum trajectory is 125 metres and, though the safety area for training is 170 metres, the projectile energy drops to about one-twentieth of its muzzle energy within about 25 metres. The MP5PT can fire single shot, sustained automatic fire or three-round controlled bursts.

Finally there is a range of shot-gun ammunition from armour-piercing solid shot through various sizes of buckshot and pellets to flechettes (miniature steel arrows fired at very high velocity). Being peculiar to shot-guns these are described with that type of weapon on p. 43.

The G11 assault rifle

One of the attempts to revolutionize small arms design was the Heckler & Koch 4.7 G11 assault rifle, which first appeared in prototype in 1977. As with any revolutionary design, there have been technical problems but, if these can be overcome, some of the new ideas it incorporates could have a profound effect on small arms development.

The 4.7 mm caseless ammunition is extremely light; 100 rounds in two magazines weigh only 0.6 kg, half the weight of 5.56 mm and a quarter that of 7.62 mm. The bullet is embedded in a solid square-sided block of propellant in the base of which the priming charge is also embedded. Everything burns up in the chamber when the round is fired. The magazine, which is the full length of the barrel and slides into the gun above it, contains fifty rounds, side by side in a single row, nose down, as they are fed by a spring downwards into the chamber.

There are two revolutionary features about the gun as a whole. First, it consists of an outer casing which includes the butt, the optical sight, the trigger and the selector; all the other moving parts (the barrel, the chamber, the firing pin and the magazine) are in one piece and recoil and return together when the gun is fired. Second, the chamber is in a cylinder, rotating about an axis at right angles to the barrel, which receives a round in a vertical position and rotates to come into line with the barrel for the round to be fired (see Figure 2).

To load, the chamber is rotated by turning a cocking handle 360°, in the course of which it receives a round and presents it in line with the barrel. (Should there be a misfire, this same 360° motion allows the faulty round to fall out base first from the underside of the gun.)

If the selector is set for single shot, the barrel/chamber/magazine assembly recoils, picks up a new round and returns, ready immediately to be fired again. If it is set for sustained fire, it operates in the same way except that it repeats the cycle automatically and continues firing so long as the trigger remains depressed or until the ammunition runs out. Each round causes a full recoil and recovery before the next is fired – as in most other guns, giving a cyclic rate of 600 rounds a minute or 10 rounds a second – about the same rate as light machine-guns at the end of the Second World War and considered ideal for covering fire at 300 metres range.

When the selector is set for a three-round controlled burst, however,

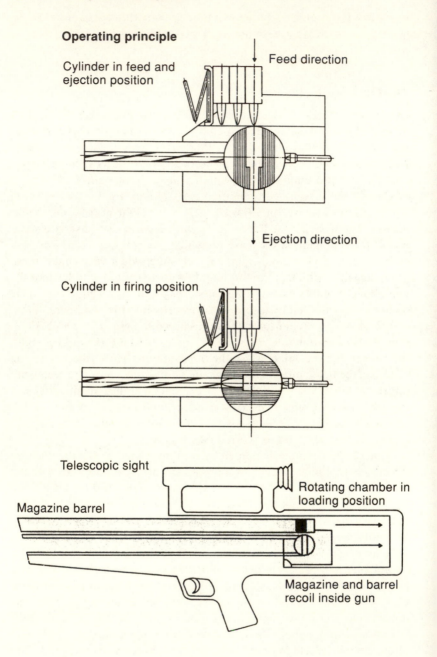

Figure 2 The 4.7 mm G11 rifle
Source: Heckler & Koch specification

the process is entirely different. The first round is loaded by rotating the cocking lever as before, but when it is fired, a second round and then a third are all loaded, fired and out of the barrel, fed by a counter within the recoiling mass, before the barrel assembly has even reached the buffer on completion of its recoil. It then returns, automatically loading another round, and is ready to fire another three-round burst.

This cycle has two main effects. Since it has to cope neither with ejecting cartridges nor a reciprocating action to reload, it produces a very high cyclic rate of 2,000 rounds per minute for the three-round burst, meaning that the three rounds are all out in less than one-tenth of a second. Since the barrel assembly, with the added inertia of the magazine and the chamber and firing mechanisms moving with it, is still absorbing the three shocks and has not even reached the buffer at the end of the recoil, the firer has felt no more than a steadily increasing pressure on the shoulder. All three rounds are on their way before the firer feels the kick when this recoiling mass hits the buffer. It is this kick which produces the reflex action causing ordinary guns to deflect up and to the right during sustained bursts, but in this case all three bullets are out of the barrel before that happens. The result is that the three rounds will fall in a much tighter grouping on the target than if there had been a full recoil between each of them, as there is when the selector is set to automatic. This is significant both at long ranges (100–300 metres), where there would be an increased probability of a lethal hit, and at short ranges in a sub-machine-gun role, where the three rounds together would give high lethality and stopping power.

Other rifles and light machine-guns

The AAI Corporation in the USA has also developed an Advanced Combat Rifle (5.56 mm AAI ACR) using caseless ammunition and this has the same high cyclic rate of fire (2,000 rounds per minute) in a three-round controlled burst mode. Like the G11, it has a slower rate of fire when the selector is set for sustained fire. The makers claim that the three-round burst increases the hit probability by 100 per cent over normal automatic fire because of the high cyclic rate and tight grouping of the shots. Trials are in progress with two different types of caseless ammunition for this gun: a conventional 5.56 mm bullet and a 4.32 mm discarding sabot bullet, both of which are embedded in a cylindrical Compressed Propellant Charge.

The British individual weapon (IW) came into service in 1987. This is the 5.56 L85 A1. A version with a heavier barrel is the current light support weapon (LSW) 5.56 L86 A1. Both are fully automatic and can be fitted with a grenade launcher but they do not have a controlled burst capability. They are fitted with an optical sight with four times' magnification, which enhances their use in poor light and is useful for surveillance. An emergency open sighting system is also fitted to the optical sight for emergency firing. An image intensifying (II) sight can quickly be substituted for the optical sight if required.

The Russian 5.45 AK74 (and AKS74 with folding butt) came into service in the late 1970s. There is also a light machine-gun version, the RPK74. All are fully automatic, but do not have a controlled burst capability. Like other Russian weapons they are robust and simple, with a foresight post and U-notch backsight. Their most interesting characteristic is the design of their bullets (described more fully on p. 30) with an air gap in the nose which causes them to distort and tumble on striking a soft target, giving them a better stopping power at short ranges.

The AK74 is also fitted with an effective muzzle brake. This reduces the recoil by diverting some of the thrust forward, and also compensates for the usual upward movement of the barrel during firing by imposing a simultaneous downward thrust. These, obviously, should help firers to hold their aim on the target during a long burst, but they make the weapon unpleasantly noisy for firers and their immediate neighbours.

One other trend which may be developed is the greater use of plastics to save weight. Thus far, plastics have been used only in such parts as the butt, hand-guard and magazine, as in the Swiss 5.6 SG 550/551 SIG assault rifle, and weight savings have so far been marginal (5–10 per cent). There is constant development in plastics so it is worth watching this trend, but there is no technological breakthrough yet in sight for substituting anything for metal in the barrels or other machine-moving parts of accurate or long-range weapons. If there is any development it is more likely to have its first effects on sub-machine-guns and pistols with their shorter ranges, reliance on a spread of burst rather than precision, and lower muzzle velocities. These are, in any case, the kinds of guns which terrorists are most likely to want to smuggle on to aircraft through magnetometers and X-ray searches at the boarding gates.

Snipers' rifles have now reached a degree of maturity in which the excellence of manufacture of barrels, ammunition and telescopic sights already matches the capability of the most skilled and experienced sniper. The accepted NATO standard of accuracy for 5.56 or 7.62 weapons is 1½ minutes of arc, that is every round should fall within 40 cm (16 inches) of a point of aim at 500 metres range. The 7.62 Model 85 Parker Hale sniping rifle is designed to give a guaranteed first-round hit *capability* on human-sized targets at ranges up to 600 metres and about

85 per cent from 600 to 900 metres. Few humans will do justice to this specification even under ideal meteorological conditions. Sterling Armaments claim that their sniper rifle with telescopic sight gives a trained person a 99 per cent capability of a hit on a point target at 400 metres in daylight. This rifle can also be fitted with an II for night use. In theory, microelectronics might enable a small projectile to be made responsive to external guidance and this could provide some new capabilities, particularly in conjunction with TI equipment, but in practice the advantages, if any, over current skills and accuracy of equipment seem unlikely to justify the expense of development and manufacture. Many experts are sceptical.

Armour-piercing bullets, though some can be fired by personal weapons, are more relevant to the discussion of other anti-vehicle weapons (see Chapter 6).

Sights and night vision equipment

The design of sights for personal weapons has been mentioned, in passing, in discussing some of the weapons above. Passionate argu-ments will continue over the pros and cons of open U-notch, aperture, optical and telescopic sights, each of which has its own advantages for certain conditions.

Night vision and night-aiming equipment are likely to be areas of continuing development. Traditional IR surveillance equipment trans-mits invisible infra-red rays which bounce back from a foreign body (as radar does). Its advantages are that a high level of power can be transmitted, giving it long range. The main disadvantage is that it is 'active': its transmissions can be detected by an enemy with the equipment to do so. This is less likely to be a disadvantage in fighting guerrillas and terrorists than in fighting sophisticated armies.

II is passive, that is nothing is transmitted. It receives the smallest trace of daylight, moonlight or starlight and amplifies it to ten or twenty times its natural intensity. Its effectiveness may, however, be reduced or even eliminated by heavy fog or rain.

TI is also passive. It receives infra-red rays – heat rather than light – and converts them to an image on a screen; it can penetrate any weather.

There are now many II sights which can be fitted to standard rifles. For some it is claimed that accurate fire is possible at 500 metres in starlight. They are also valuable for surveillance, up to 5,000 metres.

There are two other types of sights which work on a quite different principle. One is an aiming point projector which projects a narrow beam of light like a torch to illuminate the target, with a small dark spot in the centre, zeroed to the gun. A typical example is the one which can be fitted to almost all Heckler & Koch rifles and sub-machine-guns. This has a 10-watt Halogen lamp which illuminates a target for surveillance up to 120 metres and firing up to 100 metres. At this range, the illuminated circle is 4 metres in diameter, with a 60 cm black aiming spot. More practical ranges would be 50 metres (giving a 2 metres circle with 30 cm spot) or, for sub-machine-guns, 25 metres with a 1 metre circle and a 15 cm aiming spot.

The other type, likely to develop a lot further, is the laser sight, which projects a small bright orange spot marker on to the target, by day or by night, and is zeroed to the gun. As an example, the US R100 laser gun sight can be fitted to an M16 (Armalite) rifle or to a sub-machine-gun and, in normal daylight in a building, the dot may be visible at up to 100 metres. It is not, of course, much use in bright sunlight out of doors. Ranges would be longer at night but the limit would lie in the effective range of the gun. A possible application of this sight for terrorist use is discussed on p. 37.

An alternative laser sight is available in which the spot marker is invisible to the naked eye and can be used only by a person wearing night vision goggles or a weapon with a night vision (II) sight. It is totally invisible to the target and very effective for night use.

Sub-machine-guns

A serviceable and effective sub-machine-gun, albeit of a half-century-old design but unused and well maintained, can be bought for $35. There are literally millions of them in warehouses, of thousands of different models. (*Jane's Infantry Weapons* describes over 150 models still found in regular use.) 'Tommy-guns' from the 1920s and Stens from the 1940s are still used in large numbers by militias, irregular 'paramilitaries', and guerrillas. As is shown in Table 2, development over this half century has been of degree rather than of kind. Nevertheless many of the more significant developments have been since the early 1980s, particularly in the field of caseless or semi-caseless ammunition, controlled burst capability and 'double-action'. Any or all of these could burgeon into more radical development in the future.

Because they are so cheap, and in such profusion, terrorists tend to use the older designs of weapon. Of those listed in Table 2, the Uzi, Mini-Uzi and Ingram are particularly popular, along with the 7.65 mm Czech Skorpion, which is really a machine pistol but is included in the table as it has a retractable stock and is used by terrorists as a sub-machine-gun. The Ingram Model 11 is no longer manufactured but a lot remain in use by terrorist groups. It is very light (1.59 kg empty or 2.1 kg with loaded 32-round magazine) and the shortest (222 mm) sub-machine-gun available. It has the same unloaded weight (1.59 kg), is shorter than the Skorpion machine pistol, and has a very high cyclic rate of fire. The Skorpion can be fitted with a silencer and this, with the butt extended, gives it a total length of 716 mm, as long as some rifles. The Ingram can be fitted with a suppressor, which differs from a silencer in that it allows the bullet to reach its full supersonic velocity but is less silent.

Most popular with police forces and soldiers in an anti-terrorist role are the various weapons of the Heckler & Koch MP5 series. The MP5 A5E was one of the first guns to have a controlled burst facility, but this of a totally different character from that described earlier for the G11. The control is exercised simply by a ratchet on the trigger mechanism which is set during manufacture for three, four or five rounds: this ratchet holds the sear off the hammer for the indicated number of rounds. The trigger can then be released and pressed again to fire another similar burst; thus the fire is neither more nor less accurate than normal sustained firing. Firers are simply restrained from wasting ammunition by restricting each burst after which they aim and fire again. The close grouping of the burst achieved by the G11 is, however, less important for a sub-machine-gun where a degree of dispersal may be an advantage; the values of the three-round burst are mainly in conserving ammunition (to avoid having to change the magazine at the height of the engagement) and the lethal and stopping power of three rounds is better than that of one.

The MP5K series (MP5K, KA1, KA4 and KA5) were specially designed for police and military anti-terrorist squads as they are short enough for concealment under clothing, in the glove compartment of a car or in a briefcase. Heckler & Koch sell two specially designed briefcases from which the MP5K series guns can be fired.

Several of the shorter sub-machine-guns can be fitted with a laser sight (see pp. 35–6). The whole assembly could then be fitted inside a slightly larger than usual briefcase, with a porthole through which the laser beam could be directed, and triggers both for the laser sight and the gun on the handle of the briefcase.

A number of assault rifles have been adapted to produce a weapon suitable for a dual role as a sub-machine-gun. The 5.56 HK53 (adapted from the German G3 rifle) and the 5.56 Ruger AC556F (from the US AC556 selective fire weapon) are examples of this. Being of smaller calibre, however, they are thought by some to have an inferior stopping power to that of 9 mm sub-machine-guns at short range. The 4.7 G11 assault rifle is of even smaller calibre and is short enough for reasonably

Table 2 Development of sub-machine-guns

Period	Weapon	Origin	Calibre (mm)	Weight loaded (kg)	Shortest length (mm)	Muzzle velocity (mps)	Cyclic rate of fire (rds/min)	Remarks
1920s	Thompson .45	USA	11.4	5.37	810*	282	700	*cannot be retracted
1941 (WW2)	Sten, Mark II	UK	9	3.44	762*	366	550	
1949	Czech Model 23	Czech.	9	3.27	445	381	650	
1949	Uzi	Israel	9	4.10	470	400	600	
1950s	Mini-Uzi	Israel	9	3.30	360	350	950	
1956	Sterling L2A3	UK	9	3.47	483	390	550	
1950s	Ingram Model 11	USA	9	2.10	222	293	1,200	
Late 1950s	Skorpion	Czech.	7.65	2.00	269	317	840	
1960s	MP5 A5E Heckler & Koch	FRG	9	2.73	490	400	800	three-, four-, or five-round burst
1970s	MP5 KA1 Heckler & Koch	FRG	9	2.52	325	375	900	three-round controlled burst
1983	Spectre	Italy	9	3.10	350	400	900	double action

1993	FN P90	Belg	5.7	3.20	500	850	900	
1993	Steyr TMP	Austria	9	1.3 (empty)	282	380	900	

Rifles used as or adapted as sub-machine-guns

1980s	5.56 HK53	FRG	5.56	3.65	563	750	700	
Late 1980s	4.7 G11 Heckler & Koch	FRG	4.70	4.30	750	930	600 / 2,000	automatic / three-round burst
1980s	5.56 Ruger AC556F	USA	5.56	3.50	584	885	750	three-round burst
1980s	AKSU-74	USSR	5.45	3.50	420	800	800	version of AK74

Sources: Jane's Infantry Weapons 1987–88, London, Jane's 1987, and manufacturers' specifications

Note: * Manufacturers' specifications and textbooks usually quote the 'cyclic rate' i.e. the number of rounds the gun would fire in a sustained burst of one minute. This, is of course, is purely theoretical, and it is easier for the non-expert to visualize the performance of the gun in rounds per second by dividing by 60, e.g. a gun with a cyclic rate of 600 fires 10 rounds per second.

easy handling as a sub-machine-gun. Both the G11 and the Ruger compensate for the small calibre ammunition by having a three-round burst the – G11 at a very high rate of fire. The AKSU–74 is a short-barrel version of the AK74 assault rifle and is fitted with a flash-reducer.

The Italian 9 mm Spectre also breaks new ground. It fires from a closed bolt position but has a separate hammer unit which pushes the firing pin through the bolt from behind. It has no safety catch but, once the gun has been cocked and the bolt comes forward to its closed position, there are two alternative positions for the hammer unit: forward and back. It can be fired from either: by a strong pressure from the front position or by a light pressure from the back (ready for quick action) position.

The process (see Figure 3) is as follows:

1 With the gun empty, all working parts forward, a magazine is inserted.
2 The cocking handle (A) is drawn back.
3 The cocking handle is released, allowing the bolt (B) to push the first round into the chamber, but the hammer unit remains back full cock: this is the quick action position, e.g. for entering a room in which there is an adversary who is believed to be ready to fire; a light pressure on the trigger will release the hammer unit to fire the firing pin through the bolt.
4 If, having cocked the gun, there is no immediate expectation of firing, pressing a de-cocking lever (C) allows the hammer unit (D) to move forward under control behind the bolt; the gun is now in the 'safe' position but can be fired with a stronger pressure on the trigger, which takes the hammer unit (not the block) back and immediately releases it to fire.

Thus the gun offers a similar alternative to the traditional 0.38 revolver (see below), which can also be fired from the cocked (light pressure) or uncocked (deliberate pressure) positions.

Two recently developed sub-machine-guns or machine pistols are also worth mentioning. The Belgian FN P90, which went into production in 1993, uses very lightweight ammunition. Its 5.7 × 28 mm SS90 round weighs 5.5 gm (compared with 12 gm for the widely used 9 mm parabellum), and the projectile itself weighs only 1.5 gm, but it has more than double the muzzle velocity. The design of the ammunition gives it a long effective range (150 metres) and greater penetration of body armour and steel helmets. FN, the manufacturers, also claim that it has much superior stopping power and incapacitation than the heavier 9 mm round, because the bullet tumbles on entering soft targets (though it does not deform like the Russian bullet shown in Figure 1).

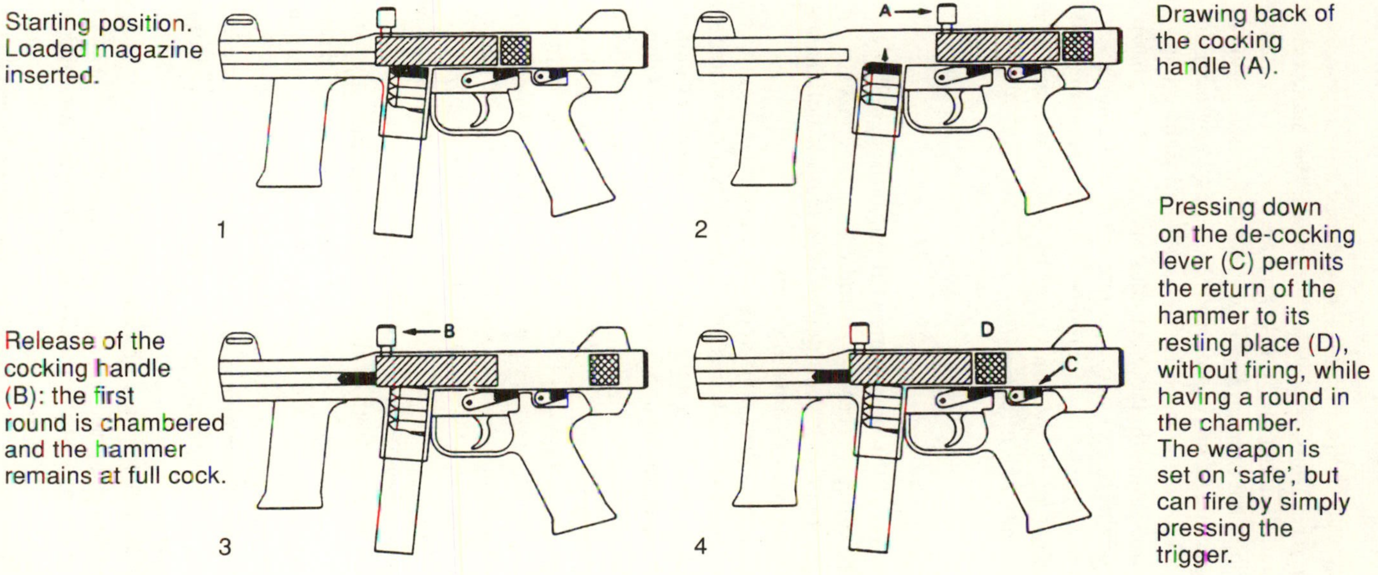

1. Starting position. Loaded magazine inserted.

2. Drawing back of the cocking handle (A).

3. Release of the cocking handle (B): the first round is chambered and the hammer remains at full cock.

4. Pressing down on the de-cocking lever (C) permits the return of the hammer to its resting place (D), without firing, while having a round in the chamber. The weapon is set on 'safe', but can fire by simply pressing the trigger.

Figure 3 The 9 mm Spectre sub-machine-gun
Source: Manufacturer's specificaiton

The Tactical Machine Pistol (TMP) developed by Steyr of Austria was undergoing user trials in 1993. This uses the standard 9 mm parabellum ammunition, but the gun is extremely small (282 mm or just over 11 inches long) and light (1.3 kg empty). It offers the option of a 15 or 30 round magazine. At its recommended range (25 metres) the two-handed grip combines the automatic firepower and tight grouping of a good sub-machine-gun with the size and weight of a pistol. It is specifically designed for quick action in unexpected encounters at close quarters, by people like tank crews, drivers, soldiers searching buildings or hunting for mines or booby traps, and by police officers or body-guards. Terrorists may like it too.

Pistols

Pistols (revolvers and self-loading) are still much used, both by terror-ists and by police officers, because of their ease of concealment in a pocket, or carriage in a hip or shoulder holster, leaving both hands free until it becomes necessary to draw the gun.

Ironically one of the oldest revolvers still in regular use, the British .38 dating from the 1930s, shares the same advantages and disad-vantages of double action firing with one of the latest sub-machine-guns just described, the Spectre, though it uses a totally different system. The .38 revolver can be carried cocked, with or without a round in the chamber aligned with the barrel. When cocked, a very light pressure will fire it if there is a round in that chamber and this could lead to accidents in moments of stress. For this reason, the hammer comb has been removed in most models. Uncocked, the pistol is safe and stable, especially if the chamber aligned with the barrel is empty. A double action is used to fire it, first to rotate the chamber and cock the action and then a second pressure to shoot. In emergency a single strong pressure will carry through both of these without significantly affecting speed of reaction or accuracy. A similar Smith and Wesson .38 revolver is still the standard weapon for Personal Protection Officers in the British police service, who regard it as the most reliable weapon on the market, with none of the propensities for stoppages inherent in auto-matic pistols, and, provided that it is never carried cocked, there is virtually no risk of accidental discharge.

Most pistols are self-loading or semi-automatic, that is the short recoil from a single shot loads the next one. Some pistols, however, are fully automatic machine pistols, that is they can fire sustained bursts. These are generally not very successful, as it is too difficult to maintain the aim of a small pistol during a burst. One of these, the Skorpion, was described under 'Sub-machine-guns' (p. 36) because it is much used in that role, as it has a folding butt and can be conveniently held in two hands. There is, in fact, no clear division between sub-machine-guns and machine pistols.

The recently developed 9 mm Beretta 93 R is probably the most advanced of the currently available machine pistols. It has a choice of self-loading single rounds or controlled three-round bursts. The magazine holds twenty rounds, and still fits into a normal-sized pistol grip as the rounds are staggered. As well as a folding stock, the gun has a folding forehand grip which greatly improves the steadiness of aim in the sub-machine-gun role.

Shotguns

Shotguns are useful both to terrorists and to police officers and soldiers, because they offer a wide choice of ammunition, some of which (with small pellets) can be fired within a small safety area.

One of the best is the SPAS (Special Purpose Automatic Shotgun) specially designed by Luigi Franchi in Italy as a riot weapon. Ammunition varies from armour-piercing solid shot (which can penetrate an 8 mm steel plate) to small pellets. Being a smooth bore weapon it spreads its pellets over nearly 1 metre diameter at 40 metres. It has an automatic action, firing about four rounds per second and, loaded with buckshot, it can put 48 pellets per second on to a 1 metre square target at 40 metres' range – each buckshot pellet having greater residual energy than a 7.65 mm pistol bullet at the same range. With seven 12-bore rounds in the magazine this gives it formidable killing power at short ranges. The gun can also project a CS gas canister 150 yards.

The CAWS (Close Assault Weapon System), jointly developed in the early 1980s by Olin in the USA and Heckler & Koch in Germany, is also a 12-bore weapon and offers two new choices of cartridge. One fires eight '000 Buck' pellets each weighing 4.5 gm and ejected with a muzzle velocity of 488 metres per second (more than most sub-machine-guns). The other fires twenty flechettes each weighing 0.376 gm, with the very high muzzle velocity of 900 metres per second. Both the buckshot and the flechettes are effective at ranges up to 150 metres.

There is great potential for development of shotguns and shotgun ammunition for use at the short ranges at which most guerrilla and terrorist actions are usually fought.

5 Missiles, longer range weapons and bombs

Free flight armour-piercing missiles (hand held)

Terrorists make increasing use of armour-piercing weapons to attack both armoured vehicles (including VIP limousines) and the walls of buildings. Thus far they have had little success against vehicles, because they have generally failed to achieve the clean hit at the right angle in the right place on which hollow charge missiles depend for their effect. The attack on the armoured limousine of the US Army General Kroesen in Germany in September 1981, for example, was made with an RPG 7 at short range while the car was stopped at traffic lights but it bounced off the boot and inflicted only superficial injuries.

The Russian RPG 7 is the hand-held surface-to-surface missile (SSM) most commonly used by terrorists, as they have been lavishly provided for Arab governments, some of whom pass them on to Arab terrorists or to the IRA and other European terrorists. Though first issued in 1962, it remains an effective weapon, able to penetrate 320 mm of armour, with its hollow charge projectile of 85 mm calibre weighing 2.25 kg. It is, however, thrown off course by cross-winds and defeated by wire mesh protection outside buildings (as at police stations in Northern Ireland), because the hollow charge relies for its penetration on detonating at right angles and the right distance from its target. It is also unsafe to fire it in confined spaces, or with a wall within 2 metres of the back of the launch tube (a fault overcome in the Armbrust – see p. 45. More modern versions such as the RPG 16 and RPG 18 are more convenient in use but generally have the same shortcomings.

The US M 72. 750 LAW (light anti-tank weapon) fires a similar projectile (66 mm, weight about 1 kg) but it has higher penetration (380 mm of armour). The makers claim that the high muzzle velocity (230 mps) and good aerodynamics give a 65 per cent probability of a hit at 250 metres, the projectile having a flight time of 1.2 seconds at this range. For moving targets, the optical sight has a series of crosses each side of the central range line, each giving the correct aim-off for a target crossing at 15 mph (24 kph). The major advantage of this weapon is its lightness: the missile and launcher together weigh only 3 kg.

The British LAW 80, which went into production in 1987, fires a bigger missile (94 mm) with very high penetration (over 600 mm – precise figure not published). The missile and launcher together weigh 9.6 kg. It is a one-shot low-cost disposable weapon and contains a spotting rifle integrated with the outer tube. This is pre-loaded with five rounds of tracer ammunition designed with the same ballistic characteristics as the missile, so that operators can get their weapon aimed accurately on to the target without giving away their position. The bullet has a flash head which indicates when it has hit a hard target, upon which the operator fires the missile. With a range of up to 500 metres, this greatly increases the probability of a hit. It can also be fired at ranges as short as 20 metres.

The West German Armbrust, adopted by NATO and by several armies in Latin America, Africa and the Middle and Far East, incorporates some major improvements: it is free of flash, smoke and blast, and makes a noise no louder than a pistol shot, and it can safely be fired from inside a room with a wall close behind it. Both of these things are achieved by the fact that the missile is projected forward and the counterweight projected backwards by pistons which effectively lock in the flash, smoke, blast and noise. The counterweight consists of some 5,000 small plastic flakes which fan out as they leave the launch tube, and fall harmlessly to the ground within 15 metres; they do not rebound from a wall as close as 80 cm behind the weapon. The launch tube, though hot and under high pressure from the gas trapped inside, can safely be discarded without risk of its exploding.

The AC 300 Jupiter is a joint Franco-German product incorporating the same flash and blast-free system (pistons and flakes) as the Armbrust. It is ejected at a lower muzzle velocity (180 mps compared with 210 for the Armbrust) but, once stabilized in its flight, is assisted by a booster rocket to 275 mps.

Heavy machine-guns

As an alternative to the shoulder-fired hollow charge weapons described above, there are signs that the medium and heavy machine-gun (HMG) with armour-piercing ammunition may be regaining popularity. A Russian 12.7 mm Degtyaref was found in an IRA arms cache in July

1988. This is an old model first produced in 1946, but improved versions with similar essential characteristics are still under active development. The US 0.50 inch (12.7 mm) GPHMG (general purpose heavy machine-gun) using Saboted Light Armour Penetration (SLAP) ammunition has completed trials; it weighs 25 kg, fires 400 rounds per minute, and has a maximum theoretical range of 6,650 metres (over 4 miles) though its effective range is probably not more than 4,000 metres. Also under development is the Belgian 15 mm FN BRG-15 heavy machine-gun, which fires 700 rounds a minute with an armour-piercing bullet weighing 70 grams (compared with 46 grams for the 0.50 inch SLAP ammunition), but the gun weighs more than twice as much (55 kg) and is twice as long (2,000 mm compared with 914 mm) as GPHMG. Both will penetrate the kind of armour used on VIP limousines at the longest ranges likely to be used by terrorists and the chances of a hit are high; they can also be used effectively against helicopters. The guns are, however, much heavier and more awkward to manhandle then either the free flight projectors above or the guided missile projectors below.

Guided armour-piercing missiles (hand held)

The earlier anti-tank guided missile projectors used the manual command to line of sight (MCLOS) system of guidance. The Russian 3M6 (Snapper) was issued to the Arab armies in the 1960s, and used in the 1967 war, but has been replaced by the AT3 (Sagger). The MCLOS missile is wire-guided, that is it feeds out a multicore cable from spools in its base, through which the operator's instructions are transmitted to two jetavator nozzles which swivel to correct its course. There is a flare on the base to enable the operator to see it. At ranges up to 1,000 metres this is done by eye. At longer ranges (3,000 metres maximum but more practically up to 2,000 metres) the operator steers it on a line above the target and guides its final approach through a ten-times magnification periscopic sight.

More modern weapons use the SACLOS (semi-automatic command to line of sight) system. The Russian version is the AT4 (Spigot), also known as Fagot. The NATO equivalent is the joint Franco-German MILAN (a French acronym) which came into service in 1985. The missile weighs 11.3 kg and the launching and guidance system 16.4 kg. The SACLOS missile is again wire-guided, but the operator has only the task of keeping the cross hairs of the optical sight on the (presumably moving) target. The guidance system follows the missile from an infra-red signature emitted from its base and corrects its flight to the line of sight. The makers claim a 98 per cent hit probability between 250 and

2,000 metres (the maximum practical range). The flight time for 2,000 metres is 13 seconds. The terrorist attacking an armoured limousine (or tank) has only to select a stretch of road long enough for it to be in view for, say, 15 seconds (250 metres at 60 kph or 500 metres at 120 kph). The weapon system will comfortably go into the boot of a car (missile 1,260 mm long and launching/guidance system 900 × 650 × 420 mm – combined weight about 30 kg). The chances of a hit are much greater than with a free flight missile at ranges over 250 metres (though at ranges less than that the advantage falls away sharply as there is insufficient time for the guidance system to be fully effective).

Mortars

Improvised mortars are very easy to make but are usually inaccurate and unreliable. The IRA regularly use home-made multi-barrelled mortars mounted on trucks to attack police and army posts in Northern Ireland, but many of the bombs fall far from the target and accidents are commonplace.

Most suitable for terrorist use are light mortars (51 mm to 61 mm). The British 51 mm Mortar weighs 6.25 kg and its bomb weighs 0.9 kg. It has a range of 800 metres and a probable error of 2 per cent in range and 3 mils (about one-sixth of a degree of angle) in line. This means that about half the rounds should fall within 15–20 metres of the point aimed at. The British 81L16 ML Mortar is much heavier (35 kg with a 4.5 kg bomb) but has a much longer range – up to 6,000 metres. Its choice of ammunition includes the Merlin 81 mm terminally guided mortar projectile, which incorporates a radar seeker in the nose which commands a guidance system directing the bomb on to any large armoured vehicle in the immediate target area; it has a hollow charge filling which will penetrate the top armour of any known tank.

Anti-aircraft missiles (hand held)

The use by guerrillas of surface-to-air missiles to shoot down helicopters and other aircraft has increased. One was found under the flight path of aircraft taking off from Rome Airport in 1973, with intelligence that Palestinian terrorists were targeting a civil airliner carrying a particular passenger. In 1978 and 1979 guerrillas in Zimbabwe (then Rhodesia) shot down two civil airliners, killing forty-eight and fifty-nine passengers respectively. And the use of US Stinger missiles by Afghan guerrillas to shoot down helicopter gunships probably accelerated the Soviet decision to withdraw from Afghanistan in 1988.

The Russian SAM 7 (Grail) was first seen in action in Egypt in 1967 and was used against US piston-engined aircraft and helicopters in Vietnam. It incorporates an infra-red seeker in the nose, which, launched into the vicinity of an aircraft, pursues the heat from its exhaust tube. More modern versions incorporate an IFF (Identification Friend or Foe) system. The launcher weighs 10.6 kg and the missile 9.2 kg (total 19.8 kg or 44 lb) and is 1,346 mm long. A first-stage motor launches the missile from the tube and burns out before the tail of the missile has left the tube, so as not to injure the operator. At a safe distance out a booster rocket is initiated from within the missile. The SAM 7 B can fly 5 km at a maximum altitude of 2,000 metres before it self-destructs. It is believed to cost less than $1,000 and a large number are in use by guerrillas all over the world.

The British Blowpipe is of similar overall weight (20 kg) and length (1,390 mm) and has two-stage firing, but its guidance system is quite different. The missile and its launching tube are contained in a single canister weighing 14 kg to which the operator attaches a 6-kg aiming unit. After firing, the empty canister is removed and a fresh one attached to the aiming unit. The guidance is by optical tracking and radio command. The missile has a flare in the back so that the operator can follow the path. The operator then has a choice: either thumb control can be used to keep the missile on the line of sight, or the automatic control can be switched off and the missile guided manually. In either case, the steering signals are transmitted by radio to a steering unit in the missile.

The British Javelin is an advanced version of Blowpipe. The guidance principle is similar but the operator does not have to watch the flare on the tail of the missile; this is tracked by a television camera linked to a microprocessor and the operator has only to concentrate on keeping the sights accurately on the line of sight. The television camera and microprocessor then send the necessary radio signals to operate the missile's steering system to keep it on the line of sight. (Compare the SACLOS system for wire-guided armour-piercing missiles described on on pp. 46–7) The range is in excess of 4 km. Blowpipe and Javelin are both manufactured by Short Brothers in Belfast.

The British Marconi close air defence weapon again uses a different guidance system, on the fire-and-forget principle. The missile incorporates its own active radar seeker. Once the operator has acquired a target visually in the aiming unit and, if necessary, identified it by IFF interrogation, the operator presses the trigger and this automatically locks the missile's active seeker on to the target, correcting any error in the aim. From the moment of launch, therefore, no further action is required by the operator. The system can track fast-moving targets advancing, crossing or receding.

The US Stinger, introduced into service in 1976 by General Dynamics, is also a fire-and-forget weapon, using a passive infra-red seeker and a proportional navigation system. The operator visually spots the target, finds it in the optical sight, initiates the missile functions, performs the IFF interrogation and, if it is identified as hostile, launches the missile which is by then locked on to the target and guides itself automatically to hit it.

Stinger POST has an improved sensing and control system which guards against infra-red countermeasures. It has a rosette-scan seeker, combined infra-red and ultra-violet detectors, and a microprocessor-controlled guidance system. The production contract was awarded to General Dynamics in 1983 and the first weapons were delivered in 1986.

Grenades

Terrorists usually use improvised grenades, for example a bunch of sticks of plastic explosive with a short time fuse, often surrounded by six-inch nails bound round the outside for fragmentation (the nail bomb).

The more sophisticated drogue grenade developed by the IRA in 1987 is a hollow charge grenade designed for use against armoured Land Rovers and troop carriers in Northern Ireland. It is shaped like the familiar stick grenade and comprises an ordinary food can with a ten-inch plastic tube emerging from a wooden block wedged into the top. The can contains a hollow charge of Semtex plastic explosive, shaped between the wooden block and a copper cone in the bottom of the can. The tube contains the firing mechanism. The initiator is housed in a wooden plug at the bottom of the tube, comprising a detonator protruding into the Semtex, its open end inserted in place of the bullet in a rimfire-type small arms cartridge above it, its rim resting on the hole through the plug. The rimfire cartridge has its priming composition packed into the extraction rim, not held in a central cap. The cartridge is fired by a chisel-edged bolt in a wooden slide, which slides down the tube against a light creep spring which collapses under the momentum of the bolt and slide on the impact of the grenade on its target. In its safe position, the bolt is held back by a detent (a transverse bar through the tube) held in position by a ring and pin. When the pin is removed, the detent is still held in by a lever, and when the thrower releases this lever, the detent is ejected by a spring and the bolt is free to compress the creep spring and strike the cartridge when the grenade hits the target.

The release of the lever also releases a polythene drogue which streams out from the top of the tube like the tail of a kite and is supposed to make the grenade strike with the base of the can square to the armoured surface of the target so that the hollow charge is properly directed. In practice, it seldom strikes squarely when thrown from the side, but it has been effective when thrown from upper windows on to the top armour of passing police and army vehicles.

Bombs and mines

By far the largest number of terrorist attacks are by bombs and mines of various kinds, almost always improvised except for standard anti-tank mines, usually of Russian or eastern European manufacture, which are delivered to Arab armies and passed on by their governments.

Improvised road mines are usually either fougasses (large charges with metal fragments in them concealed by the roadside) or bulk explosive under culverts fired by remote wire or radio control. Anti-personnel mines to catch survivors or rescuers may be fired either by military booby-trap switches (pull, press or release) or improvised switches using electrical contacts or crushable phials of acid. Improvised bulk explosives can be made by mixing certain types of fertilizer and diesel, or various other combinations of individually harmless and easily obtainable materials. Only the detonators and priming charges need to be factory-made, and these may be obtained either from sympathetic governments or by theft from mines or quarries. All of these techniques are well known and do not change very much.

Road mines, usually buried in dirt roads or verges and set off by pressure of a passing vehicle's wheels, have also changed little since the 1940s. To defeat the metal detector, plastic and wooden mines (with only the detonator made of metal) were used from 1942 onwards; so were booby traps to catch the sapper lifting them .

Improvised bombs to wound or kill are concealed in letters (normally at least ¼ inch thick), parcels, packages of goods, shopping bags, suitcases or vehicles, and may again be combined with booby traps to catch bomb disposal officers or people rescuing casualties. Again, most of them have been regularly described in the press, and ingenuity rather than technological development accounts for most of the new techniques.

Just as the radio control for toy aeroplanes was developed to fire remote-controlled bombs, so the development of timing devices for home video recorders was applied to precise delay fuses for bombs. One of these was used to blow up the Grand Hotel in Brighton in October 1984. The bomb was planted in a suitcase inserted behind the bath in a room on the fifth floor (the VIP rooms being on the first and second floors) by an IRA man booking in as a hotel guest three weeks before the Conservative Party conference. Mrs Thatcher and most of her Cabinet were sleeping in rooms below. Five people were killed (though none of the Cabinet). The IRA's expert bomb-maker tried to plant twelve more such bombs in holiday hotels (aimed to terrorize ordinary holiday-makers in the summer of 1985) but the first of these was discovered, with the plans for the rest, in time to prevent them, and the bomber was caught and convicted. This technique will be used again, and other types of electronic development will be adapted and exploited by bombers as they arise.

It is in the field of car or truck bombs that most of the current development is taking place, especially in Ireland and the Middle East. These are broadly of three types: first, those parked in advance beside a target building or on the road where a target vehicle is expected to pass (like fougasses or culvert mines) and fired by remote control or a delay fuse – huge bombs of this type were exploded in the City of London in April 1992 and April 1993 and the World Trade Center in New York in February 1993; second, those driven into the heart of a target area by 'suicide drivers' and also usually blown up (with the driver) by remote control; and third, those placed underneath cars to kill the driver or passengers when they start up or drive away.

Remote firing of static car bombs can be done in many ways. An electric detonator fired by an observer through field telephone cables is the simplest. Radio initiation using the control systems for model aircraft, cars or boats is now freely available in the shops. A new system devised by the IRA – named by the army as the Projectile Controlled Improvised Explosive Device (PCIED) – has proved cheap and effective: the bomb is in a truck or van, and a pair of metal sheets separated by an insulating layer (e.g. chipboard) are connected one to each side of an electric circuit incorporating a battery and detonator. The triple layer assembly is then set up on the side of the vehicle (e.g. casually loaded or disguised as a board carrying a company name or advertisement), so as to be clearly visible as a target visible from, say, a distant building or hillside. If it is about one metre square, any reasonable marksman should be sure of a hit from several hundred metres away. The metal bullet penetrates the three layers simultaneously, and thereby closes the circuit.

Road bombs may also be fired by the electromagnetic field from a passing metal vehicle, in the way that magnetic mines are detonated by passing ships. These, however, are not selective, though they can be made more so by reacting only to metal above a certain weight (e.g. on an armoured vehicle) but even these may be prematurely detonated by a passing truck. They can also be designed to react only to the presence of a radio transmitter or possibly to a combination of heavy metal and a radio. There is scope for inventiveness in other ways of improving selectivity by finding characteristics peculiar to the target vehicles, but complexity and uncertainty are likely to mean that remote control is more likely to remain the normal method.

Suicide bombs are almost invariably fired by radio control. It may soon be possible to obviate the need for the suicide driver as a means of remotely controlled locomotion is developed. This is already well developed for 'Goliath' and other remotely controlled bomb investigation vehicles. The advance may come with a combination of radio guidance with sensors on the vehicle itself, which enable it to 'see' and divert from obstacles such as bollards or concrete blocks in the zigzag checkpoint at the entrance to protected premises. Prototypes of such AGVs (Autonomous Guided Vehicles) are already under development for the robotization of certain factory operations. An AGV linked to an operator with radio control observing from a window or hillside may be able to guide the vehicle to 'bounce' a barrier or roadblock and drive fast into the heart of the target (e.g. under an arch to an inner courtyard) with a dummy in the driving seat. If the control equipment is cleverly sited with armoured protection, it will be less vulnerable to shots from the guards than if it were relying on even the most suicidal of drivers.

Car bombs designed to kill the driver or passengers are now most commonly put in plastic with powerful magnets to fix them under the car, or under the wheel arch closest to where the target is likely to sit. They are usually operated by a mercury tilt fuse, that is a small tube of mercury which can be rotated to vary the slope. At one end of the tube is a pair of electrical contacts linked to a battery and detonator. For normal carriage the tube is vertical with these contacts at the top. When the bomb is set, the tube is rotated to the required slope so that when the car accelerates or climbs a hill the inertia of the mercury will carry it up the slope to close the contact; the gentler the slope of the tube the more sensitive it is.

Mercury tilt fuses may be fitted with one or both of two types of safety devices (in addition to the removal of the wire or pin that sets them). There may be a test circuit in parallel with the firing circuit incorporating a torch bulb. Before the bomb is made live by removing the arming pin, the electric circuit is closed to test it and the bulb will light *unless* there is a short circuit in the parallel firing circuit: that is if the bulb failed to light in the test, the bomber would not remove the arming pin. There may also be a built-in delay of, say, twenty minutes or an hour between the time the bomber pulls the activating pin and the time the circuit becomes live. This will give the bomber time to get clear, in case the owner of the car comes to drive away earlier than expected, as well as ensuring that the bomber is far away in the event of the circuit being faulty and firing prematurely as soon as the circuit is live.

Nuclear, biological and chemical weapons

It has been feasible since the 1970s for terrorists to obtain the components of or even to manufacture a crude nuclear bomb in a university laboratory and workshop without any access to unpublished material. A public-spirited American graduate student carried out and documented each one of the processes required, to show that it could be done, though he did them separately to ensure that nothing like an actual bomb came into existence. Frederick Forsyth's *The Fourth Protocol* also describes a convincing scenario for the smuggling in and assembly of the components for a nuclear bomb.

Such a bomb could be concealed in, say, a crate of machinery or spare parts substituted for a similar crate in a stack awaiting shipment. The bomb would be tracked by radio and fitted to be fired by radio. When it had reached a port in the target country, the terrorists' accomplice would telephone an ultimatum to the government: 'There is a nuclear bomb in one of your ports. Unless our comrades are released by 12 noon it will be fired.' Would the government stand firm? Probably, because it would know that the terrorists would be reluctant to carry out the threat because of the political price they would pay. (They are all aware of the damage done to the IRA and Palestinian cause even by the massacre of ten or twenty people at Enniskillen or Rome Airport.) The terrorists themselves realize this, which is presumably why, despite its being quite feasible, none has tried it. Moreover, the operation is far more complex than a shooting, kidnap or hijack, and more likely to lead to failure or arrest – as well as being far less credible and less effective as a bargaining counter.

The argument applies even more strongly to chemical and biological weapons. It has been feasible for at least 100 years to release poison gas in suitable wind conditions, or to contaminate an entire city water supply, or to unleash a plague. Although the Iraqis used poison gas in the Gulf War, neither poison gas nor biological agents have been used by terrorists, presumably for the same reasons – even by the illusory 'mad anarchist' – so regularly cited in nightmare scenarios.

Clearly we should not be complacent about nuclear, biological and chemical weapons, both because of the need to evaluate hoax calls (there have been quite a lot of these, but none credible) and because all of them would be feasible for a group which was both desperate and suicidal. But the threat is far less, and would in many ways be easier to handle because of its lack of credibility, than the terrorist actions to which we are accustomed.

Incapacitating weapons

There are as yet no really effective non-lethal incapacitating weapons, that is weapons which render everyone in the target area, friend or foe, temporarily unconscious without inflicting permanent injury. To be effective they must be instantaneous. There are incapacitating gases and darts (used for disabling and capturing wild animals), but they do not take effect quickly enough to prevent a terrorist from shooting or throwing a grenade. Nor do low-frequency electromagnetic pulses, nor the 'sub-sound' waves which after a time have the effect of disorienting people without their realizing it. The high-voltage electric shock weapon (with a metal missile on the end of a wire fired from a generator producing an instantaneous non-lethal shock) has too short a range and its results are not sufficiently reliable for it to be effective against rioters. If, however, a non-lethal incapacitating weapon with an instantaneous effect is ever developed, it could be a very valuable anti-terrorist weapon especially to counter ambush or hijack attempts.

It may be that an instantaneous blast weapon will be developed. This at present is limited to the stun grenade, as used by the SAS, which stuns and disorients everyone in a confined space (e.g. terrorists and hostages) for a few seconds but does no permanent damage. A similar blast effect, from a sudden pulse of compressed air from emission points down the full length of an aircraft cabin, might be able to stun all those in it (both passengers and hijackers) for the few seconds needed for a simultaneous emission of a more lasting incapacitating gas to take effect.

6   Detecting explosives, bombs and guns

The developing challenges for detection

Thus far, detection of guns and bombs has largely been by detection of metal, though dogs and chemical sniffers are also now increasingly used for detecting explosives. A great deal of further development, however, is needed in the detection of plastic and other materials and of explosives by various kinds of penetrating ray or radiation, the most promising being by neutron bombardment and the detection of dielectric properties of materials. Trends and prospects will be examined in this chapter.

The wholly plastic gun has already been produced, including firing mechanism, screws, springs and bullets; many experts are sceptical, but if it does prove to be a practical and reliable weapon it would have many applications for terrorists in a hijacking, assassination or kidnap operation. There are also ways of detonating bombs, especially with rough (though not precise) delay fuses without the use of any metal. X-rays and other forms of radiation can already be adjusted to screen tell-tale shapes of plastic but, as with metal, these shapes can be concealed in metal or other containers so the various means of detection of explosives probably offer a more promising area of development.

Improvised explosives present a particular problem because there are so many pairs of innocent materials which become explosive when brought together. Well-known mixtures include fertilizer and fuel oil, and the so-called 'Co-op' mixture of nitrobenzine and sodium chlorate. Most such mixtures do, however, contain considerable quantities of nitrogen compounds and it is these which currently provide the commonest characteristics for detection either by vapour or by neutron bombardment. If sufficient effort is devoted to research, however, other detectable characteristics are likely to be discovered. Detection of regular characteristics in other components – e.g. initiating or firing mechanisms and detonating or priming materials – may well provide the best answers.

Improvised explosive devices (IED) can be fired by many different methods – mechanically, chemically, electrically or electronically – using delay or remote control systems or by booby-trap mechanisms (press, pull, release, photoelectric and so on). Areas in which IED may be concealed (e.g. behind walls, under cars) may therefore have to be subjected to several different forms of search before they can be declared safe.

Other methods of triggering which are likely to be developed include infra-red, microwave and ultrasound. Infra-red can be jammed by electronic counter-measures (ECM) and methods of detecting the others are being developed, such as the microwave 'fuzz-buster' used to detect police speed traps in the USA.

The precise delay fuse, as used in the attempt to kill Mrs Thatcher and her Cabinet with a bomb in the Grand Hotel, Brighton (described in Chapter 5) may be detected by counter-bugging techniques, vapour sniffing or gamma ray backscatter.

Bombs to attack cars can be quickly slipped underneath or in the wheel arch, held in position by magnets. They can be fired in several ways, for example by a simple pull switch operated by a wire attached to the wheel, by a pressure switch under the front of the tyre, by a pull or release switch operated by the car door or boot, by an electric detonator linked to the ignition or lighting circuits, or by a tilt-fuse (see pp. 52–3). Sharp eyes aided by mirrors, and vapour detection offer the best means of detecting car bombs.

The range of search capability required is almost unlimited. Weapons, plastic grenades or components for IED may be concealed in personal clothing or in inaccessible parts of the body (terrorists have long recognized the reluctance of searchers to probe into the private parts of the female body, especially if the woman is pregnant or carrying a small child). Weapons can be hidden in hand baggage or baggage for check-in at airports. Bombs may be inserted behind walls or easily removable panels (as in the Brighton hotel room), under floors, in cupboards, chimneys, bookshelves, piles of junk (including especially metal junk) and so on.

The two biggest limitations of detection are fatigue of the searcher and exasperation of the public, especially the travelling public. Operators can concentrate on an X-ray screen only for a limited time and even then only with difficulty if they do it every day. Few air travellers will object if they or their hand baggage have to pass the screen a second time, but they will object strongly if a false alarm reading of one of their pieces of hold baggage results in their being prevented from boarding the aircraft: for this reason the US Federal Aviation Authority (FAA) has set its specifications for search equipment at a 95 per cent detection probability (DP) and a false alarm rate (FAR) not exceeding 1 per cent.

Aids to the senses

Eyes, ears, noses, fingers, and experience leading to suspicions and hunches remain the most effective of all the armoury at the disposal of anyone searching for guns, bombs, mines or explosives. Every army sapper who has cleared mines or searched for and disposed of bombs knows this, and the first lines of hardware are those which reinforce those senses, such as stethoscopes to help detect the tiny sounds of timing mechanisms inside a device, and mirrors.

In recent years fibre optics have also come to be used when looking round corners, down holes or inside sensitive boxes or packages. Fibre optics comprise a relatively new physical science whereby light is reflected along a bundle of transparent threads of glass or plastic by bouncing between the outer walls of the thread. The threads are of minute diameter (usually between 5 and 100-thousandths of a milli-metre) so they can bend round corners without interfering with the reflection of light along them. The bundle of threads has an optical screen which resolves the images into a picture of the scene at the far end with a resolution of up to 100 lines per millimetre, that is, depending on the intensity of the illumination, a well-nigh perfect photographic image. The bundle of micro threads is encased in a larger flexible tube, the bottom of which contains a rotatable light source and lens which can be inserted into the package or bomb, enabling the operator to view it through an image intensifier and eye-piece at the other end of the tube. This technique is already much used in micro-surgery in which, instead of making an incision, the surgeon injects a very small flexible tube into the patient. Because of this obvious and widespread surgical benefit, research and development in the science of fibre optics is extremely active and well-funded; some scientists see the applications as so widespread that they believe it to be potentially one of the most dramatic areas of scientific development in the coming years. The detection, assessment and neutralization of IEDs will be among its beneficiaries to an extent as yet unpredictable.

Tagging of explosives

Tagging of explosives can achieve two aims: to enable the presence of concealed explosive to be detected and to enable the source of the explosive to be recognized and proved.

For either form of tagging to be effective, it would be necessary for a substantial number of countries (ideally all, of course, but there is little hope of that) to subscribe to the tagging system and enforce severe penalties on anyone manufacturing, distributing or smuggling untagged explosive. So long as manufacturing countries subscribed, however, it would be possible to narrow down the source of an untagged explosive to one of the few non-co-operating countries (presumably those like Libya and Iraq, which support international terrorism as a tool of foreign policy). This would improve the chances of success in detecting the individuals involved and, because of the retaliatory action thereby justified, it might make it worthwhile for more of the non-co-operators to subscribe to the system, eventually narrowing the field of those who opt out to a handful.

In view of the many forms of bulk explosive which can be improvised by combining otherwise innocent materials (as described earlier in this chapter) the most essential tagging would be of the detonators, detonating cord and priming explosives which thus far have proved more difficult to improvise effectively.

Tagging for detecting explosives would consist of incorporation during manufacture of constituents which would react to an internationally agreed form of penetrating ray (enhanced X-rays, neutron bombardment, gamma rays, and so on).

Tagging for identification can be achieved by techniques tested as long ago as 1979 by the US Government Bureau of Alcohol, Tobacco and Firearms (ATF), but not pursued – allegedly due to opposition from within the explosives trade and firearms lobbies. The method – developed by 3M in Minnesota and manufactured by the Microtrace Corporation – comprised the incorporation of 'microtaggants' in explosives during manufacture, consisting of particles of colour-coded melamine plastic. A large number of colours can be used and these are easily changed, so the number of permutations and combinations is almost infinite. This would enable the manufacturer to use a different combination of colour codes for every batch of explosives manufactured and the system would require this coding to be recorded each time any of this batch is sold to a wholesaler, retailer and user, anywhere in the world. Thus when a bomb containing tagged explosive was discovered and defused, its origin and channels of distribution could quickly be traced, greatly facilitating the process of police investigation. If – as would often happen – the explosive was found to have passed through the jurisdiction of one of a relatively small number of non-co-operating countries, the finger of guilt would be pointed firmly at that country and appropriate international action could be taken, ranging from diplomatic pressure to cutting off air traffic, economic sanctions boycott or, in flagrant cases, military action to apprehend individuals suspected of complicity in the crime.

Vapour detection

Currently the most widely used method of detecting explosives is by detection of vapour or dust particles (aromic detection) by dogs and chemical sniffers. These are also effective in detecting drugs and other illicit materials, and are in regular and successful use at seaports and airports.

Dogs can recognize astoundingly small percentages of certain vapours, especially those associated with the human body, in which their responsiveness is at least 1 million times more sensitive than that of the human nose. Bloodhounds, for example, have followed trails up to four days old for a hundred miles and can identify the hand which has touched an object from the briefest of contacts. The value of this lies mainly in helping the police to detect and identify a subject, though corroborative evidence would be needed to persuade a jury to convict. Explosives, cocaine, heroin, amphetamines and marijuana also have characteristic odours and the dog is not fooled by deliberately placed masking smells such as spices, perfumes, onions or mothballs.

The limitations of dogs are that their senses become fatigued and that, if they are hungry or thirsty, they may switch to searching for scents of food or water. Though these can be largely overcome by good training and good handling, it is not easy to tell when a dog's senses or concentration have lapsed. At their best, however, they can detect vapours better than any of the machines.

Mass spectrographic analysis is the method of vapour detection and analysis of minute dust particles mainly used by customs and security services in seaports and airports. The process involves sucking in samples of air which are then analysed in a computerized mass spectrometer. The plant is quite large and is normally housed in a building of up to 1,000 square feet, alternatively in a semi-articulated pantechnicon some 40 feet long. Samples of air from trucks, cars or containers are drawn directly into the machine through a long hose; alternatively the samples can be drawn into a separate hand-held remote sampler which sucks the air through an adsorber cartridge, which is then taken to the main plant for analysis. The maximum throughput of the system is twenty vehicles per hour and it can be combined with an X-ray plant which simultaneously maintains the same throughput.

Instant hand-held sniffers such as S&D's 97 or Graseby's GVD6 cost
£10,000–15,000 ($15,000–22,500). They will detect one part of vapour
in 100 million (some better than this) and indicate the alarm by
immediate audible or visual signals.

Heavier analysing equipments such as British Telecom's EVD1 and
Thermedics' EGIS explosive detectors cost a lot more, around £250,000
($400,000) but are about 1 million times more sensitive, detecting one
part of vapour in up to 100 million million (10^{14}). Their disadvantage is
that, as with the mass spectrometer, the vapour has to be sucked into a
sampler (or, in the case of EGIS, particles are gathered by wiping points
of ventilation, such as locks) and the analysis then takes 30 seconds –
which, allowing for handling, probably means only thirty or forty bags
per hour being searched. They are, however, sensitive enough to detect
the low vapour military plastic explosives such as Semtex, which usually
emit only one part of vapour in 1 million million (10^{12}). As pointed out
in the Preface, this is equivalent to detecting a glass of whisky in Loch
Ness. They can be set to have a very high detection probability (DP) at
the cost of a high false alarm rate (FAR); this makes them particularly
suitable for checking high-risk air baggage, such as bags requiring
special care because of the profile of the owner, the likelihood of the
flight being targeted, or doubts arising from other types of searches.
EGIS has done well under prolonged tests at Gatwick Airport, in
conjunction with VIVID enhanced X-ray (see below), checking selected
high-risk baggage. (This is discussed more fully in Chapter 18.)

An urgent aim of research must be to develop a vapour detector which
will reliably detect Semtex in real time –that is at the rate required to
check 100 per cent of baggage for a wide-bodied aircraft at peak time,
about ten bags per minute. We may be getting close to this. The
technology of the VIPER, made in the UK by Ai, Cambridge, has given
promising results. The VIPER uses gas chromatography with twin
electronic capture detection, to detect both vapour and particles. The
makers claim that it can detect the ingredients of Semtex (RDX and
PETN) with their one part of vapour in 1 million million (10^{12}) or
particle deposits of 50–100 nanograms (thousand-millionths of a gram).

VIPER is portable, comprising one or more hand samplers (each
weighing 600 gm) and an analyser. The total weight is 13 kg and the
cost about £15,000 ($22,500). The sampler sucks in vapour, taking
about 5 seconds, through a filter paper, which is then analysed in about
3 seconds. Concurrently, for high-risk baggage, another filter paper can
be used to wipe handles, zippers and locks for particles and these too are
analysed. One analyser with two samplers should, allowing for practical
handling, check the necessary ten bags per minute.

VIPER was tested at Lima Airport on five American Airlines flights on 9, 10 and 11 October 1991. All cabin and hold baggage was searched – a total of 997 bags. The FAR was 1.5 per cent (15 bags). The bags also went through an X-ray machine and, where there was any doubt, were hand searched in the presence of their owners.

This trial showed that the vapour test was quicker and more sensitive than the particle test but that both could be done on any high-risk or suspect bag without falling below the ten bags per minute rate, and that the combination with X-ray and hand search was the best procedure.

There are, however, no figures available at the time of writing for detection probability. There were no bombs or simulated bombs in any of the bags searched in the Lima test. To prove this machine it would be necessary to pass a large number of bags, including some containing 'bombs' made up of, say, 30 grams of RDX, PETN or similar low vapour explosives concealed in a tightly sealed video recorder or radio. The test would need to be under realistic conditions with enough throughput to arrive at a reliable DP. If such a test indicated a DP of the order of 99 per cent, the VIPER technology, in conjunction with other means of detecting different characteristics (e.g. enhanced X-ray and neutron) could bring us in sight of a reliable real time sequence for searching 100 per cent of baggage at ten bags per minute.

Enhanced X-rays

Enhanced X-rays detect organic material as well as metal, using a colour code, for example displaying blue on the screen for metal and orange or red for explosive type material. Machines can be programmed to indicate high or low atomic weight or density or to match a selected molecular structure. The technique was originally developed in medical research (computer aided tomography – CAT) to detect differences within bone material. One system tested successfully at Gatwick Airport in 1992 and now in regular use – VIVID – can be programmed to match particular explosives and, if one of these is in a piece of baggage, its shape will be displayed as bright red or, if it is not exact but a near match, as brown. The system can be switched at the touch of a button to pick up other characteristics (e.g. atomic weight or organic composition). An experienced operator can therefore examine a wide range of indicators for a suspect bag quickly and thoroughly and, if still suspicious, refer it for vapour test or hand search.

This reliable explosive detection, in conjunction with EGIS vapour detection (described on p. 60), is an important advance, in the light of the now common terrorist practice of defeating metal detectors by incorporating metal components such as timers, barometric devices, firing circuits and detonators among the apparently normal electric circuits in calculators, radios and cassette recorders.

Neutron detection

As with vapour detectors, explosive detection by neutron bombardment and gamma ray backscatter offers a range from relatively cheap instant hand-held detectors to more expensive permanent installations.

Gamma ray backscatter hand-held drug and explosive detectors cost around £10,000 ($15,000), for example S&D's Searcher or ABAS's Demon. These operate by projecting gamma radiation from a cobalt 57 sensor head, which is reflected back in a scattered form by dense organic material with low atomic weight. The sensor identifies the pattern of this backscatter and can be calibrated to react to the pattern of a selected drug or explosive. It indicates this with an immediate audible or visual signal. Its shortcoming is that its sensitivity falls sharply with its distance from the object. Thus a typical equipment will react to 30 grams of ammonium nitrate in contact with the sensor face but needs 1,000 grams to give a positive response at 8 cm distance.

Thermal Neutron Analysis (TNA) requires a large machine weighing about 10 tonnes, normally static with a conveyor belt running through it as part of an airport baggage search system. The cost is around £600,000 ($900,000). A number of TNA machines are under test at various airports, including New York's JFK and London's Gatwick. Experience so far suggests that, while the machine can be set to detect small quantities of explosive, it gives a high FAR if set to detect amounts less than 1 kg. Since some of the bombs used to destroy aircraft in flight (e.g. Pan Am 103 over Lockerbie in 1988) have contained less than half this amount, further development is needed.

A French company under government sponsorship has developed a fast neutron detector, EDEN, now under test at a number of French airports. This is designed to test twenty checked-in bags per minute. The machine operates two tests which measure different characteristics. If the first test indicates any doubt, the bag is automatically diverted through the second test. The machine analyses both tests and, if there is still any reason for doubt, the bag is further diverted to a belt which delivers it for hand search. Tests indicate a very low FAR but no DP figures were available at the time of writing. Also under development in the USA is the Combined Pulse Neutron X-ray Interrogator (CPNX). This is expected to cost around $1 million and the manufacturers (Oak

Ridge Laboratories, Tennessee) have published encouraging reports of its performance and reliability.

The multiple approach

No existing or potential method of detection is 100 per cent reliable. The best security will therefore come from using many methods, each detecting a different characteristic (e.g. metal, vapour, molecular structure) so that if the gun or bomb gets past one it will be found by one of the others. Where many lives are at stake, as in aviation security (see Chapter 18), this expense is justified. Would-be attackers may also judge that they are likely to fail or be caught, so they will turn away and seek a softer target.

7 Intelligence and the microelectronics revolution

The magnitude of the change

The English word 'intelligence' has at least two distinct meanings: information (about adversaries or likely events), and the faculty of understanding. This chapter is about the first of these, that is operational intelligence for police, military or political purposes; about how the microelectronics revolution can create the second, the faculty of understanding; and about how Artificial Intelligence (AI) can contribute to operational intelligence. Unless otherwise indicated by the context, the word 'intelligence' can be taken to mean operational intelligence rather than the faculty of understanding.

The scale of the changes and potential changes brought into view by the microelectronics revolution can best be illustrated by taking examples of intelligence handling since the late 1970s and looking at the prospects.

In 1977 Dr Hanns-Martin Schleyer, President of Mercedes Benz, was kidnapped in Cologne by terrorists of the Red Army Faction (RAF), who were regarded with disgust by the German public. The police were bombarded with information – 3,826 messages within a few days from members of the public anxious to help. Two of these concerned a small apartment in a nondescript suburb of Cologne, neither of which in itself seemed to have any particular significance. One of them was from a neighbour who reported that this apartment had been rented three weeks earlier by a young couple who paid a month's rent in advance in cash but had only just now moved in; the neighbour rightly thought it unusual for young people to pay cash for a place which they were not going to use for three weeks. The second message, about the same apartment, was that a furniture van had delivered a single large box to it. The police intelligence records were at that time kept in card index and filing systems and, although Schleyer was probably held in that apartment for a week or more, by the time the police had spotted the significance of these reports and the link between them, he had been moved. They missed him by a day.

As a result of this and other terrorist incidents at that time, the German police installed a sophisticated computer system which would have drawn attention to those reports – and especially to the link between them – immediately.

This computerized system led to a series of successes over the next seven years which resulted in numerous arrests and such pressure on the RAF that they were unable to achieve any successful operations (other than stealing enough money to keep alive) until 1985. One of these successes occurred in Frankfurt in 1979. The police had information that an RAF safe house was operating in the city. They deduced that semi-clandestine terrorists would not risk paying bills using cheques or credit card transactions which could be traced; they therefore asked the electricity authority to provide a list of names of all those who had paid their electricity bills in cash. There were 18,000 names. They then approached other organizations (e.g. hire purchase companies) and ran all the names of people paying bills in cash through the computer. Only two of the 18,000 fitted the criterion in every case, and both were clearly paying their bills in false names, so their apartments were raided. One was occupied by a drug-dealer, the other by Rolf Heissler, an RAF terrorist on the wanted list. Heissler obliged by drawing a gun and was arrested.

The traumatic experience in the case of Britain was that of the 'Yorkshire Ripper', Peter Sutcliffe, who brutally murdered thirteen young women in Leeds and neighbouring areas. There was a clear connection between these crimes. Large numbers of police officers obtained vast amounts of information from witnesses and from door-to-door enquiries. During the case, the weight of information on paper reached 24 tons, far beyond the ability of any human being to sift and correlate. Eventually Sutcliffe was caught, largely by luck, in a neighbouring police force area by two quick-witted traffic policemen whose suspicions were aroused when checking his car on some quite unconnected matter.

As a result of public disquiet over this case, the British equivalent of the German system was developed: the Home Office Large and Major Enquiry System (HOLMES), which can within 30 seconds correlate facts whose links would otherwise not be immediately apparent. It has proved particularly useful in solving 'serial crimes' like sequences of rapes or child murders.

In both HOLMES and the German system, however, the decisions are still human. The computer simply makes binary yes-or-no decisions. By taking about 4 million binary decisions in a second, it helps the humans to make their decisions by tirelessly sifting data faster than people could do it, so contributes in efficiency, speed, convenience and economics.

Other systems have been developed for assisting in identification from photographs, for example the Facial Analysis Comparison and Elimination System (FACES). This is based on forty-nine characteristics, each categorized on a 1 to 5 scale. This can be enriched by the 'Photo Retrieval from Optical Disc' (PROD), in which the data are held in digital form and characteristics can be projected pictorially on a screen. As witnesses describe a person they have seen, the picture can be amended – 'No, his mouth was a bit smaller' – until gradually the synthesis from several witnesses takes shape. In due course, this can be compared, both digitally and pictorially, with a small number of pictures of known criminals or terrorists. Positive identification is far more likely to be achieved by these means than by bemusing the witness with a continuous succession of photographs, which experience has shown results in positive identification in only 5 per cent of cases and in an even smaller percentage of convictions.

FACES proved particularly successful in trials in a group of towns around Blackburn in Lancashire, with a population of 250,000, where 82 per cent of the reported crimes in 1986–7 were committed by local criminals. The number of photographs held in police records pictorially or on the computer is of manageable size and can be quickly narrowed down as witnesses eliminate certain characteristics in turn. In due course only a handful remain, from which a positive identification by several witnesses can be made.

These systems are relatively new and there will no doubt be fresh applications and further developments.

Similar developments can be expected in the matching of fingerprints. Currently these are matched better by human beings than by computers, but The Automatic Fingerprint Recognition (AFR) system can link every police force in Britain to a central fingerprint collection. Police records contain some 40 million individual fingerprints and palmprints from 3.5 million people with criminal records. The hope is that it will become possible for detectives at the scene of a crime to feed in a fingerprint on their terminal from which the central AFR system can match it to a shortlist of three or four candidates, after which more detailed analysis and other evidence will in due course provide enough material for an arrest and conviction.

The successors to HOLMES, FACES, AFR, and so on will be built round parallel computer systems in which there may be, say, six computers, each one doing a number of things simultaneously. Such a system can make about 25 million decisions per second and can also make logical inferences (of which more to follow). In the laboratories, and in sight, are massively parallel computers which may be able to handle 25,000 million decisions per second. These will add a qualitative element as well as a quantitative one. They will be thinking machines and certain scientists do believe (and have believed since the earliest days of computers) that they may, within the foreseeable future, be able to rival the human brain in their capabilities – though others doubt if they will ever quite do that.

The computer and the brain

Alan Turing, who invented the computer which broke the apparently impregnable German 'Enigma' code system in 1940–1, forecast that 'within fifty years a machine may be able to fool people that they are talking to a human being', that is, by the early 1990s. We are not quite there yet but Turing may not have been far out.

The human brain, which the computer hopes to match, comprises a huge number of brain cells (neurones) and cell junctions (synapses). There are about 1,000 billion such junctions in each brain. With Turing's computer in the 1940s, relying on thermionic valves and metal grids, a system with 1,000 billion electrical contact points capable of taking binary decisions would have required premises as large as Greater London. The transistor which replaced the valve in the 1960s would have reduced this to the size of the Albert Hall. By 1980 the microchip could have assembled these 1,000 billion within a small room. Microprocessors now in the laboratories should be able to fit them at last into something the size of a human brain.

This does not necessarily mean, however, that they will be able to make all the logical, qualitative, intuitive and emotional judgements that the brain can make – though some believe that one day they may (perhaps in another thirty years?).

The way in which a brain does these things is through its ability to learn by experience. Some of its qualitative powers are built into a brain at birth: a human baby and a kitten both know instinctively that their food comes from a nipple to which they are guided by scent. They are then taught certain skills and judgements by their mothers; others they may teach themselves without knowing precisely why; and others they learn from experience, such as that some things are prickly or taste nasty so that they give them a wide berth.

Environment and artificially imposed experiences can distort the learning process: kittens denied access to their mother and brought up from infancy with a certain species of rodent will never hunt that particular species, though their mother would have taught them to do so if she had been with them.

These learning processes, whether induced by instruction or by experience, seem to come about from the ability of the brain to strengthen the relevant cell junctions (synapses) when a number of experiences pass a certain threshold. In laboratory tests, animals with much simpler brains, such as slugs, have been given access to a plant which has an unpleasant effect. Eating it once does not noticeably change their behaviour but, when the experience has been repeated a number of times, they learn to avoid that plant 'instinctively'. This 'instinct' has in fact been programmed into the electrical contacts in its brain – its memory – by experience. A computer memory can be similarly programmed to learn by experience to an increasing degree each time that experience is repeated. This is the beginning of the process of instructing it to make 'logical inferences'.

The nature and development of the computer

Turing's computer – and indeed every computer – was based, like the brain, on a number of electrical points of contact, each capable of taking a binary decision, that is to close or not to close the circuit. The development of digital computers has been in terms of speed (number of decisions per second) and reduction in size from the conductor grid to the microchip.

The digital principle of selection has been used for more than two centuries, in the form of the punched card machine. The machine is asked, say, to select a person fitting a specific profile. A personnel manager may specify fifteen ideal qualifications for a job, such as (1) under 25, (2) unmarried, (3) in good health, (4) holds a driving licence, (5) speaks fluent French, and so on. Only if the candidates' cards have holes punched to indicate 'Yes' to every one of these fifteen qualifications will the machine put their names forward for consideration. Experience shows that a potential terrorist or criminal may also have a similarly quantifiable profile from which a short list of suspects can be distilled.

The limitation of the card system depended on the number of holes it was possible to punch in a card – the number of bits of information the card could hold. Today a common silicon chip, a few millimetres square, can hold 250,000 bits of information (250 K-bit) and those under development can hold 1 million (1 M-bit).

In essence, the binary decision is made by currents passing along an intersecting grid of conductors and it has only one possible route, when the circuit is closed at one particular intersection, which thus holds one bit of information, like the hole in a punched card. The early computers did comprise a large stack of such grids, until the ever-shrinking microchip took their place.

The principle of this kind of decision is familiar to anyone accustomed to finding a grid reference on a map. A normal map sheet at 100,000 scale, say 50 cm × 100 cm, contains 5,000 squares each 1 cm × 1 cm. A four-figure reference, say 47–23, indicates square number 47 along and 23 up. The eye can then subdivide each square into 10 each way, estimating, say, 6 out of 10 along and 9 out of 10 up – a six-figure reference of 476–239. This fixes a point within 1 millimetre on the map or 100 metres on the ground. On one such sheet there are 500,000 – half a million – different six-figure references, and the limitation is that the eye perusing the map cannot in practice judge differences smaller than one-tenth of the square (1 mm) each way. Experienced map-readers can find a six-figure reference on the map in about two seconds and, in so doing, they are choosing one intersection out of half a million.

This is what a computer does and it does it a good deal faster than the human eye picking out coordinates in this way. It can also be programmed, depending on its yes-no choice from the quarter million on the first 250 K chip, to ask another question and make a choice from the next quarter-million chip, then another, then another. Whether it makes a choice from 4 million (16 × 250 K) or 25,000 million alternatives in a second, the basic nature of its decisions is binary – yes or no – and is made by the intersection of conductors, whether on an old tangible metal grid or a modern microchip, or a linked series of such grids. It is very fast and (provided it is programmed to answer the right question) very reliable; but, as so far described, it is still strictly 'data-based', rather than 'knowledge-based'.

The human brain, even if a little slower and less reliable over automatic data-based decisions, can go a very great deal further than the computer. Reverting to the map squares, human map-readers may not know the exact map reference but they may remember that the place they wanted was, say, just outside a village, after crossing a bridge over a stream, by a road junction; a quick sweep of the eye and – 'Ah, here it is!' People can also judge quality from the map – 'That hill-top should give a fine view of the village. I should be able to pick out the house.'

Taking another example, instead of looking at a map, some people might be looking at a painting on which, without any grid references, they can instantaneously pick out a fieldmouse nibbling at some seeds on the ground; then they can see a cat about to spring out of the bushes at the mouse; then there is a dog coming round the corner and experience tells them that, when the cat jumps out, the dog will be jerked into action and chase the cat. They need no conscious yes-no decisions; they spot the three animals and instantly judge their relationship; in a single glance at the picture as a whole they can predict what is likely to happen, not for certain, but in all probability. An immediate logical inference has been made from a picture which in fact consists of millions of blobs and pinpoints of pigment, each contributing its bit to the story.

Teaching a computer to make logical inferences

The purely data-based computer can be programmed to make a whole series of specific 1-in-250,000 binary choices, each depending on the answer to the last one. To approach the human brain, however, it has to become knowledge-based, that is to make logical inference based on experience. (For the non-professional, the most understandable book on the subject is Yazdani and Narayanan 1984.) Each logical inference is a series of choices, each based on an 'if-then' rule, which lead to a *probable* conclusion, just as a child learns to recognize, say, a duck: 'If it looks like a duck, waddles like a duck, and quacks like a duck then it probably is a duck'; if, however, there are other non-duck-like characteristics – too big, wrong colours, long neck – then on balance the child learns that it is probably not a duck after all, but maybe some kind of a goose. Unlike the simple binary decision this is a muzzy one – a balance of evidence and a probable conclusion. Children of 3 or 4 years old, long before they can explain why in words, can tell the difference between a duck and a goose or between a horse and a cow, or between an Austin Maestro, a Vauxhall Astra and a Volkswagen Golf – even if some mischievous hand has switched over the names, because children can tell the difference before they can read the words.

A computer can similarly be trained to make logical inferences. Each inference may be based on 100 or 1,000 individual machine instructions or binary decisions, some of them grouped into key words or concepts. Current knowledge-based computers can work through 30,000 LIPS (logical inferences per second) each one involving (at 100 to 1,000 each) 3 million to 30 million binary decisions. Coming on stream now are parallel computer systems capable of 200,000 LIPS (that is making 20 million to 200 million binary decisions per second). This is what the human brain is doing, albeit unconsciously.

Such systems are already in use to assist certain commercial processes and medical diagnoses. A diagnosis can often be made from fewer than 500 sequential rules ('Is the pain in your chest?', 'Is it a steady pain?', 'Is it a stabbing pain?') provided that the questions were selected by an expert doctor. A preliminary questionnaire on these lines leading to a conclusion before a consultation can save the doctor a lot of time. A similar set of rules could be applied to a computer interrogation before clients talk to their lawyers. But the idea that a computer system could become a chess grand master is not yet in sight: it is estimated that grand masters have some 50,000 rules in their brain – a far cry from 500 or 1,000.

A computer can be trained to try every possible solution – every permutation and combination in turn – until it finds the best. This can be useful to, for example, tour operators who wish to include thirty places in their itinerary and to pick the route which involves the minimum travelling time. Throughout the process, the computer retains the best so far. If the next is worse, it is rejected; if better, it supplants the reigning champion. For a complicated itinerary the computer can do this far more quickly than a human brain. A computer can also be programmed so that, when it tries something which fails and is rejected, it propagates the error backwards into its programme so that it is avoided next time – as the slug does with the nasty plant.

To supplement the 'if-then' rules, a number of other schemes can be used to assist computers to make logical inferences. Two in particular are worth mentioning: semantic networks (with key words) and frames. Key words have long been an aid used on normal computers: of millions of words recorded on floppy disks by a word processor, a computer can call up every page containing, say, the word 'bomb'. This can be carried further by programming it to link synonyms or associated words – e.g. pub, bar, inn, hotel – or to link concepts or relationships – e.g. Bogotá (as capital of) Colombia.

'Frames' are what psychologists call 'schemata' to represent stereotyped situations. A house, for example, almost always includes certain rooms – kitchen, bathroom, bedrooms, living-rooms. Someone who owns a car will normally have bought a driving licence, a tax disc and an insurance policy, and will buy petrol and tyres from time to time. If one of these is missing, the computer will draw attention to it. It can be programmed to pursue the matter further, acting on incomplete knowledge in much the same way as a person reasons. If it is equipped with a hierarchy of frames, it can do a lot of things a human cannot, or at least can do them more quickly and reliably. Looking further into the future, there is current research into the automation of 'hunches'.

Expert systems for police intelligence

The knowledge-based computer will be a particularly useful tool for police or military intelligence handling. The ability of a computer system to make logical inferences makes it possible for ordinary police officers, not trained in computer technology beyond knowing which keys to press, to have immediate access to an expert system which is able to provide them with judgements and knowledge far wider than they could carry in their own head; it can also prompt them on the questions they should ask. The officers can carry a simple terminal with its keyboard and visual display unit and link it either by radio or with a modem through any telephone to the mainframe computer at police headquarters; better still, they can carry a portable intelligent computer containing a large memory of its own, able to tell them most of what they want without reference to headquarters. There are now such computers, about the size of a pocket book and costing less than £100, whose memory contains information equivalent to that in a 300-page reference book, which people can call up far more quickly than if they had to hunt through an index and 300 pages. If they are equipped with a portable briefcase-sized desktop machine, they can have in their hands information equivalent to that in a thirty-volume *Encyclopaedia Britannica*. If, by any chance, the information is not there, the 'intelligent computer' will tell them so and they can still tap in to their station or force computer and thence, if needed, to the national police computer system.

This gives the police officers the option of making straightforward decisions themselves or, if they wish or in the event of the answers not being clear, to refer the question to a higher level, where there is a more complex system working to more complex rules.

When they arrive at the scene of a crime (e.g. of a murder, kidnap or robbery), they will feed into the headquarters mainframe computer all the evidence they see and obtain from neighbours, and so on. This computer will also, however, have information from other sources, including the past, which human beings will not know or, if they do, the relevance may not strike them. Any linkages between such things as car registration numbers or telephone numbers found in diaries will at once be thrown up by the computer. If it is properly programmed, however, it will also draw attention to linkages with 'shadow events' having no apparent connection, such as a red Ford Cortina hired in a town one hundred miles away. It can do this because of its ability to sift vast amounts of data automatically at lightning speed and spot relationships. The more data which are recorded and the more the computer is capable of logical inference, the more quickly and surely it will build up a meaningful picture, giving clear signposts for further investigation.

Among the leaders in research of the potential of Artificial Intelligence (AI) for acquiring and handling police intelligence against crime and terrorism in 1987 were Chief Superintendent John Hulbert and Superintendent David Webb, the head and deputy head respectively of the Operational Research Department of the Devon and Cornwall Constabulary. Dr Hulbert, with degrees in computer science and psychology, must have been one of the best qualified police officers in his field before his retirement to the commercial world in 1988. David Webb, who also now has a PhD, encapsulated some of their ideas in a presentation to a symposium on International Terrorism at the Office of International Criminal Justice at the University of Illinois in Chicago in August 1987. He took as his theme a quotation from Douglas Hofstadten.

> The aim of AI is to get at what is happening when one's mind silently and invisibly chooses, from a myriad of alternatives, which one makes most sense in a very complex situation. In many real-life situations, deductive reasoning is inappropriate, not because it would give wrong answers, but because there are too many correct but irrelevant statements which can be made; there are just too many things to take into account simultaneously for reasoning alone to be sufficient.

Though still far behind the human brain in other respects, parallel computer systems can simultaneously take account of more factors and inferences, thereby eliminating the need for consideration of whole ranges of enquiry, more quickly and surely than the brain. The process was described on pp. 70–1 in the already familiar context of medical diagnosis. In the field of criminal and anti-terrorist intelligence, this instant elimination of superfluous lines of enquiry can release the human brain from wasted time and exhaustion to concentrate on what it can still do better than the computer.

There is still no substitute in sight for the human expert who (like the diagnostic doctor) feeds into the computer the 'if-then' rules on which its inferencing depends. It is rare, however, for someone who is a leading expert in one field (medical, behavioural, psychological, economic) also to be a trained computer scientist. It is necessary to have a 'knowledge engineer' who acts in effect as an interpreter. They discuss together the line of reasoning, and the knowledge engineer programmes the computer in accordance with the expert's logical sequence of 'if-then' rules and inferences.

The greatest value of the resulting expert system is that it saves future, less expert users from wasting time in proceeding down a cul-de-sac. This has a particularly strong application to police and military intelligence organizations, in which officers' postings change fast. This is healthy in almost every other way: constant input of fresh ideas, new challenges and stimuli preventing staleness and boredom, and building up a breadth of varied experience for senior officers. The price to be paid is that outstanding people often take their expertise with them. Operating an expert system, with the aid of knowledge engineers, they will now be able to revise its programming week by week as their own experience and ideas evolve and new technology develops. Thus, when they leave, the system will have in its memory the best of their expertise on call to their successors. This should provide the best of both worlds.

This may be particularly valuable in such fields as hostage negotiation and prediction of political and security risks. The London Metropolitan police have an outstanding record in hostage negotiating, built up over some years of experience from the Spaghetti House and Balcombe Street sieges in 1975 to the Iranian Embassy siege in 1980 and some other, less spectacular cases. The number of actual cases, however, is relatively small, so every one is likely to contribute a considerable advance in at least some areas. Access to 'state of the art' advice should therefore be instantly available to all when the next emergency arises.

Parallel computer systems should in future enable past predictions of political and security risks to be exhaustively analysed against the way events actually did unfold. Analysis of the factors affecting success or failure of the predictions will be more surely identified and made conveniently available to guide (though not to direct) others in avoiding mistakes in future predictions.

This ability to amass and correlate data at a speed and scale beyond human capability will similarly place a powerful tool in the hand of those searching for a pattern and a *modus operandi* in the data from past terrorist acts and other crimes. The human expert will be able to amend the rules and frames to enable the AI system to decide when certain data and inferences cease to be relevant and to feed in new ones with appropriate weighting. As AI develops, the system will develop a growing capability of learning from its own experience to eradicate error and improve judgement.

Risc

The prospects ahead for computer-aided intelligence may be quite revolutionary as technology develops, particularly in the field of fine-grained parallel computers (Risc). They may at last begin to emulate the brain in its instant recognition capability – spotting a face or picking out a familiar voice in a crowd. The brain clearly uses quite a different system from that used by the present generation of AI systems. The author asked Dr John Hulbert – now managing director of a research and development firm (Cogitaire Ltd) – if he could explain this in terms comprehensible to the non-professional and his reply was so clear that it is repeated here, with his permission, unaltered.

The current AI frame and rule-based systems were extremely power-ful logical analysers, but suffered from the defect that the operation was essentially sequential. This can be improved to a large extent by the application of what is termed coarse-grained parallelism. This essentially means modest numbers of parallel computers, such as the famous 'Transputer' produced by the UK firm Inmos. However, these machines are still essentially sequential (Von Newman machines in the jargon) computers, operating in some degree of co-operation: they naturally increase the power available just by the fact that there are a lot of them. It is however apparent that such an approach will not be totally successful for all aspects of information manipulation.

How does an observer recognize the face of a friend from a glimpse lasting a fraction of a second? Nobody knows for certain; however, answers are beginning to emerge. The well-known '100-step rule' is beginning to have dramatic effects on computer design in the high volume information-processing area. The 100-step rule is based upon some fairly simple arithmetic. It is well known how fast the average neurone in the brain can fire. It is also known how long it takes for complex recognition tasks to be completed by the human being. It only requires secondary school mathematics to work out that each brain computing element can have fired only a small number of times, hence the 100-step rule. This rule essentially says that the human computer cannot have taken more than 100 pro-gramming steps in order to achieve the complex recognition that we all personally experience. Recognition systems in military, police, and other areas involve programmes with millions of lines of code, large amounts of which are used for every recognition event. Obviously therefore some parts of the human brain must approach the recognition problem in a fundamentally different way. This fundamentally different approach is known as fine-grained parallel or neural computing. The essential difference here is that instead of designing parallel computers in terms of hundreds of computing devices, the design objective is to produce parallel computers numbering thousands if not millions on a single board. Each of these computers has a very reduced capability (the technical term is Risc: reduced instruction set computers). However, each of these low Risc machines can be connected to an arbitrarily large number of other computers or neurones (as the researchers in this area tend to call the ultra micro computers), and can affect the behaviour of the other computers to which they are attached. This arrangement is very reminiscent of what we know about the brain, hence the reasons why this research area is redolent with a combination of physiological as well as computer terminology.

This science fiction prospect is nearer than one might imagine. Dramatic advances in the electronics industry have made available at an economic cost facilities which can be used for these new 'neural computers'. This type of facility will be of particular value in sensory systems, systems which have to sift through vast amounts of information in large data banks, and of course within the intelligence community, both military, police, and commercial.

Dr Hulbert stressed in his future prognosis that in the next few years, intelligence systems are likely to incorporate a mixture of the current artificial intelligence paradigms using sequential and moderately parallel computers, with much of the information fed by parallel facilities using the latest neural technology.

The Economist on 14 November 1992 gave an indication of the speed of progress in mircroprocessors. The Californian-based firm Intel invented microprocessors in the early 1970s, with 2,300 transistors on a single microprocessor. Their Pentium model, launched in March 1993, has 3.2 million. Their P7, under development for launching in 1996, is planned to have 15 million.

8 Physical security

Access control

'The strongest castle walls are not proof against a traitor within.' This ancient proverb applies more strongly each year with growing scope for treachery as electronic technology develops. So the control of access and the identification of moles, sleepers, intruders, impersonators, criminals and terrorists have become more crucial than the efficiency of perimeters, surveillance systems and alarms. The main risk is of entry through the front door.

Access control requirements include vetting and selection; control of admission of staff by a guard checking identification or by electronic locks operated by a key card; checking credentials of visitors and contract workers and tying down responsibility for their supervision while they are inside; detecting impersonators and spotting would-be terrorists or criminals, including hijackers, by detecting suspicious personal characteristics or weapons or explosives.

Access and parking of vehicles is equally important. Tagging is the best way, for example with a coded tag on the windscreen, which is read by a surveillance beam, or the tag can be under the vehicle to be read by a coil buried in the roadway. Each tag can be unique, enabling the vehicle's authorization and movement to be recorded and cross checked. The tags can also be used to operate automatic gates or to lower a robust road-blocker which is normally kept raised from the road surface.

The traditional pass or identity card, relying on a photograph, a signature, and sometimes a thumbprint, is no longer good enough for sensitive premises. Watermarks, metallic strands and holograms make forgery more difficult, but none of these provides a reliable guard against impersonation.

In recent years, various forms of machine-readable card have been developed, some passive and some active (i.e. with a power source, transmitting, receiving and processing signals recorded). The simplest passive cards contain a strip of electronically recorded data, as on the familiar key card and credit cards with their black strips. The 'smartcard' is better, incorporating its own microprocessor – a small computer memory activated when the card is placed in the slot of a host computer terminal, in an entrance lobby or checkpoint. Alternatively, authorized persons can be issued with uniquely coded tags, like those for vehicles, clipped to their lapels as an identity badge, and checked by a reading head built into the wall by the door (invisible if necessary), so that they can pass without pausing or putting down what they are carrying. If required, the system can be programmed to record each occasion and the time when someone goes in and out, which could be useful for any subsequent investigations. Active cards or tags, transmitting their own signals and processing signals received, need be no more than 4 mm thick, like the smallest pocket calculator. Passive smartcards, with a lot of data in the memory of their microprocessor, are no bigger than a credit card and some cost less than £2. The simplest machine-readable card system is that now issued on European passports and on a growing number of EC identity cards on which the data can also be read by eye.

Identification and impersonation

International travel by drug smugglers, terrorists and other criminals has become easier, because they can merge into the ever increasing land, sea and air tourist traffic, or among the flow of refugees and illegal immigrants. The wealth now acquired by terrorist movements (especially from the Middle East) and by narcotic and other criminal gangs enables them to travel at will. Due largely to the political and economic turmoil in eastern Europe, nearly half a million refugees entered Germany alone in 1992. Not all of these will have been as genuine and innocent as they seemed.

On 1 January 1993 the EC opened its internal frontiers. Though external borders have been strengthened, it is not difficult to find ways across the thousands of miles of rocky coastlines, forests and mountains which make up most of these borders. Once in the EC, illegal visitors are able to move freely between the twelve member countries to dodge the attention of national police forces.

It is therefore highly desirable for police, immigration and customs officials to be able to check anyone's identity anywhere, any time, and to detect impersonation. In a free society, people do not have any need to conceal their identity from a police officer unless they have done or mean to do something illegal; they certainly have no right to impersonate someone else. The ability to check identity will contribute not only to combating terrorism, drug trafficking and international crime, but also to curbing the growing wave of ordinary crime – assault, rape, robbery, theft and fraud.

Aviation security depends on access control, identification of passengers and reconciliation with their baggage, and on the detection of guns and explosives. The application of technology for these purposes will be discussed more fully in Chapter 18.

Thirty countries of the world, including Germany, Ireland, the UK and the USA, now issue machine-readable passports (MRPs). These carry standardized data agreed by the UN's International Civil Aviation Organization (ICAO) and the International Standardization Organization (ISO). MRPs contain both the normal photograph and two lines of machine-readable data – name, date of birth and passport number with expiry date. This is sufficient to refer to the national police computer (NPC) from any police checkpoint to check that the holder has no restriction on movement. These data are in normal lettering (optical character reading – OCR) which the holder can read as easily as the machine can. There is space for the issuing country to add any other data it wishes (e.g. national insurance number) but this too would be in OCR lettering for the holder to read. There are no other data, secret or otherwise.

Germany issues machine-readable visas (MRVs) on the same system and others will follow suit. The Germans also have machine-readable identity cards (MRIs) and the Dutch will have them by 1995. Seven other EC countries have ID cards, but not yet machine-readable ones. The British, Danes and Irish have no ID cards at all.

The fact that the German MRP, MRI and MRV can activate the NCP does not, however, prove that the person presenting it is its lawful owner. In the airport context, the Dutch (at Amsterdam-Schiphol) and the Germans (at Frankfurt) are testing the use of biometric data, which give a far more reliable identification than any photograph. The trials have so far been open only to volunteers – mainly business people who travel regularly through that airport – who then get 'fast stream' access through automated gates for embarkation and disembarkation, instead of having to wait in the queue. This also releases airport security staff to concentrate their attention on passengers more likely to pose a threat. If successful, this system could be applied to all EC airports and more widely still, with enormous benefits to security and to the convenience of the travelling public. These two experiments and their potential extension are more fully described in Chapter 18. Similar trials have begun in Newark Airport, USA. Biometric data are also used by some corporations to restrict access to sensitive areas; staff members often welcome it and are proud to be on the access list.

Biometric cards are cheap, reliable and quick to use. There is a choice of data suitable for preventing impersonation. The most commonly used are finger-prints or hand geometry. The data can be recorded digitally on the card and/or on the computer memory. Recording it – 'enrolment' – takes only about half a minute. Once enrolled in this way, cardholders place the hand or finger on a scanner and their card in the slot. If the two match, the gate will open automatically in a second or two. The data, in fact, need not be on the card at all if the owner has an MRI, since the OCR data on this can call up the data to match the hand on the scanner, which again takes only a few seconds. This is the method being used in the Frankfurt trial, and is even more reliable, since imposters could not get their hand geometry data on the computer, though they could conceivably get it recorded on a forged card.

To allay any public anxiety about hand geometry recording, the Frankfurt system records only a limited number of characteristics, enough to give the match needed, but not enough to enable the print to be reconstructed, nor to be matched with any fingerprint data which may be held on normal police files.

Having tried fingerprints and hand geometry, both Schipol and Frankfurt have opted for hand geometry. Both are equally simple: the finger or hand is placed on a scanner and matched to the data on the card or in the computer in a few seconds. The hand geometry is more difficult to forge (e.g. with a plaster cast) than a fingerprint. It is also more user-friendly.

Retina reading is used by some corporations and is reputedly as reliable, but there is some consumer resistance to having an infra-red gun aimed point blank into the eye.

Voice matching can be used to control sensitive access for a limited number of staff for whom a choice of words for matching is recorded on the computer. The same applies to signature dynamics.

The vein pattern on the back of the hand or wrist can be as quickly read by a diode as the bar-code on a bottle of sauce in a supermarket, but the veins are not parallel so they must be read in two dimensions, like a map, and further development is needed. If successful, this could be the most user-friendly of all.

DNA molecules – 'genetic fingerprints' – are unique and reliable, but matching needs a laboratory test, so this is unsuitable for instant access control.

Biometric smartcards or databanks are much more reliable than a guard looking at a photograph on a passport or ID card; they can operate access gates automatically with only the lightest supervision, releasing security personnel for more serious threats. In the face of growing violence, drug trafficking and other crime, we can really no longer afford the emotional prejudice against citizens having to be identifiable, as they are in most other EC countries.

Perimeter security, surveillance and alarm systems

No barrier, surveillance or alarm system can provide 100 per cent security. The best that a security system can offer is concentric rings of protection, each of which detects and delays intruders and which, collectively, may present enough visible and perceived hurdles to deter them from attempting to break the system at all.

The outer concentric rings are procedural, including selection and vetting of staff, location and design of buildings (security advice at that stage can avoid expensive and often insoluble problems later), training of staff, and active liaison with the police. Access control at authorized points of entry, aided by reliable means of identification and technical aids, have been discussed earlier in the chapter: they are the most important of all security measures.

The biggest problem in perimeter security, in both outer and inner concentric rings, is the false alarm rate (FAR). Police records show that 98 per cent of automatic burglar alarm calls have been false. As well as wasting time and money, a high FAR dulls the alertness and response of staff and produces dangerous complacency. The astounding story of the intruder who got into the Queen's bedroom at Buckingham Palace early one morning gave an awesome warning. A passing policeman happened to see him jumping from the wall and reported it, but his report was ignored. The intruder jumped over an 'impregnable' beam, triggered two other alarms (both quickly dismissed as false) and was finally seen in the corridors (staff assuming that he must be an authorized maintenance man). The Queen had to keep him talking on the edge of her bed for some time before help came. No one believed it could happen.

The outer physical concentric ring, that is the perimeter fence (barbed or razor wire, chain link, or solid wall with wire on top), will impose no more than a few minutes' delay, when the intruder may be observed by human, canine, electrical or electronic eyes. Dogs are probably the best, but for an airfield with a ten-mile perimeter a large number would be needed. Where there are long straight lengths of fence on level ground, narrow line-of-sight beam coverage is practicable, but there may be false alarms from animals or large birds. Patrols by security guards require good lighting – effective (especially as a deterrent) but expensive. There are various alarms which rely on changes in the tension of the wires between special fence posts. The problem of tensions changing with temperature variations (very large in a hot continental climate) can be overcome by building in a system which eliminates such gradual changes and reacts only when they are abrupt.

Another method is for two of the fence wires to radiate and create a capacitance field between them. When any foreign body enters this field, the alarm is triggered. The limit of length of these wires is usually about 200 metres but the Canadian Sentrax system, for example, incorporates a controller which can read and analyse 32 lengths each of 150 metres – a perimeter of more than 3 miles.

A variant of this system is for the radiating cables to be buried, up to 9 inches deep and about 5 feet apart, arranged so that anything passing over the ground above them triggers the alarm. This, for economic and maintenance reasons, is usually more suitable for inner perimeters round key points (e.g. a pumping station, main switchboard or computer centre) rather than for a long outer perimeter.

The innermost ring for key points will be robust walls and doors and windows, possibly using bullet-proof glass or Kevlar screens.

Closed circuit television (CCTV) is widely used but to be effective it is expensive in personnel. No one can remain alert enough to be sure of spotting movement for more than about ten or fifteen minutes on end, and even then the boredom is such that there is a risk of its being missed. There are various means whereby the system can be made to react to movement automatically but these usually have a high FAR because, for example, strong winds may cause trees and bushes to move or, by turning up the underside of the leaves, can change the light pattern enough to trigger the alarm.

Volumetric alarm systems using radar or infra-red transmissions can detect intruders either in the open or within a designated area indoors. There are some free-standing models, each with its own power and radio link. One successful application of this is to dispense a number of such units on the tarmac where aircraft are parked.

Pilkington have developed an alarm system based on fibre optics, which is triggered only if an optical fibre is actually broken, which should have a low FAR. They also have a covert version in which the fibres are buried and react to pressure without being broken.

Generally, however, progress in perimeter surveillance and alarm systems has been less dramatic than in, for example, computerized intelligence analysis and collation, vapour detection and neutron bombardment (discussed in earlier chapters) and seems likely to remain so. The biggest challenge is to provide an economic system with a low

FAR: large rewards should come to the firm which makes the first practical and significant breakthrough in this field. Meanwhile, and still thereafter, the best security will be achieved by presenting the intruder with a succession of many hurdles to jump, some not easily recognizable as a hurdle, each one in itself cheap and simple, and with a combination of automatic and human responses. With reasonable luck and an alert staff, the intruder should trip up on at least one of them.

Travel and VIP security

The most vulnerable time for VIPs is when they are travelling, and especially on regular journeys between home and work. The most effective protection is procedural, that is making it difficult for the would-be assassin or kidnapper to predict their routes and times of travel, or to recognize their cars, that is to maintain a low and unpredictable profile. It may well be better to travel inconspicuously in a junior-level company car, frequently changed, than in an armoured VIP limousine which will be easier for terrorists to recognize. These aspects are discussed more fully in Chapter 17.

Vehicle armour obviously gives some protection but if terrorists know that it is armoured they can employ a big enough weapon to pierce it (see Chapter 5). Other aids will include internal and simultaneous locking of doors and windows, two-way radio, alarms, tracking systems and smoke projectors. Robust construction and bumpers will assist escape from an ambush, given an expertly trained driver. No major technological development is likely, however, which will defeat a well-planned attack in strength using heavy enough weapons. The root of the danger is the stricture of being on the road.

The prime targets – presidents, ministers and chief executives of very large corporations – can often travel by helicopter from within one defended landing zone to another, travelling by road only in well-populated areas and where heavy protection can be given for a short distance. But this can be only for very few.

The development of microlite and of short (STOL) and vertical take-off and landing (VTOL) aircraft offers a ray of hope for widening the scope for local door-to-door air travel. (This is further discussed in Chapter 17.)

Part III

Drugs, political violence and crime

9 Cocaine

The narcotic supply chain

The cultivation, processing, transport and distribution of narcotics is probably the greatest single generator of political violence and crime in the world. Its profits are used to finance and arm rural guerrillas, urban terrorists and criminal gangs; also to facilitate the trade by intimidation and corruption and by keeping the army and police away. In certain countries it is now a far more potent motivator of terrorism than Marxist ideology or religious fundamentalism. In some of these it dominates the national economy and governments govern by its leave. Almost all of this is ultimately financed by the money extracted from drug addicts on the streets of the western world, so this is where the problem must be tackled.

There is a small, lawful production of narcotics for medical purposes – e.g. cocaine as an anaesthetic, morphine processed from opium – but this can be tightly controlled and is quite insignificant in relation to the quantity of drugs used illegally.

The annual world profits from drug trafficking have averaged about $300 billion; there has been an estimated rise of 10–15 per cent per year and possibly a great deal more than this. Precise estimates are difficult because, if traffickers are blocked in one area, they switch to another. This could prove to be the most dangerous of all the threats to the democratic way of life in both rich and poor countries. The cocaine trail permeates and poisons the societies of the main producing countries (Bolivia, Peru and Colombia), through the transit areas (mainly in the Caribbean and Mexico) to Florida and thence to the rest of the USA and Europe. The peasants who cultivate the coca get a price sufficiently attractive for them to resist any attempt to force them to grow other crops instead, and in this they are assisted by guerrilla movements who gain their support by protecting them from the army. The growers' price is, however, only a fraction of the pickings of the traffickers and dealers on the way, and of the street value. The whole process is organized by huge international drug 'corporations' based mainly in Colombia and the USA, where a new narcotics millionaire is created every day.

A similar situation prevails over the heroin trail in Asia, which will be discussed in Chapter 10.

Bolivia

One-third of the world's supply of cocaine comes from Bolivia, where coca production is not illegal. Its cocaine trade is officially estimated at $3.6 billion. This amounts to ten times as much as all the legal exports put together, so no one need be surprised that Bolivian governments have sometimes seemed to be half-hearted in their determination to stamp it out. Coca plants are hardy and not generally susceptible to herbicides. The only effective one is Tebuthurion, known as Spike, but environmentalists point out that it also seriously damages other plant and animal life, and might also damage human health; thus far, it has been used only for brush clearance on land not destined to grow crops in the USA. Cutting back the coca plant acts as pruning and enhances future yield. The growers deter spraying by growing alternate rows of coca and other plants. It is very time-consuming to dig out coca roots in remote areas not easily accessible to mechanical plant. Moreover, 23,000 Bolivian peasants and their families depend for their livelihood on 60,000 acres of coca cultivation. Their rural dwellings are basic so they can easily move – as they have done when soldiers have been sent in to uproot their plants – whereafter they have been that much more hostile to government and welcoming to anti-government guerrillas. Political pressure and aid from the USA to promote crop substitution has some effect but will never cure the problem. Most of the Bolivian coca goes to Colombia for processing, though an increasing amount is going out through Paraguay, Brazil and Argentina.

Peru

Peru grows 50 per cent of the world's coca plant, the main centre being in the Huallaga valley on the eastern side of the Andes Mountains, some 250 miles north-east of Lima. From here it is transported, mainly in light aircraft from tiny, often temporary, airstrips, to Colombia, where the main processing plants are located. Though Peru is not as dependent on coca as Bolivia, coca still makes up about 50 per cent of Peru's exports.

As in Bolivia, coca is by far the most profitable crop which peasants can grow wherever the soil and climate are suitable. In response to the demand from addicts in the west and encouragement from the drug barons, the area under coca cultivation in the Huallaga Valley increased tenfold between 1970 and 1985. Attempts to induce Peruvian peasants to co-operate in crop substitution have, not surprisingly, met with no more success than in Bolivia. The drug barons employ armed gangs to encourage this resistance and the drug traffickers provide money and arms for one of the most fanatical terrorist movements in the world, *Sendero Luminoso* (SL, the Shining Path), which will be described more fully in Chapter 12. SL not only keeps the army and police tied up, but also reacts violently to any attempt by government forces or agencies to dig up the coca or encourage crop substitution.

One of the problems is the ambivalent attitude of some of the army and police officers. If they turn a blind eye to the growing of coca and its conversion on the farms to the transportable paste base for cocaine, the *campesinos* (peasants) will be more ready to co-operate in getting rid of the terrorists, whom they greatly fear. So the officers get credit for making progress against SL. Moreover, their pay is dismally low, so they are prey to corruption.

It was estimated in 1993 that one light aircraft could carry coca paste worth about $300,000, of which the drug barons were willing to pay a fee of $20,000 for each flight out of an airstrip prepared and secured by SL. There were more than twenty flights per day, so this could bring SL an income of up to half a million dollars a day or over $100 million in a year. With big money like this available, there was a strong temptation for a corrupt official, police officer or soldier to ask a similar fee for the use of a municipal or military airstrip. The drug barons were, of course, happy to pay this because, once he had accepted their money, the officer was in thrall to them for blackmail. For junior officers earning $100 a month this was good business – and they could salvage their conscience with the thought that otherwise SL would get the money, both swelling their funds and developing their three-cornered relationship with the drug traffickers and the *campesinos*.

The capture in September 1992 of Dr Abimael Guzman, the founder and leader of SL, did not have an immediate effect on drug trafficking, as he had shifted his focus to Lima, delegating much autonomy to his provincial leaders. And there was growing disaffection among army officers because of the government's failure to improve their pay.

Colombia

While some of the coca paste is processed in Bolivia and Peru, the majority goes north into Colombia for refinement into cocaine. This is very big business indeed run by two cartels, based in Medellin and Cali. The Medellin cartel was dominant but began to split and 1992 and its leader, Pablo Escobar, was killed in December 1993 (see p. 92). The better organized Cali cartel quickly seized the lion's share of the market.

The leaders of these drug cartels exercise an enormous influence on the whole fabric of Colombian government, business and journalism, and on terrorism and crime. Due in great part to the huge inflow of drug money, Colombia has one of the healthiest balance of payments figures in the world. It has, at the same time, one of the strongest democratic traditions in Latin America and, for many of its people, a good life. On the other hand, Colombia has an appalling history of violent crime, with by far the highest kidnap rate in the world. In the long run, the power of the drug barons is such that the country *could* fall completely under their control, with government and industry subservient to them.

The production of coca in Colombia itself, as in Bolivia and Peru, has been increasing but Colombia's really big business comes from the refining and marketing of the crops from all three countries. Though the price is falling, the output is rising.

The scale of the problem was illustrated by a helicopter raid by the Colombian police on a coca-refining plant on the Yari River, 700 miles south of Bogotá, in March 1984. After a two-hour battle they secured the perimeter and then repulsed a counter-attack by an estimated force of one hundred men from a jungle guerrilla base nearby. The plant consisted of forty-four buildings and other structures, ten cocaine-processing laboratories, seven aircraft with a runway equipped for night landings and six months' supply of food for eighty people. The police seized 13.8 tons of cocaine, with a street value of $1.2 billion. But even this, the biggest cocaine seizure in history, was a mere drop in the ocean.

As in Peru, the expansion of the cocaine industry in Colombia was closely linked with the growth of political terrorist movements, and especially of FARC, whose organization and techniques are examined more fully in Chapter 12. FARC was founded in 1966 and was making no great political impact until the end of the 1970s, when it began to raise a 10 per cent levy on peasants growing coca in exchange for 'protection' from the police and military. This was estimated to produce a revenue of about $40 million per year. The big drug rings saw huge profits in keeping the government out and the movement grew rapidly under their patronage. In May 1984 (shortly after the Yari River raid described above), FARC and two other movements, M19 and EPL, signed a truce with the government, but there were suspicions that this was as much a live-and-let-live agreement as a cease-fire, and drug-running seemed to continue unabated. M19 and EPL soon dropped out of the truce. FARC continued to observe it to some extent, though not at the expense of the continued flow of cocaine and the prosperity of the Medellin drug rings with whom FARC have a good working relationship for mutual benefit. Medellin is totally dominated by the drug trade and there are few of its inhabitants, police officers included, who do not have some family links with people involved in it. As in any community involved in big money crime, there are many gang murders. The homicide rate per thousand is reputed to be three times as high as anywhere else in the world: one murder every three hours in a city with a population of about 1 million.

Up till 1992, the leaders of the cartels lived like robber barons, moving freely between heavily guarded ranches and alternative bases in suburban areas where they could rely on the population to give warning of police operations. They had ample money both for guards and for bribing politicians, judges, police officers and other officials, which only the most courageous dared refuse, because they knew that the next stage would be intimidation and, if that failed, murder or kidnap of themselves or their families. It was said that judges had to choose between silver and lead: most chose silver.

The barons also used their wealth to cultivate a Robin Hood image. In Medellin, for example, they owned one of the leading football teams; they provided other sports grounds with lighting systems and they financed hospitals and schools. They were also major employers. In some places the government would have been very unpopular if it had acted too firmly against them.

On 18 August 1989 the drug Mafia made what may well prove to have been their greatest mistake, when they murdered Luis Carlos Galan, the potential presidential candidate to succeed President Barco. Galan was a popular leader and there was a surge of public support for an intensive crackdown by the government on the drug barons. Large numbers of the Medellin and Cali cartels were arrested and their bases, laboratories and aircraft seized. President Barco reinstated the procedures for extradition to the USA, which was particularly feared by the drug barons. On 15 December 1989 one of the three most wanted leaders of the Medellin cartel, José Gonzales Rodriguez Gacha, and his son were killed when police raiding his ranch pursued them by helicopter as they tried to escape in a truck and shot them.

On 27 May 1990 Galan's replacement as Liberal candidate, Cesar Gaviria, was elected President. He took office on 7 August and continued the campaign vigorously. On 22 November 'the Extraditables', an association of drug barons who were liable to extradition, offered a cease-fire during the constituent assembly elections in December and for

200–300 senior drug traffickers to surrender if President Gaviria would undertake not to extradite them to the USA. The government agreed to this on condition that they confessed to some of their crimes and served sentences for these in Colombia. In January and February 1991 another three of the most wanted leaders – the Ochoa brothers – surrendered on these terms. After long and highly publicized negotiations through intermediaries, the most wanted of all the Medellin leaders, Pablo Escobar, surrendered on 19 June and was incarcerated in a specially constructed prison after the constituent assembly had voted to end the extradition of drug traffickers. It seemed to be a fair compromise.

In the security of his 'prison' Escobar lived the life of a millionaire, surrounded by his aides (fellow prisoners) and prison staff doubling up as servants. Through visitors he was able to continue to direct the Medellin cartel and, above all, to arrange for the murder of a number of his rivals. His surrender may, in fact, have been because he himself feared assassination, and preferred to eliminate his rivals from a secure base. He was no doubt confident that he would be able to escape when it suited him and, in July 1992, after a little over a year in captivity, he did so, along with his colleagues and aides. He continued to direct the cartel's drug and terrorist operations, probably from a secure base in one of the poorer suburbs of Medellin where he could rely on the population.

Escobar resumed terrorist operations with increasing violence for sixteen months until he was killed by police in a gun battle in Medellin on 2 December 1993 at the age of 44. At his peak in 1989, *Forbes Magazine* estimated his wealth at £3 billion and he was alleged to be responsible for the deaths of over 1000 civilians and 500 police. He was, however, regarded as a hero by many of the poorer people in Medellin. His drug trafficking drew in most of the region's wealth from the USA and Europe and they benefited from it. The Cali cartel will seek to satisfy the rich world's demand for cocaine in a less violent and more businesslike way.

Central America, the Caribbean and Florida

Across the Caribbean and the Gulf of Mexico the cocaine has traditionally gone mainly to Florida, though the activities of the US Drug Enforcement Administration (DEA) have forced more of it to go directly to other distribution points stretching from New Mexico to Maryland. The primary market-place is unquestionably Miami.

The Panama–Colombia border is only 150 miles from Medellin, and Panama has been a staging post both for drugs and for laundering money. As long ago as 1983, a light aircraft about to take off from Miami for Panama was found to contain $5 million in cash. Further investigation revealed that this one aircraft had carried over $150 million to Panama over an eight-month period.

Panama was, until 1989, under the dictatorship of General Noriega, who had long had links with the drug trade and had cleverly used his contacts to gain acceptance by the CIA as a source of information while continuing to make huge sums from it. In May 1989, under US pressure, he held a general election monitored by a team of international observers which reported that the opposition candidate, Guillermo Endara, had comfortably won, upon which Noriega declared the election void. The USA, which had by treaty a garrison on the canal, flew in extra troops and installed Endara as President. Noriega was arrested to face charges for drug and other offences and sentenced to a long term of imprisonment in the USA. Drug traffic, however, continued across the mountainous Colombian frontier and so did money laundering.

Mexico is the home of large-scale wholesale brokers for cocaine from Colombia, and the business brings about $1.25 billion a year into the Mexican economy. Most of this is illegal money, which provides ample means of corrupting government officials, fuels inflation and destabilizes the economy. Yet Mexico, like Bolivia and Colombia, is now so addicted to this money that there would probably be even greater disruption if the flow were suddenly cut off. Mexico is also heavily involved in producing and smuggling heroin into the USA (see Chapter 10).

Cuba, under a 1979 agreement negotiated with a Colombian emissary from M19, has sometimes provided transhipment facilities for cocaine at a charge of $500,000 per ship. Ships from Colombia would hoist the Cuban flag in international waters and on reaching Cuban waters would tranship their loads to small fast motorboats from Florida or the Bahamas, which would quickly transport the loads to any one of numerous beaches and inlets on the Florida coast, a mere 90 miles away. Geographically, Cuba is ideally placed for this, and was happy both to gain hard currency and to help to destabilize US society but, probably for political reasons (i.e. the image she wishes to present to the world) she had never played more than a minor and discreet role in the gigantic capitalist enterprise of drug trafficking.

Jamaica, however, provides a major transit route, with forty registered and thirty unregistered airstrips. The traffickers have become adept at filing legitimate flight plans and then diverting en route. After clearing US customs in Puerto Rico, for example, an aircraft diverts to an unregistered airstrip on one of the many other Caribbean islands to load drugs and continue its journey to the USA.

The administration of the tiny Turks and Caicos Islands has in the past succumbed to the bribes of the traffickers and in 1985 the Chief Minister, Norman Saunders, and two senior officials were arrested in Miami and convicted of participating in drug smuggling through its airstrips to the USA. Within a year, the British government removed his successor and took over direct rule of the Islands.

The Bahamas are even closer to Florida and, with a mass of islands and numerous harbours and airstrips, provide another ideal transhipment area, particularly from light aircraft to speedboats for the final dash to the Florida coast. The DEA has estimated that the value of drugs shipped through the Bahamas runs into many billions of dollars each year.

The DEA admits that only about 1 per cent of the 18,000 illegal flights in the USA each year are stopped and a similar percentage probably applies to speedboats and other means of smuggling. This traffic probably comprises Florida's largest single industry, with a turnover estimated at $15 billion a year. One Colombian businessman, for example, took a commission of 2 per cent for delivering US dollars in Miami and writing cheques in pesos, which could be cashed with little risk in Colombia. During the eight months before he was caught $242 million had passed through his bank account in Miami. With banking regulations only loosely enforced, and a huge Caribbean and Latin American immigrant population, laundering of money is big business in Florida.

10 Heroin and hashish

Opium and heroin

Heroin is more addictive and more damaging than cocaine. It is produced by processing opium poppies – ten tons of opium produces one ton of heroin. There have at last been a few encouraging developments. In Britain, for example, the number of new addicts registering with the authorities has declined and heroin seizures have fallen. Nevertheless, not too much weight should be given to this as not all addicts register and the seizures are only a small percentage of the drugs actually smuggled into Britain.

There are two main areas of opium production: the Golden Triangle (Myanmar, Laos and Thailand) and the Golden Crescent (Iran, Afghanistan and Pakistan). As was described for cocaine in Chapter 9, there is a well-developed chain for processing, trafficking and marketing, leading primarily to the affluent streets of the west, in which Hong Kong and Lebanon both play key roles. Over the years, the Golden Triangle and the Golden Crescent have each produced about half the world's opium and heroin.

The Golden Triangle

Myanmar is the world's largest single source of opium, producing 80 per cent of the Golden Triangle's output. This is grown mainly in areas outside government control, because a large part of the country, especially that in the north and east occupied by the Kachin and Shan peoples, is controlled by large insurgent armies or warlords. The Burmese Communist Party (BCP), 10,000 strong, operates in the northeast of the country along the Chinese border, having strong links with China. Another ten insurgent organizations, of which the largest is the Kachin Independence Army, form the National Democratic Front

(NDF) with a total strength of 17,000. Mayanmar's most powerful warlord, Khun Sa, has a private army of 2,000 (he says it is 8,000) and controls a large part of the border with Thailand, including the drug traffic across it. He claimed in a press interview that he makes $8 million a year from this.

The drug business was originally built up to finance these armies, particularly those of the BCP and Khun Sa. None of the hill tribes has ever accepted Rangoon's authority since Mayanmar's independence in 1948. Now opium cultivation and trading has become the main purpose for some of them, and they have become extremely wealthy and well armed – much more so than the government army of 170,000, which is very unlikely to gain control of the insurgent areas other than the main towns and the roads between them.

The government has attempted to curb opium production by military operations and by aerial spraying, but this has had only limited success, and has naturally had a very hostile reception from the inhabitants. So long as the demand for opium and heroin persists, the opium growers of Mayanmar will meet it.

In Laos the cultivation of opium poppies was officially banned in 1975 but government control of the rural areas is tenuous; the country is so poor that the government is suspected of quietly encouraging opium production in order to help the economy. Laos produced about 150 tonnes of opium per year.

In Thailand the government has welcomed international assistance in cutting opium cultivation, and production was down to 15 tonnes in 1988, most of this being produced in inaccessible country along Myanmar's border, which is virtually outside government control. In February 1988 the Thais reported the seizure of 1.3 tonnes of high-quality heroin consigned from Bangkok to the USA, with a street value of about $2 billion. This was hailed as one of the largest heroin seizures ever, but it amounted to only about 1 per cent of the heroin produced each year in the Golden Triangle, of which about 75 per cent probably passes through Thailand.

From the Golden Triangle, the drugs are transported through China, Vietnam, Malaysia, Indonesia and Hong Kong. Addiction in all of these countries takes some of it on the way, but most of it is destined for Europe and the USA. In February 1988 seven small statues sent from Thailand to Chicago were found to contain heroin to the value of $1.8 billion and another $1.8 billion consignment was found by Chinese customs officials in Shanghai en route from Hong Kong to San Francisco. Malaysia has some 180,000 addicts of its own, consuming between 4 and 5 tonnes of heroin a year. Another 4 tonnes are smuggled through the country. Mandatory death sentences (so far carried out over sixty times) have been a deterrent to drug smugglers, but this tends to catch only the couriers, not the big dealers.

Hong Kong has 45,000 addicts, but it is also a major transit route to the western world. Hong Kong has some fifty triad secret societies with a membership of 300,000; their tentacles extend to Europe, where they control a large part of the heroin trade. Because of pressure by the Royal Hong Kong Police, some of the big drug dealers and traffickers have moved to Thailand and northern Europe and this drift can be expected to continue as the return of Chinese sovereignty over Hong Kong approaches in 1997. There are also well-established contacts between the triad societies and international criminal networks, including the US Mafia and the Yakusa gangs in Japan.

For the present, however, Hong Kong still provides an ideal transit area for heroin. Most of it comes in fishing boats and small coasters from Thailand. On an average day there are about 5,000 boats in Hong Kong harbour, and many are turned round in a few hours. The triad network is adept at altering shipping manifestos so that goods concealing heroin do not appear to have come from suspect countries. It has been estimated that the triads collect protection money from 80 per cent of Chinese businessmen in Hong Kong. They also monopolize gambling, and a common technique is to trap gamblers into debts which they cannot repay except – under threat to their lives – by serving them as heroin smugglers. The triad societies probably now provide about 50 per cent of the heroin consumed in the USA and an even higher proportion in Europe, where Amsterdam is a major distribution centre through its Chinese community of 20,000. As an illustration of the scale of the problem in the USA, 838 lb of heroin (90 per cent pure) was seized in Queens, a suburb of New York City, in February 1989, concealed in a consignment of wheelbarrow tyres. It was valued at $1,000 million and would have supplied 200,000 addicts for six months. There were simultaneous arrests of seventeen people in New York and nine in Hong Kong.

Hong Kong is also a major centre for laundering money: some of the banks are reluctant to co-operate in enforcing the British and US laws enacted in 1987 for seizing assets and authorizing police access to bank accounts where there is a prima-facie case that they may contain money acquired by criminal means. Hong Kong is a huge financial centre, handling some 40 per cent of the flow of foreign exchange into China, so it abounds with international banks and trading, shipping and insurance agents, giving enormous opportunities to conceal unlawful transactions. China is likely to maintain Hong Kong as an international

financial and trading centre in its own interests, so these opportunities
may remain after 1997.

The Golden Crescent

The Golden Crescent produces as much opium as the Golden Triangle,
but less of it is consumed locally than in the Far East. Most of its exports
are shipped through Pakistan.

Afghanistan became the main opium producer in the Golden Crescent,
and its production may have overtaken that of Myanmar. This resulted
from the urgent need of the rival *mujahideen* groups to finance their
guerrilla campaigns, both during and since the Soviet occupation (see
Chapter 13). This is likely to continue.

Opium production in Iran is also centred on the traditional insurgent
areas of Kurdistan and Azerbaijan, bordering Turkey, Iraq, and the
former Soviet Union.

Pakistan plays a role in the heroin trade similar to that of Colombia
with cocaine. Again, the cultivation of opium is mainly in the remote
areas of the North-West Frontier bordering Afghanistan, where no
government, including that of the British Viceroys, has ever maintained
permanent control. Tribal leaders have a great deal of autonomy, and
government incursions can only take the form of strong military
columns, which seldom venture far from the roads. The growing of
opium and, more important, its processing to produce morphine and
heroin have always produced a large slice of local income and made it
possible for the tribesmen to be well armed. The increasing use of
helicopters by government forces will result in their needing ever more
money to buy expensive surface-to-air missiles.

Opium production in Pakistan was 800 tonnes in 1979. A government ban on opium cultivation coupled with a severe drought in 1980
reduced this to 60 tonnes in 1983 but by 1986 it had risen again to
between 100 and 160 tonnes. In October 1986 the government enacted
harsher laws, imposing sentences of from seven years to death for
cultivation of opium and life imprisonment for the use, sale or
smuggling of narcotics. The government is also co-operating fully with
the UN Fund for Drug Abuse Control (UNFDAC) in crop-substitution
programmes. As elsewhere, aerial spraying arouses intense hostility
among the tribesmen and, as they are heavily armed, this can be
extremely hazardous. Up till now, both the opium-heroin business and
the tribal insurgencies have been supported by the Kabul government
because of the Pakistanis' harbouring of mujahideen bases amongst the
millions of Afghan refugees.

Despite the Pakistani government's determined efforts to combat opium and heroin production, the demand at the two ends of the chain – for heroin by the addicts of the USA and Europe and for money for arms by the dissident tribesmen in the North-West Frontier Province – is going to be difficult to eradicate.

Lebanon, Syria and West Africa

Lebanon is a major transit route for Asian opium and heroin, for refining heroin and cocaine and for producing both hashish (cannabis) and opium in its own right. The drug trade in Lebanon is not new. Soon after the Second World War the Italian Mafia set up heroin-refining laboratories in the Beka'a Valley to process opium from Iran and Turkey. The start of the civil war in 1975, with Christian and Muslim militias fighting each other and the Palestinians, set in motion the drugs–money–arms cycle.

Syria has thus far made only half-hearted efforts to deal with the widespread and blatant cultivation of opium and hashish since her army moved into the Beka'a Valley in force in response to the Israeli invasion in 1982; they have done very little better since extending their military control over much of the remainder of Lebanon in 1987. About 80 per cent of land in the Beka'a Valley is now believed to be under cultivation of opium and hashish. Hashish production is at least 700 tonnes, valued at $100 million, and may be as high as 2,000 tonnes. There is virtually no interference with its cultivation and export.

The Islamic fundamentalist Hezbollah was sponsored and trained by the 1,000 Iranian Revolutionary Guards who have been based with the Syrian Army in the Beka'a Valley since 1982. Hezbollah justify their participation in the drug trade as a means, not only of financing their terrorism, but also of furthering the advance of Islam by fostering the weakening of western societies through drug addiction.

The Syrians currently feel the need to co-operate with the west. If future world events demand more such pragmatism, Syria may try to curb the drug trade which, in theory, they should easily be able to do in a country without inaccessible cultivation areas but, with Lebanon's drug barons maintaining their large heavily armed militias, the Syrian army would have to expect a tough battle.

As pressure has grown elsewhere, the international drug rings have recently developed increased traffic along the West African coast, mostly coming from Pakistan and Lagos, Abidjan and Accra, and thence to Europe and the USA. The three governments concerned, of Nigeria, Ghana and the Côte d'Ivoire, are generally co-operating with the west to stamp this out but, if they succeed, the traffic may simply switch to other routes. There are people everywhere willing to make big money quickly, and the international drug rings have plenty to offer. This is a problem the world can tackle only as a whole.

Mexico – and black tar

In 1975, 87 per cent of the heroin smuggled into the USA came from Mexico; by 1981 this percentage had fallen to 36 per cent as a result of determined action by the Mexican government, with US financial aid. They eradicated more than 20,000 acres of poppy fields using the herbicide paraquat. Cultivators responded by growing poppies in small patches and interspersing them between rows of other crops. The battle continues and overall the quantity of heroin crossing from Mexico into the USA is probably increasing again. There have been disturbing increases in heroin overdose deaths and hospital admissions. These figures are more convincing than mere estimates of tonnages seized or of new addicts; the increases have been particularly high in areas where a new form of Mexican heroin – 'black tar' – is available.

Black tar is so called because it is like coal tar in colour and consistency. Being almost solid, it is more difficult to dilute than the conventional heroin, which is a white powder, often heavily diluted with other powders by the dealers. Black tar is usually sold at 60 per cent purity or more, and is therefore extremely potent – hence the hospital admissions and deaths. It is also cheap, because the farmers can process it and smuggle it across the 950-mile border themselves or with the minimum of middlemen and couriers.

11   The consumers

The multinational narcotic corporations

The two previous chapters have dealt with the influence of drugs on guerrilla warfare, terrorism and crime on the upstream or supply side; on the corruption by the cocaine trade of government and business in Bolivia, Peru and Colombia and the nurturing, financing, and arming of terrorist groups like SL and FARC, causing tens of thousands of violent deaths each year; and the corruption and intimidation of politicians, officials and business people across the Caribbean and Central America. In the same way, the heroin trade finances the continuing insurgency by warlords and guerrilla armies which have helped to make Myanmar one of the poorest countries in the world; the financing of dissident tribesmen in Pakistan, Kurdistan and Afghanistan is likely to dog the efforts to restore stability. The drug traffic also finances the horror of Lebanon, where warring militias have maintained chaos in the country for fourteen years.

This chapter examines the downstream side, handled by the main broking centres in Miami, Mexico, Lebanon, Pakistan and Hong Kong, with their offshoots elsewhere in the USA and Europe. They organize the distribution of the drugs through traffickers, couriers and pushers to the addicts on the streets, mainly of the USA and Europe, but increasingly in other countries as well, especially in Asia; and they organize the contraflow of money, partly to the distributors and traffickers, but mainly to the drug barons themselves, with only a small proportion reaching the peasant farmers who grow the narcotic plants in Latin America and Asia.

The big headquarters in Miami (now increasingly dispersing to other parts of the USA) are organized like any other giant multinational corporation, with departments for purchasing, transport, marketing, finance, international political risk analysis and public relations. Like the multinationals, some run the equivalents of charitable foundations, to finance 'good works' to retain the goodwill of the people in the areas where that is important to deter government interference with their operations. And few multinationals could match them for 'slush money'.

The drug multinationals run large 'subsidiary companies', each with their own operating, finance and public relations departments as appropriate; for purchasing, refining and transportation in Colombia; and for smuggling, distribution and retailing in Los Angeles, New York, London and Amsterdam.

At every level they have loads of money, both upstream and downstream, to finance political terrorists or criminal gangs to protect and further their business. If at any time there is a temporary cash-flow problem, they can rectify this with a lucrative kidnap and ransom, or a demand for protection money from a businessman whom they have ways to persuade that it will be cheaper to pay.

The distribution chain

The downstream distribution is by a mixture of large consignments and small amounts concealed on the bodies or baggage or cars of individuals. Refined drugs have a huge dollar-to-weight ratio. At $24 for a few milligrams of heroin, couriers can carry a thousand dollars' worth in the soles of their shoes, tens of thousands of dollars' worth sewn into their clothing, or millions of dollars' worth in a false bottom in their suitcase or in the seat of their car. Sniffers, and especially dogs (see Chapter 6), are excellent for detecting any of these, but not every car, every bag or every person can be sniffed. Even this risk has been overcome by 'body-packing', whereby the courier inserts one or more strongly sealed capsules of high-grade cocaine into the rectum and excretes them a few hours later in the USA. Risky but, with several thousand dollars in one piece of excrement, the courier is no doubt well paid for it.

Addicts

In the USA there are about 5 million cocaine and heroin addicts and over 20 million more have tried one or the other. Malaysia, despite the death penalty, has 200,000 heroin addicts, with another 200,000 using opium. Pakistan has 300,000 and Italy 350,000 hard drug addicts.

As described in Chapter 10, there is an alternative version of heroin – black tar – which costs only one-tenth of the price of Mexican heroin. There is also an alternative version of cocaine – 'crack' – which first appeared in the USA in 1981 and its use spread rapidly in Britain. It is more powerfully and instantly addictive than cocaine. It is made by heating cocaine powder with water and baking powder, which removes the impurities put in by dealers to dilute it and the result is a hard rock, easily split into chips, which contains 70–90 per cent pure cocaine. Local dealers can do this and its popularity is such that, with cocaine costing them £1,000, they can produce crack with a street value of about £3,000.

In Europe and the USA the average addict has to find at least £100 ($150) per week to finance hard drug addiction. Some spend three or four times as much as this. Some of the addicts are the unspeakable playboy sons and daughters of millionaires and the yuppies who find that drugs help them to relax after a day in the exchange market. The majority, however, are people who, if they ever could earn that much spare money, certainly cannot do so now. If they cannot or will not seek help to break the addiction they have only two alternatives: crime or pushing drugs themselves. Most of them do it by continuous shoplifting until they are caught, whereafter they face two problems instead of one. If they have been caught and served time (and, to the disgrace of the prison service, prison spreads addiction rather than suppressing it), they may fear re-arrest and probably turn to the second alternative – to recruit new addicts and sell drugs to them to buy their own. Thus drug addicts, like animals and plants, have a powerful urge to reproduce the species. So this is where the tackling of this global problem must begin – at the level of the pusher and the addict on the street.

The cure at the demand end

Of course the drug chain must be fought all along the line from the producers through the barons and the traffickers to the addicts, but ultimately the battle can be won only if the source of all the hundreds of billion dollars can be cut off – the payments by addicts to pushers on the streets.

Many people support the view that suppression will never work and that hard and soft drugs should instead be legalized, strictly licensed and heavily taxed, in the same way that alcohol is controlled. They argue that Prohibition (of alcohol) in the USA in 1919–33 was a failure; that drinkers who wanted alcohol found a way to get it; that providing the alcohol created a huge network of criminal gangs; and that the inflated price that people paid for it financed these gangs and led to violent battles on the streets. They argue that this is exactly what the current attempts to prohibit drugs are doing; that if the huge profits now made by the drug barons were removed, the terrorism and international crime they finance would decline; and that the crimes committed by addicts to pay for their drugs, or their compulsion to recruit new addicts to whom they can sell drugs to raise the money, would also decline. The heavy tax revenue would be available to the government to finance their licensing and control of distribution of drugs and of weaning substitutes like methadone; also for expenditure on curing addiction through bodies such as Narcotics Anonymous.

There is great strength in these arguments, and they could prove to be the only answer if all else fails. Society would, however, pay a heavy price in other ways. With hard drugs costing as little as 5 per cent of present prices, very many more people would become addicted. These would, as now, be either inadequate people seeking an escape from problems they cannot solve, or affluent people seeking fresh excitements. Though some addicts have been cured, the majority, even if temporarily cured, revert to the addiction under stress. The drugs, over the years, make them more inadequate or irresponsible; in most cases, their lives are irrevocably ruined. Hard drugs are much more damaging and addictive than alcohol, and making them more readily available at a vastly reduced price would greatly increase the number of lives that would be ruined.

It has also been proposed at various times in the US Congress that aid should be cut off from Third World countries which fail to prevent the export of drugs to the USA. This would be counter-productive, because most of their governments are doing their best, bearing in mind the constant threat to the lives of the politicians, officials, judges, police officers, journalists and people who work loyally with them; also the financial power of the barons and the consequent strength of the guerrillas and terrorists they support. Cutting off aid would merely ensure that these governments would either face collapse or have to live-and-let-live with the barons and the terrorists. Aid to the hard-pressed governments should continue, so that they can fight and defeat the terrorists. It is the far, far more lavish 'aid' to the barons and the terrorists, flowing from the evil fringe of addicted citizens on affluent western streets, which must be cut.

The suffering inflicted on the ordinary people in the producing countries, as well as on those who try to govern, administer, and protect them is intolerable. The heroism of the many Colombians who have died resisting the drug barons should shame the west. The flow of 'evil aid' from their streets has financed and prolonged the terrorism in Peru and Colombia; the corruption in Central America, the Caribbean and Hong Kong; the fifteen-year agony of Lebanon (1975–90); and the insurgencies in Myanmar and Pakistan; it also looks set to destroy any attempt to restore stability to Afghanistan. It is hypocritical of the western powers to preach sermons to these countries, who are their victims. They must attack the real villains – their own traffickers, pushers and addicts.

Malaysia, a major consumer country, has attempted this by hanging couriers and distributors to deter others, but these people produce neither the drugs nor the contraflow of money; they merely batten on them. Moreover, the death penalty is in practice counter-productive because it scares potential informants and witnesses away; it leaves the big fish and the addicts who provide the money untouched.

The US and British laws to freeze assets of people arrested for drug offences and confiscate them if convicted (including any which their colleagues and families cannot prove were obtained by legitimate means) will help, provided that the bigger fish can be detected and convicted. But are their sentences long enough? The middleman who laundered $242 million of drug money, taking $4.8 million himself, got only six years (see p. 94), yet he must have known that he was contributing to the ruin of millions of lives of previously innocent people all over the world.

Any person who knowingly contributes to ruining a substantial number of other people's lives may or may not be morally entitled to stay alive, but he certainly has no moral right ever to be free again. One way of shutting them out is the Malaysian death penalty for anyone found in possession of more than 15 grams of hard drugs. A better alternative would be perpetual imprisonment for drug traffickers, couriers and pushers found in possession of or proven to have distributed more than, say, 50 grams (which is 5,000 shots of heroin) – and it should be known that there will be no remission. The same penalty should be imposed on those proven to have carried out organizational or anciliary tasks (e.g. laundering money), knowing that this was for the purpose of distributing drugs. For them too, the sentence must be for ever and they must know it. The only candidates for remission might be those prepared to give direct information leading to police action, which would fully compensate for the total damage to which they had been a party.

The strongest opposition to 'life-meaning-life' sentences would come from the prison officers, wondering how they could ever control prisoners to whom they could offer no incentives. The answer would be for the prisons concerned to provide a range of three regimes. First, a really harsh regime, with solitary confinement, which they already need for recalcitrant prisoners; second, the normal punitive regime, with prisoners in cell blocks but allowed out for a number of hours each day to associate, play games, work for money or learn a trade; third, a relaxed regime within a totally secure building inside the prison, as has been successfully tried at Barlinnie in Scotland and Bullwood Hall in Essex. In the relaxed regime, six to twelve prisoners would be allowed to live a relatively normal life, with open dormitories, each with three or four beds, within the secure building, with access to a central recreation area and, if possible, a secure sports area on the roof. They would have almost unlimited scope for association, and facilities for studying, writing or other activities as nearly as possible according to their choice. Regular visits (without physical contact) would be allowed. All of these privileges would be dependent on continued good behaviour, and there must be no hope whatever of escape or release.

'Life-meaning-life' prisoners in the second – normal – section would be threatened with the harsh regime if they were recalcitrant or rewarded with the relaxed regime if they earned it; but any abuse of the privileges would at once mean transfer to the harsh regime.

What of the addicts? Addiction is not a crime but addicts will fund their addiction either by crime or by recruiting other addicts. People identified as hard drug addicts must therefore be kept off the streets except under supervision; they must be subject to compulsory treatment, where possible living at home and attending regularly at a clinic; any who failed to co-operate in their cure would have to be treated in custody. In either case, when medically passed as cured, they should be required to visit the clinic at regular intervals to be tested and their treatment resumed if they have relapsed. No person known to be addicted should ever be at large unlicensed on the streets, putting other members of the community at risk.

It is urgent to arouse public opinion to the implications of our tolerance of drug pushers and addiction. Most people in the west would agree that drug barons, traffickers, and pushers are among the most loathsome of all criminals in the ruin they inflict on other people; we must also accept the corollary that, having done it, they should never be free again. We are more compassionate about addicts, but they are not so much pitiable as despicable; more important, so long as they remain addicts, their urgent need to steal or recruit more addicts means that they carry a virulent contagious disease and must be kept in quarantine until cured.

Two countries have bucked the trend, in very different ways. First, Turkey, which used to supply 80 per cent of the heroin reaching the USA and had itself a major opium and heroin addiction problem, broke both production and addiction by a degree of ruthlessness which would not be acceptable in the west, but a positive feature of the government's success was that it did mobilize a massive public revulsion against drug abuse to support its campaign. Second, Japan, despite its affluence and its proximity to the opium trails, has succeeded in preventing any substantial addiction to hard drugs, again by mobilizing the public behind the judiciary and the police and convincing them of the dire consequences – for individuals, their country and the world – of failure to stem the tide which they have observed flowing into Europe and the USA. Even the Yakusa, the Japanese Mafia, have failed to overcome the power of the eyes and ears of the people and their readiness to report what they see and hear.

If the USA and Europe, by tolerating a dangerous form of individual greed, lust and libertarianism, allow the growth of drug abuse on their streets to continue, the consequences will be dire not only for them, but even more so for the poorer countries in which their illegal money finances large-scale criminal and political violence.

Part IV

Rural guerrilla warfare

12 Rural guerrillas – Latin America

Rural guerrilla conflict, though largely driven off the front pages of western newspapers by the spectacular fashions of urban terrorism (see Part V), is still very much alive and probably accounts for many more deaths, though these are in the less developed parts of the world and are usually of local people.

Chapters 9, 10 and 11 examined the involvement of the cocaine traffickers in maintaining rural guerrilla movements in Peru and Colombia and of the heroin and hashish traffickers in Myanmar, Pakistan, Afghanistan, Kurdistan and Lebanon.

Chapters 12 and 13 look at how some of these guerrilla movements are organized and how they operate. Those selected are the ones which seem to teach the most useful lessons, and which cover a wide range of terrain and political background. There is no attempt to chronicle every rural guerrilla movement – nor every terrorist movement – in the world.

Peru

As was described in Chapter 9, *Sendero Luminoso* (SL, the Shining Path) has many of its strongest rural bases in the areas where coca is grown. Having a somewhat puritanical ideology, it does not get directly involved in the drug trade, but this does not stop it from extorting a levy on the cultivation and movement of coca, or from accepting substantial contributions of money and arms from the drug traffickers to prevent or deter the army, police and DEA from interfering.

Potentially SL's rural guerrilla organization and techniques may prove to be the most significant in the world in the 1990s. It is the first revolutionary movement which has aroused any enthusiastic response from Amerindian peasants so, if it is successful, it could be copied in other Latin American countries with a high Indian population. It has no external or internal political allies, scorning all other Peruvian left-wing movements and all other Communist countries including China and Cuba. Having begun as a rural movement, SL has in the 1990s been operating equally successfully in the shanty towns around Lima. It is extremely violent and vicious, terrorizing the people with public mutilations and executions. More than 25,000 have been killed since their terrorist phase began in 1980. The aims and organization of SL will be described in the next section.

Peru has a population of 22 million, of whom nearly 7 million live in Lima (5 million of them in shanty towns); 12 per cent are white Europeans, 39 per cent *mestizo* (mixed race) and 49 per cent Quechua Indians – the highest percentage of Indians in any Latin American country. The country comprises an arid coastal plain and the complex ranges of the Andes Mountains, whose eastern slopes drain into the rain forests of the Amazon basin in Brazil. The Quechua Indians live mainly in the temperate and fertile highlands above 7,000 feet. Peru's major exports – copper, silver, zinc, lead and iron ore – are mined among the western foothills of the Andes, which are peopled mainly by *mestizos* who regard themselves as Peruvian rather than Indian. Peru also has a large educated *mestizo* middle class, known as *mistis*, who historically provided the middle and lower management for the Spanish settlers. Professor Abimael Guzman, founder of SL, comes from a *misti* family.

The main coca-growing area is the Huallaga Valley (see Chapter 9). By late 1993, SL competed with the army for control of the whole valley, having ousted their rivals, the Tupac Amaro Revolutionary Movement (MRTA) from the southern half.

Peru's last foreign wars were over 100 years ago but, because these wars had a traumatic effect, the governments have remained obsessed with their frontiers and have maintained a large army, which has regularly seized political power. There were military coups in 1930, 1946 and 1968 and the country was under military rule for twenty-eight of the fifty years from 1930 to 1980. The most recent military coup (1968) was by radical army officers (best described as national socialists) who nationalized the big corporations, dispossessed the landowners and turned their estates into giant collectives, but in doing so wrecked the economy. Unable to cope with the economic problems they had created, the soldiers abandoned the attempt and called an election in 1980. President Belaunda was elected from 1980 to 1985 and Alan Garcia from 1985 to 1990 but the economy, despite the country's natural resources, showed no sign of recovery, due largely to corruption. By 1990 inflation had reached 7,000 per cent; the people turned their backs on their traditional political parties and elected a Peruvian businessman of Japanese descent, Alberto Fujimori, as President.

He appointed Carlos Bolona, who has an Oxford DPhil, as Finance Minister and by 1993 they had brought inflation down to 56 per cent. Fujimori, however, was frustrated by a hostile Congress, still dominated by the traditional political parties, and by a corrupt and intimidated judiciary. In 1967 only 6 per cent of prosecutions for terrorism had resulted in convictions; by 1991, the great majority of cases were never even coming to trial, the judges ruling that there was 'insufficient evidence'. Of those which were tried, only a derisory number resulted in convictions. On 5 April 1992 Fujimori secured army support in dissolving the Congress and the judiciary in a 'self coup' (*autogulpe*).

The *autogulpe* increased Fujimori's popular support, which rose still further when, in a brilliant intelligence operation led by General Antonio Vidal, Abimael Guzman was captured on 12 September 1992. On 22 November a seventy-seat constituent assembly (CCCD) was elected. The traditional parties, knowing that they had lost public support, boycotted the election. The CCCD gave Fujimori some legitimacy by confirming him as President by forty-nine votes to twenty-eight.

The army, however, was becoming disenchanted. Though there were many rich business people in Peru, public officials were notoriously badly paid. Junior officers in the army and police in 1992 were paid as little as $100 a month and generals about $200–400; they could live their middle-class lifestyle only in one of two ways: by devoting part of their time to their jobs and the rest to moonlighting; or, more commonly, by corruption. Although the Fujimori government attempted to provide more for them in kind (cars, fuel, servants, and so on) many remained frustrated; on 13 November 1992 the government had to pre-empt an attempted military coup. Nevertheless, Fujimori narrowly won a referendum on 31 October 1993 with 52 per cent of the vote in favour of his proposals for a new constitution giving strong powers to the President.

The war against *Sendero Luminoso*

Ironically, a military coup was what Abimael Guzman had been hoping to provoke all through his campaign. He knew that, historically, Marxist revolutions generally succeeded only against autocratic rather than democratic regimes – as in Russia, China and Cuba. The military coup in 1968 tempted Guzman to start on what he expected to be a long march to seize power. He was at that time Professor of Philosophy at the University of San Cristobal de Huamanga in Ayacucho in the old Inca country where almost all the students were Quechua Indians or *mestizos*. During the next ten years he built up his revolutionary infrastructure in the neighbouring villages with an agit-prop campaign.

He found his fellow *mistis* particularly responsive to his idealism. When they graduated, they found little outlet for their ambitions, often finding themselves back in their own villages as primary school teachers. Guided by Guzman, they were able to build on the resentment of their Quechua and *mestizo* neighbours against the injustices of their society and created SL's underground organization.

Guzman's philosophy was puritanical Maoist, which he coupled with the traditional values of the Inca society. He rejected all contemporary Communist movements as revisionist, including that of China since Mao Zedong's death in 1976. His plan of campaign, based on the early writings of Mao, was in five phases:

1 mobilization, agitation and propaganda
2 sabotage and rural guerrilla activity
3 generalization of violence into guerrilla warfare
4 establishment and expansion of bases and liberated zones
5 the blockading of towns and cities by peasant armies leading to collapse of government.

Phase 1 lasted from 1968 to 1980. The restoration of democracy in 1980 signalled the start of phase 2. The first acts of sabotage were, significantly, against polling stations in the first democratic election, which Guzman denounced as a fraud. From 1982 the violence rose rapidly through phases 2 and 3 to reach a peak in 1984. The numbers killed each year tell the story (see Table 3). The war is believed to have cost over $20 million million.

Table 3 Deaths arising from terrorism in Peru

1980	3	1987	697
1981	4	1988	1,986
1982	170	1989	3,198
1983	2,807	1990	3,452
1984	4,319	1991	3,180
1985	1,359	1992	3,101
1986	1,286		
		TOTAL 1980–1992	25,554

Source: Peruvian government figures, March 1993

President Belaunda had not taken the threat seriously and had allowed SL to reach phase 4 by 1984, with large no-go areas under their control, especially in the Huallaga Valley. President Garcia introduced states of emergency in these areas to recover control; these soon covered more than half the country. Some of the better generals and colonels succeeded in winning the co-operation of the *campesinos* (though in some cases turning a blind eye to the growing and sale of coca – see p. 89). This led to rising government confidence in 1985–7 but in 1988 Guzman announced that his campaign was ready to move into its final phase 5, and that its focus would shift to the cities, especially to Lima. Between 1989 and 1992 more than 3,000 people were killed every year. Most of those killed by SL were civilians, as always with terrorists. Army and police casualties were only 10–15 per cent of the total – 348 killed in 1989 and 455 (a peak) in 1992.

SL's organization was modelled on Mao Zedong's. There were six military regions, each with its 'principal force' for large-scale operations. Regions were split into zones, each with a 'local force'. These in turn were split into villages or urban communities, each of which had its own people's committee, comprising a committee secretary and usually four other commissars – for security (i.e. military), production, communal affairs and people's organization. Many of the most militant terrorists and leaders were *mestizo* women, combining the fiery and passionate Spanish character with Indian stoicism and resilience. The organization, most of it part time, probably involved about 20,000 people, many of the rank-and-file acting under coercion. Its funds came mainly from the Colombian drug Mafias, as described in Chapter 9. Other sources were bank robberies and 'revolutionary taxes', a bland term for extortion of protection money and blackmail.

Lima offered Guzman an ideal field for developing his urban infrastructure. The city was ringed by a barren desert hinterland on which some 5 million squatters had settled in 'new towns' (*pueblos jovenes* – PJs). Compared with the shambles of shanty towns elsewhere in Latin America, these PJs are remarkably well organized. The inhabitants of each PJ normally come from a specific rural area. Organized by an elected committee, as many as 1,000 families (perhaps 5,000 people) travel on a single night in buses to a secretly selected piece of open ground on the outskirts of Lima, where the committee will have marked out a 90 square metre plot for each family. Next morning, the police find a tent city of several thousand people, initially under temporary matting shelters but laid out in orderly rows with wide spaces for roads in between. Within a few weeks, they will have organized factories for baking mud bricks and built brick houses – often with second storeys added within a few months. They will have prepared in advance for developing means of livelihood, and the committee will quickly organize markets and workshops to make goods for which they believe there to be a demand in Lima, and garages from which to operate transport. Hernandez de Soto, in his book, *The Other Path*, describes how 90 per cent of the public transport in Lima is operated by the technically illegal 'informal economy' from the PJs. Some of the people do, of course, live by begging, hawking and crime, and at every traffic light there is a swarm of children trying to sell things to the car drivers. But generally the inhabitants do more to help themselves than those in other Latin American shanty towns.

The Peruvian authorities will give land title to a PJ only if it does have an elected committee to represent it. These PJ committees, however, also provide SL with a ready-made structure if they can infiltrate them. It is easy for SL to find grievances to exploit; the municipal authorities are hard pressed to provide all the services that 5 million squatters require – access roads, links to water supplies, electricity, and so on. If SL can incite a riot, this will polarize the people against the soldiers and police sent in to repress it.

From 1988 until his capture in 1992, Guzman was usually based in Lima, heading his Metropolitan Committee which directed the revolutionary structure in and around the city. In 1991 and 1992 large car bombs in the business and residential districts became more frequent – in the pattern which developed in London, New York and Northern Irish towns in 1991–3 (see Chapter 3). On 12 September 1992 most of the Metropolitan Committee were arrested with Guzman. Exploiting the intelligence they gained, the police and army arrested some 200 more SL organizers in the following few weeks.

Throughout Fujimori's campaign there were two schools of thought about how the war could be won, which the Peruvians referred to as the 'French school' and the 'British school'. The French school follows the example of Algeria, where the French army largely ran the civil administration through its *cinquième bureau*, which produced a 'seamless' campaign. The army provided local government, public services, roads, education, recreation facilities – everything. It could use the provision or denial of these facilities as a carrot or stick. These activities also offered opportunities for gaining intelligence. Coupled with the traditionally robust methods used by French troops against rebels, this approach had proved highly effective in the short term, for example in suppressing bombing and other terrorist activities in the city of Algiers. But in the end the French alienated the people and lost the war in Algeria, as they had lost it in Indo-China.

The British school refers to the methods used by General Templer and his successors in Malaya in the 1950s. The aim was to establish and support a working structure of civil officials, and the task of the army and police was to enable them to run their administration and to provide the services the people needed. Working contacts between officials, the police and the public was the basis on which the intelligence system – the battle-winning factor – was built. It also provided, ready for when the terrorist organization in the district was destroyed, a functioning and legitimate local government in being.

In 1991–2 some of President Fujimori's advisers commended the British school and others the French. By 1993, however, his principal adviser was of the French school. Apart from its proven failure in Algiers and Indo-China, and the danger of it alienating the people and their elected committees, the overriding military authority in emergency areas could strengthen the army's ability to attempt another military coup.

Peru has the resources and its people have the democratic instincts to revive the economy and to win the war. This will necessitate giving scope to the commercial potential of the 'informal economy', building on the successes of the police intelligence and establishing local government answerable to the people.

SL have many determined leaders still at large, and the murder rate has increased since Guzman was captured. They have also developed organizations in neighbouring states and even in Europe, mainly for propaganda. Their puritanism and the racial basis of their appeal (to restore the Indian Inca philosophies and root out those of the descendants of the Spanish invaders) could strike a chord not only amongst Quechua Indians but also among radicals embittered by the decline of far left politics world-wide. If SL were to prevail in Peru, their philosophy might find fertile ground for expansion.

MRTA declined in 1992–3 with the arrest of its key leaders. It split, some of its rank and file joining criminal gangs in extortion attempts. Its more ideological members may try to take it into Peruvian politics as M19 did in Colombia (see p. 119).

Colombia

Colombia has one of the most politically stable democratic systems in Latin America, with one of the strongest economies, but has been constantly plagued by violence. It is only in recent years that Colombia has largely been financed by the international drug trade, as described in Chapter 9. The billions of dollars coming into the Colombian economy each year (albeit much of it clandestine, untaxed and therefore inflationary) probably accounts for the fact that Colombia is the only country in the area which has not had to reschedule her foreign debt. Despite this alluring bonus to her balance of payments, however, and despite the constant threat to the lives of politicians, judges and others, the governments and security forces have courageously fought both the drug barons and the terrorists they support.

The murder and kidnap rate, both by terrorists and criminals, is horrific. The homicide rate in the drug capital, Medellin, was mentioned in Chapter 9 – three times the highest rate anywhere else in the world. There were 666 kidnaps in 1989, 1,322 in in 1990, 1,717 in 1991 and 1,320 in 1992, mainly of local people for ransom but with a sprinkling of expatriates; about half were by political terrorists and half by criminal gangs. Altogether, 27,000 people were killed in Colombia in 1992, by terrorists and by drug-related and other crime.

The biggest and oldest terrorist movement is FARC (Armed Revolutionary Forces of Colombia). This is a nation-wide rural group operating in thirty-nine 'fronts'; its politics are orthodox Communist. Founded in 1966, it remained only a few hundred strong until 1980 but, since receiving support from the drug trade, it has grown to several thousand active guerrillas with many more thousands of supporters. There is no firm demarcation between guerrillas and supporters, as the movement acts more openly than any of the others and has an open political front (Patriotic Front – UP), which stands in elections.

FARC goes to considerable lengths to enlist local popular support in rural areas by applying pressure on the multinational companies. Typically when a foreign company's planning team moves into an area to prepare for a project, the local authorities, such as the mayor and the police, will approach them (with FARC approval) and ask them to employ local people to the maximum possible extent (e.g. junior management, staff, labour, and subcontracting locally for construction, transport, etc.). It is made clear that if they do this, they will have no trouble from FARC, and this promise is honoured.

If the company declines to accept this proposal, its next callers will be from FARC members, stating themselves to be 'representatives of the people' but leaving no doubt, from their guerrilla-style dress and demeanour, who they really are. They issue a warning, and if the company then fails to fill every possible post with a Colombian, it will be attacked. Most foreign companies do comply, and integrate well with the local population. If the people say that they are happy with the company because it is bringing them work, FARC know that any attacks would be unwelcome, which is why the number of expatriate victims of murder and kidnap is relatively small.

ELN (National Liberation Army) is a Castroite rural guerrilla movement operating in the main oil-producing areas in north-east Colombia up to the Venezuelan border. Their aim is mainly to drive out the foreign oil companies. These companies, however, have largely

Colombianized both management and labour, and expatriates maintain a very low profile, keeping their movements unpredictable, when they do visit the oil fields. Most of the attacks are therefore on their installations, not people.

EPL (People's Liberation Army) is a movement with roughly Maoist ideology, which operates both in the countryside and the cities (notably Bogotá and Medellin).

M19 (April 19 Movement) was primarily an urban, intellectually based movement, having rural fronts mainly in the south, with links to sympathetic movements in Peru and Ecuador. M19 changed its policy in 1989, abandoned terrorist activity and decided to stand as a lawful political party, AD M19, in the 1990 election. It emerged as the second largest political party after the ruling Liberal Party.

Only FARC now continues even to pay lip-service to the truce begun in 1984, and continues to attack army posts and other government targets. Some of these attacks are in co-operation with the other three movements which, since September 1987, have all been allied with it in the CGSB (Simón Bolívar Guerrilla Co-ordination). The very active participation by FARC in protecting the drug business – cultivation, processing and trafficking, including running a number of cocaine laboratories themselves – brings them into constant conflict with the army and the police: the level of violence and kidnap is such that a great deal of protection money is paid to the guerrilla movements. The government will be hard put to do more than contain the guerrilla activity until the western countries cut off the flow of drug money to the drug traffickers who finance them.

As an indication of the scale of the killing, an independent church study estimated in August 1988 that there had been 1,500 political murders in the first six months of 1988, of which only 212 could at that stage be specifically attributed: 46 by ELN, 92 by FARC, 52 by EPL, 22 by CGSB and 9 by M19; in the same period there had been 256 army guerrilla clashes, in which 208 security force personnel, 234 guerrillas and 55 civilians had been killed. The infrastructure and the oil industry are the main targets.

The election of the new President, Cesar Gaviria, in 1990, the surrender of the leader of the Medellin drug cartel, Pablo Escobar, in June 1991 and his escape in July 1992 were described in Chapter 9. Escobar's weakened narco-terrorist organization resumed violence but suffered further blows when security forces killed his military leader, Brances Munos Mosquera, on 28 October 1992 and Pablo Escobar himself on 2 December 1993. The political terrorist organizations, increasingly co-ordinated under CGSB, continued their attacks, especially on the oil industry, and the government trained a 5,000-strong professional force to guard oil installations and pipelines. Though the drug money contined to flow into the country and there seemed to be no sign of the violence subsiding, there were growing signs of public exasperation with the instability. The success of M19 in entering the democratic process won it many new adherents and government successes against the Medellin cartel have increased confidence. There may be a long way to go but there are probably more grounds for hope in Colombia than at any time since the 1950s.

El Salvador

For a tiny country of about 5 million people, El Salvador has suffered horrific casualties from a long-running insurgency: 10,000 people were killed in each of the years 1980 and 1981 and the total killed in the period 1980–91 was over 75,000.

One of the unusual factors was that the guerrillas began their campaign in 1978–80 by building up a $40 million 'launching fund' by kidnapping expatriate executives from five multinational companies based in different countries, and skilfully playing off one against the other. After that there was no kidnapping of expatriates; the guerrillas continued to finance their campaign by the more normal local kidnaps, robberies, extortion, and payment of protection money. The priming of the pump with the original $40 million, however, enabled them to build an infrastructure and maintain their initial momentum with an adequate cash reserve.

In 1980 six Marxist guerrilla groups joined forces in an umbrella 'National Liberation Front' (FMLN) which, with Cuban support, tried unsuccessfully to bring down the government which was formed after the overthrow of the repressive President Romero in October 1979. The guerrillas had an army of about 10,000; it was supplied from Cuba and Nicaragua. For the first two years (1980–1) the new government, seeking a broad range of support from hard-line military men and Christian Democrat politicians, was unable to control either the FMLN or right-wing death squads taking the law into their own hands. Democracy was established with painful slowness, with the election of a constituent assembly in March 1982 but, although the Christian Democrats emerged as the biggest single party, they could govern only in coalition with four other parties, including some of those suspected of collusion with the death squads. The guerrillas claimed to have killed or wounded over 7,000 soldiers and captured some 1,700 more in 1983.

José Napoleon Duarte, a Christian Democrat of long standing, was elected president in June 1984 with enough political strength to remove some of the more unsavoury army officers, but the FLMN rebuffed his proposals for negotiations and still held about a quarter of the country. Operating in groups of 400 or more, they aimed their attacks at disrupting communications and the economy – especially through damaging the electric power systems. Only US Aid (reputedly amounting to $2 million per day) enabled the country to survive. There was little to encourage investment and there was a continuing flight of capital, now estimated to have reached $3 billion. The economy went into serious decline, as the FMLN intended.

In 1985 the Christian Democrats obtained a parliamentary majority but peace talks again proved abortive. Ambushes, sabotage and road mining reduced transport in the east of the country to about 10 per cent of normal, with continuing paralysis of the economy in many of the provinces. President Duarte's prestige was further damaged in September 1985 when the guerrillas kidnapped his daughter and to secure her freedom (along with that of twenty-four abducted mayors) he had to agree to the release of twenty-two prisoners and safe conduct for ninety-six wounded guerrillas.

Gradually, however, army tactics improved and by 1987 the FMLN could no longer operate in large units. In August 1987 the Presidents of El Salvador, Nicaragua, Honduras, Costa Rica and Guatemala agreed to cease supporting gueriila activities and to reject military aid 'beyond what was normal and reasonable' from foreign powers, notably from Cuba, the USSR and the USA.

In March 1988, Duarte's Christian Democrats lost their congressional majority in the mid-term elections to the conservative ARENA Party. Duarte, who was dying of cancer, went to the USA for treatment and did not stand at the next presidential election in March 1989, which was won by the ARENA candidate, Alfredo Cristiani. In November 1989 FMLN responded with a final offensive and in several weeks of intense violence 3,000 people were killed. But by February 1990 FMLN's support, inside and outside the country, had begun to collapse, with the defeat of the Sandinistas in the Nicaraguan election (see next section), the revolution in the USSR and the consequent cutting of aid to Cuba. President Cristiani, under conflicting pressures from his hard-liners to be more ruthless and from the USA to observe human rights or lose US Aid, was unexpectedly moderate and conciliatory. In January 1992 a peace treaty was signed and in February a UN-supervised cease-fire. Cristiani agreed to halve the size of his army within the coming two years and to dismiss or transfer one hundred senior officers of human rights violations. The FMLN agreed to disarm and to hand in their weapons by 15 December 1992, which generally they did, though inevitably some arms caches remained. March 1994 was agreed as the date for a general election in which FMLN would stand as a political party.

Many problems remained. The economy and the infrastructure had been weakened by fourteen years of violent conflict. Some 9,000 ex-guerrillas needed resettlement and there were disputes over land. Both ex-soldiers and ex-guerrillas had developed the habit of reaching for guns to resolve their disputes and there were plenty of guns still lying around. Violent crime also increased for the same reason. There were the usual accusations by both sides that the other was dragging its feet but there was discreet co-operation between Cristiani and the FMLN leaders, who tried to restrain their more violent supports. They knew that the people were thoroughly sick of the war.

Nicaragua

The Sandinistas in Nicaragua were an amalgam of Marxist and non-Marxist resistance movements against President Somoza, whom they ousted in 1979 with the support of almost all elements of society. This resulted from a classic rural guerrilla campaign, for which they started organizing from a base in Honduras in 1962. Working up from small-scale guerrilla attacks, they built up cadres in the villages and in the shanty towns around Managua. By 1978 they were able to organize mass demonstrations in the cities and the guerrilla units coalesced into large units which defeated the National Guard as Somoza fled the country. The present head of state, Daniel Ortega, was leader of the moderate wing of the movement, and had a Marxist Interior Minister, Tomas Borge.

The Sandinistas assumed power with their own junta in coalition with liberal politicians, with support from the church and the business community, both local and expatriate, who were encouraged to continue functioning. President Carter tried to help the new regime with aid but by the time President Reagan assumed office in 1981, the US had become disenchanted with the ousting of the liberal wing of the Sandinistas. A new resistance movement, the 'contras', was founded in November 1981 and gained US support. The contras were based on and across Nicaragua's northern frontier with Honduras, with some co-operation from the Miskito Indians in the under-developed Atlantic coast provinces.

The contras had a peak strength of about 18,000 in 1984–5, falling to

12,000 in 1987. They were not able to gain permanent control of any territory inside Nicaragua. They conducted raids into the northern provinces in strengths of 200 or more, ambushing government troops, destroying the infrastructure, kidnapping and terrorizing villagers, as the Sandinistas used to do in the 1970s and as other guerrilla groups did in El Salvador, Colombia and Peru. The inability of the US military advisers to restrain them from these kinds of tactics caused the US Congress to limit funds for aiding the contras.

The numbers killed in Nicaragua between 1979 and 1987 (i.e. after the Sandinistas seized power) probably exceeded 70,000 out of a population of 4 million and the damage to the economy was about $4 million. As in El Salvador, things began to improve with the agreement in August 1987 by the five Central American Presidents not to support guerrillas in each other's countries and then by the revolution in the USSR and the cutting of Soviet aid to Cuba. (In the period 1981–6 the USSR had provided $500 million in direct aid to Nicaragua and $4 billion to Cuba.)

On 25 February 1990 the Sandinista government called a presidential election which they were confident that they would win. Both the Sandinistas and the rest of the world were astonished when Daniel Ortega was decisively defeated by the middle-of-the-road UNO opposition candidate, Violeta Chamorra. The result was declared fair by the Supreme Electoral Council and by a foreign observer team, and was accepted by Daniel Ortega, who promised his co-operation. Mrs Chamorra, who had been one of the liberal ministers in Ortega's earlier coalitions, was equally conciliatory and, perhaps because she was especially anxious to avoid a breakdown of order, she agreed to keep the Sandinista command structure in the security forces, including the army chief of staff, General Humberto Ortega. President Chamorra took office on 25 April 1990.

US sanctions were lifted and the contras completed disbandment by June 1990, though a number of dissidents clandestinely rearmed. Violent crime increased. Both Chamorra and Ortega were plagued by their right and left-wing extremists respectively. By January 1993, forty-four of the fifty-two UNO deputies had deserted Chamorra and became the opposition in the national assembly. She could govern only with the support of the thirty-nine Sandinista deputies, the eight UNO deputies who remained loyal to her, plus one independent, giving her a slim majority over the forty-four UNO defectors.

Violence continued, though not on a scale comparable with that of the 1980s; Chamorra and the two Ortegas did their best to co-operate in keeping the peace.

Prognosis for Latin America

Despite the horrific slaughter in the 1980s and the ongoing violence and terrorism financed by the drug cartels in Colombia and Peru, there have been three deeply encouraging developments in Latin America. First, after years of predominantly military rule, almost every Latin American country now has a democratically elected government. Though many are plagued by corruption, this is no worse than in some European countries, such as Italy. Second, with the end of the Cold War, the guerrillas and governments are no longer armed and financed by the rival superpowers, directly or indirectly via Cuba. Third, the two bloodiest conflicts, in El Salvador and Nicaragua, have largely blown themselves out and there has been a remarkable spirit of conciliation among the rival leaders in both countries.

Latin America has had very few interstate wars in the twentieth century, in stark contrast to Europe and Asia, where deaths have been measured in tens of millions rather than tens of thousands. But individual Latin American activists have turned readily to the gun when they could not get what they wanted, under both authoritarian and democratic governments; the quality of their domestic rule of law has not coped with this.

Central America, Argentina, Brazil and Chile were by 1993 enjoying unusual peace and democracy. Colombia remained intensely violent though there have been some encouraging indications, for example the transition of M19 into a lawful and successful political party and the government's success against the terrorism sponsored by the drug cartels. Peru, at the time of writing, remains in the balance, despite the capture of Abimael Guzman.

The ultimate financiers of terrorism in Colombia and Peru are the drug addicts, affluent or inadequate, on US and European streets. Only a tiny proportion of the huge sums they pay for their shots goes to the farmers who grow the coca; all the rest goes to finance the terrorist movements which facilitate this and the international criminal gangs which process and distribute the cocaine. It is hypocritical for western governments to criticize the Colombians, Peruvians and Bolivians for producing cocaine when they make only half-hearted efforts to prevent their own drug addicts from buying it, financing the international Mafias and the terrorist movements which have killed tens of thousands of Colombians and Peruvians. It is the fault of the west that these are the two countries in which terrorism is most likely to persist.

13 Rural guerrillas – Asia and Africa

The Asian rural guerrilla heritage

Whether their ideology is Marxist, nationalist, religious, or a mixture of these, most rural guerrilla movements, past and present, follow the Maoist revolutionary strategy. First, the guerrillas deploy cadres to organize popular support in remote areas, to make them a 'friendly sea in which the fish can swim'. Thereafter they terrorize any who do not co-operate, establish liberated or no-go areas, and extend their influence into the more prosperous areas to isolate the cities in whose shanty towns they can develop the organization for an uprising when the time is ripe. In some cases, as in Peru and Colombia (see Chapter 12) the violence in the cities runs in parallel with the rural campaign, in close co-operation with big criminal gangs, usually those financed by drug trafficking.

The successful defeat of rural guerrillas has almost always been founded on three pillars: village security, enlightened government so that people have more to gain by getting rid of the terrorists and – the ultimate battle-winning factor – intelligence.

One of the classic successes was in Malaya, where a guerrilla army of 8,000, with a strongly established village cadre organization built up during the Japanese occupation, was worn down and broken in 1948–60. The crucial battles were fought around 400 'New Villages' in which their 400,000 strongest supporters were resettled. None was resettled until a secure village perimeter had been built and a resident police post established *inside* the village. As confidence was restored, the decisive flow of intelligence built up, handled by a unified and highly sophisticated intelligence organization.

By contrast, in Vietnam there were no resident police or army posts in the villages so that, despite a façade of government control during daylight hours, the people were unprotected by night from the avenging cadres, who did live and sleep in the villages. As a result, no one dared give decisive information and, in any case, there were eleven rival intelligence organizations (US and Vietnamese) so the cadres could play off one against the other to keep out of trouble.

There is a myth that the winning side always has 'the support of the people'. In practice, 80 per cent of the people do not want to get involved with either side for fear of retribution by the other side against themselves or their families. They prefer to see and hear nothing. Usually 10 per cent at most will actively support the guerrillas (though more may be coerced by terror into doing so) and 10 per cent at most will actively support the police, army and local government, often encouraged by incentives and rewards.

The real breakthrough usually comes when guerrillas or their active supporters defect and give inside information. Of the 4,000 guerrillas who surrendered or were captured in Malaya, 2,700 were willing to co-operate in this way. They were known as 'Surrendered Enemy Personnel' (SEPs) and were encouraged by generous rewards and, when they so wished, resettlement, with their families, under a new name in a new country with the resources to start a new life. At the end of the campaign, a number of 'Super SEPs' – including the second-in-command of the guerrilla organization, Hor Lung – surrendered, and co-operated in persuading others to follow suit. What had started as a trickle became a flood and the whole organization quickly crumbled away. The experience in Italy with the *pentiti* (in an urban setting – see pp. 162–3) taught the same lesson.

One other part of the rural guerrilla heritage is worth mentioning. Refugees from internal conflict or oppression have often been trained in neighbouring countries to go back as guerrillas. The Indians did this to train a guerrilla force to assist their invasion of Bangladesh in 1971; and the Pakistanis, with US support, gave sanctuary, training and support to Afghan mujahideen. They are still fighting each other.

Cambodia

In 1975–8 Cambodia was subjected to the most vicious regime of government terrorism ever recorded, excelling even Stalin's terror in the 1920s and 1930s (he killed 19 million Soviet citizens to enforce his will), in terms of deaths in proportion to the population. After the final withdrawal of US troops from South Vietnam and its take-over by the then Soviet-supported North Vietnamese in 1975, the Lon Nol government in Cambodia was ousted by the Khmers Rouges (KR), a Chinese-oriented Communist Party with Khieu Samphan as President and Pol

Pot as Prime Minister. They introduced a ghastly parody of a puritanical Maoist society. The entire populations of the capital, Phnom Penh, and of other towns, were driven out to work in the fields, where large numbers were summarily killed. A million people died – one in seven of the population. These included almost all the professionally and technically qualified people in the country. Factories, laboratories, hospitals – all manifestations of commercial, industrial, scientific and urban civilization – were gutted. KR officials used every conceivable technique to terrorize the survivors.

In 1978 the Vietnamese invaded Cambodia and ousted Khieu Samphan and Pol Pot, who withdrew with the KR army to the north-west of the country and into camps in east Thailand. The Thais had long been subjected to a Communist guerrilla insurgency organized by the North Vietnamese – those same Tongkingese who had historically tried to subjugate the Thai and Khmer peoples – and they feared the Vietnamese army's approach to their borders as a prelude to a renewed version of this threat. They therefore preferred to maintain KR as a buffer. The former ruler of Cambodia, Prince Norodom Sihanouk, also threw in his lot with KR and both were supported by China. The Vietnamese, with Soviet backing, installed a puppet Prime Minister, Hun Sen, and supported him with an army of occupation while they helped him to form and train his own army and to form a Communist political party, the Cambodian People's Party (CPP). Cambodia suffered thirteen years of civil war before a UN brokered peace plan was signed in Paris on 23 October 1991, with Soviet co-operation.

Under this plan, all parties agreed to dismantle their armies and prepare for an election in May 1993. The country would meanwhile be governed by a Supreme National Council (SNC), to include Hun Sen and Sihanouk and also Khieu Samphan representing KR. This was to be supervised by a UN Transitional Authority for Cambodia (UNTAC), headed by a Japanese diplomat, Yasushi Akashi, and supported by a UN peacekeeping force of 22,000, with a budget of $2 billion.

KR, however, having signed the Paris agreement, refused to disarm their 35,000 strong army or to allow UN staff to enter their occupied areas to register voters for the election. The UN therefore decided to go ahead with the election in the remaining 85 per cent of the country. In April 1993 Khieu Samphan and his KR delegation walked out of the SNC and left Phnom Penh. KR was consolidated along the Thai border, where they were financed by a lucrative cross-border trade in gems and timber. The KR soldiers pursued their own version of ethnic cleansing, attacking members of the large ethnic Vietnamese community, many of whom fled to Vietnam. This, of course, gained KR popularity among some Cambodians. They also murdered several UN officials, announced their intention of disrupting the election and warned the people not to vote.

In the event, the disruption was minimal and about 90 per cent of the eligible voters turned out, some walking from KR areas, where there were no polling booths, to vote in neighbouring districts. The royalist party, FUNCINPEC, led by Sihanouk's son, Prince Ranariddh, got 46 per cent of the vote, and CPP 38 per cent. This gave them fifty-seven and fifty-two seats respectively in the assembly, with a balance of eleven for minor parties. CPP complained of irregularities but UNTAC declared the election fair and confirmed the results on 11 June. Prince Sihanouk had announced a coalition with himself as Head of State and Prime Minister and with Ranariddh and Hun Sen as deputies but this quickly broke up. Ranariddh was reluctant to share power, and the CPP bureaucracy, after fourteen years of privileges as a Communist *nomenklatura*, did not want to give these up; they also controlled the army. But KR, still aggressively hostile to CPP as the 'Vietnamese party', threatened to resume the war unless the election verdict was accepted – Sihanouk having earlier hinted that he might offer them some form of participation. A hard-line wing of CPP (bizarrely under the leadership of another of Sihanouk's sons!) tried to set up a secessionist state but this quickly collapsed. On 15 June 1993 Ranariddh and Hun Sen, with the moderate wing of CPP, agreed to set up a coalition under Sihanouk and to co-operate in working out a new constitution.

The election was a major achievement by the UN but long-term stability must remain in doubt. The most encouraging feature is that the Cambodian people have shown that they are thoroughly sick of the war.

The Philippines

There have been two main guerrilla groups fighting in the Philippines since the early 1970s the Maoist New People's Army (NPA) and the Muslim secessionist group MNLF fighting for an independent Islamic state in the Southern Islands – Mindanao and the Sulu Archipelago. When the corrupt dictatorship of President Marcos was overthrown by Mrs Cory Aquino in February 1986 amid massive public acclaim, she hoped that the guerrillas would join in the rejoicing and respond to offers of an amnesty. They, on the other hand, thought that, with her liberal policies and a weakening of the suppressive police-military-intelligence structure, she would be an easier proposition than Marcos. Both were wrong. The army generally remained loyal to Mrs Aquino despite a number of attempted coups, and she retained the support of the great majority of the people.

The guerrillas played little part in the overthrow of Marcos, except that he had used their activities as an excuse to clamp down on free speech, demonstrations and civil rights and this made him still more unpopular with the public. He called the 1986 presidential election in response to US insistence, tried quite brazenly to manipulate the results, and was swept from power by a massive and generally peaceful flood of public demonstrations in the streets. The Americans, along with the people, clearly wanted him to go and he went.

The NPA does still constitute a serious threat, even though its sympathizers have dwindled to about 100,000 out of a population of 62 million. There are some 14,000 guerrillas, based mainly in the northern part of the main island of Luzon, in the shanty towns which make up 2 million of the 6 million population of Manila, in the peninsula in the south of the island and in some of the other islands. The plan for their campaign – which began in 1969 as a resumption of the defeated Huk rebellion of 1950–3 – follows the traditional Maoist strategy of the protracted war: building cadres to organize support in the remote villages and working inwards to control the more prosperous areas until the cities, starved of supplies and raw materials for their industries, are ripe for an internal rising.

NPA 'sparrow squads' aim to spread terror by assassinating local officials, police officers, and soldiers (they killed 100 in 1987). In 1993, they were about 300 strong and were financed mainly by the extortion of protection money from local and multinational businesses, who transfer the money to banks in neighbouring Asian countries where no questions are asked. NPA propaganda is conducted both in rural and urban areas by a front organization, the National Democratic Front (NDF). They were, however, set back by the initial popularity of President Aquino. After she came to power they accepted a sixty day cease-fire, presumably to gather strength and lull the government, but they broke it early in February 1987. Mrs Aquino, whose power was endorsed by a landslide victory in the Senate and Congressional elections in May 1987, hoped for regional cease-fire agreements, which the public certainly wanted. The NPA's cadres in rural areas, however, are well organized and exercise discipline by terror both in the villages and in the shanty towns, so their threat must still be taken seriously.

The MNLF, led by Nur Misuari, has about 5,000 armed guerrillas. It is supported by Iran and Libya, and sometimes offered sanctuary, if needed, by sympathetic Muslims in the neighbouring territory of east Malaysia. Their insurgency has cost about 60,000 lives since 1972.

Now facing strong resistance from the Christian majority in Mindanao, they have been more amenable to truces than the NPA but, again, the insurgency is not likely to disappear.

Mrs Aquino decided not to stand for re-election in May 1992 and her Defence Minister, Fidel Ramos, was elected President, taking office on 30 June. He and Mrs Aquino had been forced to bow to the Senate refusal to ratify the treaty for US bases to remain in the Philippines. The Clark Air Force Base had already been abandoned in June 1991 due to damage suffered in a volcanic eruption, and the Subic Bay Naval Base was evacuated at the end of 1992. This meant a serious loss of revenue and employment in an already troubled economy but for the Senate it was a matter of national pride.

President Ramos initiated peace talks with the right-wing army rebels who had staged six attempted coups against Mrs Aquino. The rebel leader, Colonel 'Gringo' Honosan, emerged from hiding under a negotiated truce and talks began on 22 January 1993. Ramos also tried to start peace talks with the NPA, which had begun to fragment, with local warlords conducting lucrative operations such as kidnap and ransom for criminal gain. So, whatever may be agreed with any NPA leadership, many of its members are likely to continue as armed criminal gangs.

Factional fighting also continued among rival movements on the island of Mindinao, where there were believed to be some 52,000 weapons at large.

Sri Lanka

Sri Lanka has been plagued by civil war since 1983. The country has an explosive population mixture, with 74 per cent Sinhalese (mainly Buddhist) and 12.5 per cent Ceylon Tamils (1.8 million, mainly Hindu). The remainder include 5.5 per cent Indian Tamils descended from migrants working in the tea plantations in the Central Highlands, who have taken no part in the civil war, and a number of mainly Tamil-speaking Muslims. The Ceylon Tamils have an overwhelming majority in the Northern Province around Jaffna and have 42 per cent of the population of the Eastern Province, where the remainder comprise 33 per cent Muslims and 25 per cent Sinhalese. There is also a substantial minority of Tamils in the capital, Colombo.

The insurgency in the north, led by the Tamil Tigers (LTTE), began in 1983 with communal massacres by both sides. Initially the Tigers received some support from their 55 million cousins in Tamil Nadu in southern India. This was largely cut off after Mrs Gandhi's assassination in 1984 because her son Rajiv Gandhi, who was elected to succeed her, feared that supporting secession of Sri Lanka's Tamils might encourage other secessionists, such as the Sikhs in India.

By 1987, the Tamil insurgency had cost some 6,000 killed and at the end of July Rajiv Gandhi persuaded the Tigers' leader, Vellapillai Prabhakaran, to accept an agreement for autonomous government in the Northern and Eastern Provinces. With the approval of President Jayawardene, the Indians sent a 7,000 strong peacekeeping force (IPKF) to whom the Tigers would hand over their weapons, but Prabhakaran did not keep his agreement and fighting intensified. The IPKF grew to 50,000.

Meanwhile another insurgency had begun in southern Sri Lanka by a radical Sinhalese nationalist movement, the JVP (People's Liberation Front), which had failed in an earlier attempt at an insurgency in 1971. JVP resented what they saw as an Indian take-over in the North and directed a campaign of terror against local government officials and citizens who collaborated with them. They killed some 1,500 people between the decision to deploy the IPKF (August 1987) and the end of 1988.

A presidential election was due under the constitution and was held on 19 December 1988. President Jayawardene, aged 83, decided not to run again and his Prime Minister, Ranasinghe Premadasa, was elected. Premadasa was committed to insisting that the Indians withdrew the IPKF and made conciliatory gestures to the JVP, but these were rebuffed, as JVP's real aim was to seize power. Premadasa realized that he must first destroy the JVP insurgency in the south, since he would otherwise not have enough soldiers to replace the IPKF in the north, so the Sri Lankan army mounted a ruthless offensive which allegedly included extra legal killings of JVP suspects and supporters. There are no reliable figures for casualties but the total killed is believed to have run into tens of thousands. In November 1989 the army and police finally captured or killed the entire JVP leadership and that war was over.

The IPKF left in March 1990, having themselves launched a final offensive hoping to ensure the survival of the provincial government which they had established in the Northern and Eastern Provinces, at a cost of more than 1,000 Indian soldiers' lives. The Tigers, however, quickly re-established their control in the north, though the Sri Lankan army, following up the IPKF offensive, drove most of them out of the Eastern Province.

On 21 May 1991 Rajiv Gandhi was assassinated in Madras by a suicide bomber with explosives strapped round her body; there was strong evidence that the Tigers were responsible. This caused outrage throughout India: support and supplies for the Tigers from Tamil Nadu virtually ceased. The Sri Lankan army redoubled its offensive and claimed to have killed 2,000 Tigers in a battle for the Elephant Pass, which controlled access to the Tigers' stronghold in the Jaffna peninsula. By 1992, the army had cut off the Peninsula from Tiger bases further south. There was, however, a substantial Tamil population in the east as well as in the north and in Colombo, many of whom sympathized with the Tigers.

On 1 May 1993 President Premadasa was assassinated in Colombo by a suicide bomber who, like Rajiv Gandhi's assassin, had explosives strapped round his body. There was again strong evidence that this was the work of the Tigers. Only a week earlier, one of the leading opposition politicians, Lalith Athulathmudali, had been assassinated. At the end of May, however, the provincial elections (with the north and east excluded) went ahead peacefully, resulting in a fair mixture of seats for government and opposition parties – an encouraging proof of the health of Sri Lanka's democratic process, which had operated continuously since 1931.

The Tigers have lost ground, especially in the east, and have suffered heavy casualties, but their more fanatical members still resist in the north. Whatever political or military solution is reached, the legacy of hatred is such that some terrorism will almost certainly continue.

India

In the eleven years up to 1993, about 15,000 people had been killed in the Sikh–Hindu violence which began in 1982. This must be seen in the context of communal violence in India as a whole, including that between Hindus and Muslims and high-caste and low-caste Hindus; and in separatist violence by Gurkhas, Nagas and others. Casualties run into hundreds or more in a single incident. The Sikh violence is mainly urban-based, though it extends to massacres of Hindus in the villages and in buses on the roads. It could be covered in either Part IV or Part V but is included here because of its similarities with the communal violence in Sri Lanka.

The 16 million Sikhs comprise 2 per cent of India's population of over 800 million; nearly half of these are in the state of Punjab, where they have a narrow (51 per cent) majority. This majority used to be bigger. but there has been an immigration of Hindus seeking work and an emigration of prosperous Sikhs seeking business opportunities in Delhi and elsewhere in India. It is this decline in the Sikh majority that the militant Sikhs are trying to reverse, by terrorizing Hindus to leave, and by provoking a Hindu backlash against Sikhs elsewhere so that more Sikhs return. They also demand independence for a new state of Khalistan.

The Sikh militants operate in a loose cell structure in about six main organizations, which mix open violence on the streets with individual murders and massacres. The most important is the All India Sikh Students Federation (AISSF), whose militancy is influenced by there being 100,000 unemployed graduates in Punjab.

The first terrorist killings were in 1980 but began in earnest when the leading militant, Sant Bhindranwale, established his headquarters in the sanctuary of the Golden Temple in Amritsar in July 1982. He continued to direct operations from there until the Indian government (which had suspended the Punjab state government and imposed direct rule in October 1983) sent in the army, which assaulted the Golden Temple on 5 and 6 June 1984. Bhindranwale was found dead inside and another 400 Sikh militants killed. This was highly emotive, not only because the Golden Temple is the Sikhs' holiest shrine, but also because 10 per cent of the Indian army are Sikhs, many of whom took part in the assault.

As a direct result of this the Prime Minister, Mrs Indira Gandhi, was murdered by two of her own Sikh bodyguards on 31 October. In the Hindu backlash, over 2,000 Sikhs were killed in New Delhi in the next three days. Her son, Rajiv Gandhi, was elected in her place.

On 23 June 1985, 329 passengers and crew were killed in a mid-air explosion of an Air India jet, which had taken off from Montreal (see pp. 167–8) and the cycle of violence and backlash was given another twist. Violence escalated further in January 1986 when Sikh militants reoccupied the Golden Temple, which was recaptured by state police in April. Killing continued at a rate of 1,000 or more every year, rising to higher peaks in 1991 and 1992. The murder of Rajiv Gandhi in May 1991 (see pp. 131–2) was by Sri Lankan Tamils but it further increased the tension.

Meanwhile there was a steady rise in public support for the militant Hindu revivalist Bharatiya Janata Party (BJP). In the 1984 election BJP won just 2 seats. This rose to 88 in 1989 and 119 in 1991. Opinion polls suggested that BJP might have won 170 seats if there had been an election in 1993. This would still have been well short of the 273 needed for an overall majority but 83 per cent of Indians are Hindus and communal strife with Muslims (11 per cent) and Sikhs (2 per cent) could drive enough of them into BJP to secure a parliamentary majority. By 1992 BJP held four of the state governments, including that of Uttar Pradesh.

Hindu–Muslim violence is endemic in India and the estimates of the numbers killed in communal violence in the period of partition in 1947 vary from hundreds of thousands to millions. There was an explosion of violence in Uttar Pradesh in December 1992 which probably cost about 1,700 lives in the following few weeks. For some time militant Hindus, encouraged by the BJP state government, had been demanding that the small sixteenth-century Muslim Babri Mosque in Adodhya must be demolished and replaced by a Hindu temple, as it was allegedly built on the site of the birthplace of the Hindu God Ram. On 6 December 1992 a rally of 200,000 Hindus overpowered the police guard and demolished the Babri Mosque. The BJP state government, if not actually encouraging the rally, did not stop it. The Indian Prime Minister dismissed the state government and assumed direct rule, later doing the same to the other three BJP state governments. This, however, did not prevent the killing of at least 1,200 people in communal rioting during the next seven days and, after a brief lull in mid-December, another 500 in January 1993, and probably more. These killings took place all over India, but especially in Uttar Pradesh, Gujerat and Bombay. In Bombay the violence took on a form of terrorism similar to that in Bosnia: gangs of Hindus looted Muslim shops and forced some 20,000 Muslims to flee from their homes, which they sold in panic for whatever they could get for them – another horrible manifestation of the fashionable scourge of ethnic cleansing. But BJP support declined in the 1993 elections.

Against this dark background, however, the early months of 1993 saw an encouraging decline in Sikh violence in Punjab, thanks largely to public exhaustion and exasperation with the bloodshed (see Table 4). Nearly 5,000 people had been killed in 1991 and 4,000 in 1992; as a result, there was popular support for a robust and sometimes ruthless police campaign against the militants.

Table 4 Fatal casualties in Punjab, 1991–3

	1991	*1992*	*1993 Jan–Mar*
Civilians killed by terrorists	2,094	1,226	7
Police killed	497	252	17
Terrorists killed	2,177	2,113	270

Source: Punjab Police, cited in *The Economist* 22 May 1993

If the Hindu–Muslim violence can be similarly contained, India's eleven years of terror (1982–93) could subside, as did Central America's. The risk remains, however, that communal terrorism, if not restrained, could one day cause the largest democracy in history to disintegrate or become an autocracy.

Afghanistan, Central Asia and Kurdistan

The North-West Frontier of Pakistan and Afghanistan has a long tradition of a particular type of highly effective rural guerrilla warfare. It is dependent on their rocky mountainous terrain and their tribal structure, and has been mirrored in the Kurdish areas of Iran, Iraq, Syria and Turkey, and to some extent in the southern part of the Arabian Peninsula (Yemen and Oman).

In recent years the conflict has been intensified by the Soviet invasion of Afghanistan and by the flow of money from opium and heroin trafficking (described in Chapter 10). The character of fighting, however, continues to be shaped on the unchanging character of the people and the terrain.

Generally the tribesmen have been operating against regular armies of governments from which they want to be independent, such as the British and now the Pakistanis in the North-West Frontier, the Russians in Afghanistan, and the four countries between which Kurdistan is split.

The regular armies have had to depend on roads for the movement of heavy weapons, ammunition and supplies, because without these the guerrillas, in their own terrain on equal terms, could beat them. This applied both in the nineteenth century, with wagon trains, and in the twentieth, when helicopters, despite their other values, cannot move or maintain tanks or heavy artillery. The wars remain focused on control of these roads and of the villages through which they pass. Tiny groups of tribesmen with snipers' rifles and (now) shoulder-fired missiles have been able to wreak havoc on wagon trains and mechanized convoys on the roads (even tanks can seldom move far into the rocky hills) and the helicopter gunships have brought a change of degree rather than kind from the biplanes of the 1920s. The shoulder-fired missiles have to some extent neutralized even this change of degree.

Success for the road-based armies has always depended on two things; on occupation of the commanding heights flanking the road by leapfrogging infantry trained in mountain warfare skills matching those of the guerrillas (and often recruited from rival tribes); and on intelligence. New technology has improved airborne-surveillance even of the elusive mountain guerrillas but the decisive intelligence must come mainly from the villages on which the guerrillas rely for supplies – one of the lessons which does seem to apply world-wide. Because of strong tribal cohesion and loyalty, no government's writ has extended into these villages beyond doing deals with the leaders.

President Brezhnev sent the Soviet army into Afghanistan in 1979 lest the quarrelling Afghan Communist factions opened the way for an

Islamic fundamentalist regime which might arouse echoes in his own Central Asian republics. The Soviet army was bitterly if somewhat chaotically resisted by a large number of rival *mujahideen* guerrilla groups. Eventually, the Soviet army had 100,000 troops in the country and, in ten years, suffered 15,000 killed before President Gorbachev withdrew them in 1989. By then, 1 million Afghans had died, 2 million refugees had gone to Iran and 3 million to Pakistan. The Soviets had installed President Najibullah, whom the *mujahideen* continued to resist; Gorbachev supported him with economic aid and military equipment until the end of 1991. In March 1992 Najibullah's army commander, General Dostam, joined forces with the *mujahideen* and Najibullah declared that he was willing to hand over power. The UN sent a special envoy, Benon Sevan, to try to work out an orderly transfer of power.

The sixteen *mujahideen* guerrilla groups had conflicting strands of relationships and rivalries – religious (nine Shia, seven Sunni) and tribal (e.g. Pathans and Baluchis bordering Pakistan, the Shia Hazaras linked to Iran and Tajiks, Uzbeks and Turkmen adjacent to their cousins in the ex-Soviet Central Asian republics).

The UN special envoy moved fast. Najibullah stood down and on 15 April 1992 took refuge in the UN office in Kabul. A temporary head of state, Sibghatullah Mujaddidi, who later handed over to Burhannuddin Rabbani, was backed by an uneasy council of rival *mujahideen* commanders. The most successful guerrilla fighter, Ahmad Shah Masoud (a Tajik), became Defence Minister, and was sporadically supported by General Dostam (an Uzbek), whose army was north of Kabul. They occupied Kabul in April but were immediately challenged by Masoud's strongest rival, Gulbuddin Hikmatyar, a fundamentalist Pathan who had spent most of the war in Pakistan. Hikmatyar occupied the hills to the south of Kabul from which he could bombard the city. While still unable to enter the capital and still at war with the Defence Minister, Hikmatyar was appointed 'Prime Minister designate' – a bizarre situation symptomatic of the situation in Afghanistan. But occupation of Kabul has never signified control of the whole country and is unlikely to do so.

The more serious prospect in the region as a whole comes from the ambitions of the big neighbouring powers to extend their influence in Turkmenistan, Uzbekistan, Tajikistan, Kazakhstan, Kirghizstan and Afghanistan. The Russians will try very hard to retain their influence through the Commonwealth of Independent States (CIS), their trading links and the large ethnic Russian minorities in some of their former republics. Turkey's hopes lie in the fact that many of the people are racially Turkic, and their Muslim faith is generally not fundamentalist. Iran has designs on the Shia communities, such as the

Hazaras, and on other Pharsi speaking peoples like the Tajiks. Pathans have traditionally dominated Afghanistan, and Pakistan acted as host to many of the *mujahideen* groups after 1979. The likely pattern will be for all these countries to support, discreetly or otherwise, the internal groups that they hope to see prevail. Where this succeeds, other groups will take to the hills and resist, as displaced tribes have always done in Afghanistan.

There are 16 million Kurds, of whom about 10 million are in Turkey, with smaller numbers in Iraq, Iran and Syria. They will continue their prolonged campaign to unite their mountainous landlocked heartland into an independent Kurdistan. Saddam Hussein decimated the Kurds in northern Iraq with chemical weapons in 1988 but, after he lost the Gulf War in 1991, he had to concede them virtual autonomy. The Iraqi Kurds were reasonably content with this as their real fear was of being taken over by Turkey. Saddam Hussein would certainly re-establish his control if he could, both for his own prestige and because so much of his oil is in that area. The Turks have been unwilling to grant any form of autonomy to their own Kurds.

There is going to be a great deal more guerrilla warfare, no doubt combined with ethnic cleansing, in Central Asia. The centuries old echo of small arms fire through the mountains has been reinforced by helicopter gunships and hand held surface-to-air missiles.

Sudan

The Sudanese People's Liberation Army (SPLA) is based in the southern – black (animist and Christian) – half of the country. The Muslim Arabs in the northern half have always dominated, but only 39 per cent of the 27 million population are Arabs and 52 per cent are black. The SPLA was formed in 1983, led by Colonel Dr John Garang, and soon had about 20,000 fighters. In 1991 SPLA split into two factions. The Torit faction led by Garang aims for a federal Sudanese government which, in view of the population mix, would in theory mean black control. The Nasir faction seeks independence for southern Sudan.

The Prime Minister of Sudan, General Omar Hassan al-Bashir, seized power by military *coup d'état* in 1989 and is backed by the fundamentalist Islamic National Front (INF). He governs with a military junta; he has close ties with Libya and Iran but he alienated other Arab countries by supporting Iraq's seizure of Kuwait in 1990–1. He introduced strict Islamic law, including the traditional punishments such as flogging, amputation and public execution. Though initially Bashir exempted the south from this, he later applied it throughout the country, and Arab and Islamic studies became compulsory in all the schools, including those in Christian areas.

The civil war in the south followed an established pattern. The dry season (normally October to April but extending into July in 1992) favours the government's heavily armed and mechanized offensives; in 1992 they captured most of the main towns in the south, including Garang's base in Torit, and they relieved the siege of Juba, the southern capital. When the belated rains came, the SPLA were able to besiege these towns and re-establish their domination of the countryside in between.

This pattern is likely to persist unless Bashir's control of the Arab north is eroded, which is quite possible. The repressive fundamentalist regime is unpopular and there is unrest over food shortage in the cities and in the densely populated areas around Khartoum, Omdurman and Wad Medani. Shortages approach the levels of the 1984–5 famine in the eastern Red Sea provinces and in Kordofan and Darfur in the west, where millions of refugees have been displaced, nearly 1 million of them to camps around Khartoum alone.

Order is maintained by intense repression by the army and police, but they are stretched with continuing guerrilla warfare in the south and unrest in the north so Sudan could explode into chaos at any time, throwing its almost insoluble problems into the lap of the UN.

Somalia

Somalia did explode into chaos in 1991 and independent intervention by US troops set a new pattern which may well reappear elsewhere.

On 26 January 1991 Siad Barre, after twenty-one years of dictatorial Communist rule, was ousted in a coup by General Mohamed Aideed on behalf of the United Somali Congress (USC). This was followed by an immediate split between Aideed and Ali Mahdi, whom the USC had appointed President of Somalia. For the next two years they ran separate private armies. In the first year 25,000 Somalis were killed, another 250,000 made homeless while 800,000 more fled to Ethiopia. In March 1992 a UN-brokered cease-fire was agreed and a special envoy was sent in with 50 observers to monitor it – with very little success.

The UN made no attempt to organize distribution of food, on the grounds that it could intervene only with the agreement of the 'local authority'. General Aideed, who controlled the southern part of the capital, Mogadishu, including its airfield, refused this, claiming that his own army could maintain order. The two private armies – and later a third one under the deposed Siad Barre's son-in-law – consisted mainly of scarcely controlled gangs of young men, often in vehicles mounted with machine-guns and rocket launchers (known as 'technicals') who ranged the countryside looting food supplies.

Heroic efforts were made by non-government organizations (NGOs) such as the International Red Cross, the British Save the Children Fund and the French *Médecins sans Frontières* to run food kitchens and health centres, usually making private deals with the local warlords to provide gangs of their gunmen as guards, paying them in the only currency worth anything – food. Thus, between 15 and 50 per cent of the food had to be handed over as the equivalent of protection money. Members of NGOs took huge personal risks but they could provide only a fraction of what was needed; at one time 5,000 Somalis, mainly the old and the very young, were dying every day.

The UN made a further futile intervention in July 1992, negotiating with Aideed to send 500 UN troops (Pakistanis) to guard food distribution but this tiny force could do no more than guard the airfield; little of the food reached those who needed it.

By November 1992, 300,000 Somalis had died of starvation and it was clear that this figure would reach half a million unless something drastic were done. The US government therefore obtained UN Security Council approval to send a predominantly US force, with other small contingents, to take the situation in hand. The force totalled 35,000, of whom 28,000 were Americans, and it was under US command. The warlords bowed to *force majeure* and agreed to co-operate. The US troops were generally welcomed and they quickly showed that they meant business; individual gunmen and 'technicals' who shot at them were drenched with return fire, often from helicopter gunships. Substantial numbers of weapons were seized, though many more were hidden away in the countryside for future use. Within a few weeks, food was flowing and being distributed; in fact, after a few months, the farmers complained that there was so much food that the rural economy was being undermined – a common result if food aid goes on for too long. But the private armies were not disarmed.

In May 1993 the US force was relieved as planned by a multinational force of 28,000 UN troops under a Turkish general, with an American deputy who had call on a force of US Navy and Marines lying offshore.

Under normal UN peacekeeping rules – to act only with the agreement of the local government – peace would never have been restored. The US force acting under US command with UN approval created a valuable precedent, but no single country is likely to take on such a commitment unless she is sure that it is within her power to succeed; any countries doing so may, as the Americans did, undertake it only if the operation is under their own direction and control. No single country would take on peacemaking in Bosnia or Sudan because of the terrain and the scale and extent of the fighting. The possibility of NATO undertaking such operations for the UN is discussed in Chapter 19.

The warlords soon showed their contempt for the new UN force. On 5 June 1993 gunmen loyal to General Aideed ambushed a UN contingent attempting to continue the unfinished business of finding and confiscating weapons. They killed twenty-three Pakistani soldiers and wounded fifty others. The warlords would not have dared to do this against the US force for fear of the immediate and devastating retaliation, especially from helicopter gunships. A measured response following Security Council discussions in New York has not the same psychological effect. It will be unfair to ask soldiers to face these risks unless the UN delegates to its field commanders the power to react promptly and effectively on such occasions.

Southern Africa

During a brief spell of Communist government in Portugal in 1975, her two main African colonies, Angola and Mozambique, were given independence in some haste under the Marxist movements which had long been fighting colonial rule – MPLA and FRELIMO respectively (see List of Abbreviations). In both cases these new governments were opposed by guerrilla movements supported by South Africa – UNITA and RENAMO. The MPLA and FRELIMO governments were in turn supported by the USSR, which did so by financing large contingents of the Cuban army. UNITA and RENAMO both held substantial amounts of territory and the conflicts could better be described as civil war than guerrilla warfare, though they involved some fairly large-scale terrorist incidents aimed at intimidating the villagers or tribesmen.

In the late 1980s, due to President Gorbachev's policy of running down Soviet overseas involvement and especially subsidies to Cuba, both the MPLA and FRELIMO governments moved away from Marxism in order to encourage investment and trade with the west. South Africa also withdrew its support from UNITA and RENAMO.

In May 1991 a cease-fire was agreed in Angola and in September 1992 a presidential election was held. The first round was won by the incumbent President, José de Santos, with 49.57 per cent of the vote compared with 40.07 per cent for the UNITA leader, Jonas Savimbi. MPLA won the election for the legislative assembly more comfortably, with 124 seats to 67. Savimbi, however, refused to accept the result, pulled out of the second round of voting in the presidential election and resumed the civil war. Despite no longer having any outside support, Savimbi still had the loyalty of many of the larger tribes and controlled 70 per cent of the country, including some important towns.

In Mozambique, a General Peace Accord and cease-fire was signed on 4 October 1992. It was agreed that both the government forces and the RENAMO guerrillas (who held 85 per cent of the country) would disarm over a period and form a combined army of 30,000. This was supervised by a team of 7,500 UN observers. In view of the experience in Angola, there was some caution about naming a date for elections but it was agreed that RENAMO would stand as a lawful political party.

The prognosis for Mozambique is reasonably hopeful but there seems at the time of writing (late 1993) to be little hope of an end to the civil war in Angola. UNITA continues to hold a large part of the country, populated by tribesmen who do not wish to be governed by the urban-based MPLA. Assuming that the government is able to hold the capital, Luanda, and most of the oil-producing areas in the north on which the economy depends, UNITA is likely to try to disrupt these areas by terrorist activity, including the kidnap of foreign technicians working in the oil and other industries. UNITA is also co-operating with an independence movement in Cabinda, a rich enclave of Angola surrounded by Congolese territory.

In South Africa, President de Klerk and Nelson Mandela, the moderate leader of the African National Congress (ANC), are working together towards a constituent assembly, leading to full majority-rule elections preceded by a period of multiracial coalition government. Both are hampered by violent extremist fringes, Afrikaner nationalists determined to maintain white rule, at least in certain specified Afrikaner republics, and ANC militants objecting to the slow transition and demanding immediate black majority rule. De Klerk and Mandela are well aware that the South African economy, in which black South Africans are far more prosperous than any other Africans in Africa, will continue to depend on white know-how, management and investment and that, if this is not to explode or collapse beyond recovery, a gradual transition of power is essential. Nevertheless, whatever the pattern of political progress, and whatever the final result, it will probably be disrupted by violence and terrorism by one or both extremes.

14 Development of rural guerrilla warfare

This chapter deals with the way that current and future developments, particularly technological ones, are likely to affect rural guerrilla warfare. The technological trends and developments were discussed in Part II (Chapters 3–8), and their effect on urban terrorism will be assessed in Chapter 17, in the light of urban political and tactical factors in Chapters 15 and 16. Where the effects on rural and urban terrorism are relatively similar (e.g. in certain weapons, access and perimeter protection and search techniques) these will be deferred to Chapter 17 with only a brief reference in this chapter as it is better to go into detail only once, in the light of both rural and urban factors. This chapter will therefore attempt only to highlight the effects peculiar to rural conflict, on both terrorist and security force tactics and techniques.

The psychology of rural terrorism

The rural populations are psychologically very vulnerable to terrorism as encapsulated by Sun Tzu: 'Kill one – frighten ten thousand'. When there are terrorists prowling their villages at night, or liable to jump out of the bushes when they are at work in the fields, the people feel very insecure – far more isolated than someone moving among the bustle of a city or a shanty town. This particularly applies to local government officials, village police officers, and to villagers accused of co-operating with them. Among the most chilling of stories was the treatment of one village chief in South Vietnam. North Vietnamese guerrillas entered the village at night, assembled the villagers, subjected the chief to a public trial, then mutilated each of his children, disembowelled his wife in front of him, castrated him, and let him go, *pour encourager les autres*. Recent experience in Peru, Bosnia, Sudan, Somalia, India, Sri Lanka and Cambodia suggests that this kind of terrorism is growing rather than declining.

So too is the ambushing of buses on country roads, in all these cases and also by various Arab terrorists and the IRA. This tactic is considered in Part V as an offshoot of urban terrorism. Extortion of protection money and revolutionary taxes is also practised by both rural and urban terrorists. The conflict in Bosnia is as much urban as rural and will be discussed in Chapter 15 (pp. 163–6).

Growing rural affluence, as in the drug-producing areas of Peru, Colombia and Lebanon, makes people psychologically more vulnerable, not only to extortion but also to physical intimidation, because before a better standard of hygiene and better medicine had reached them they were more philosophical about deaths in the family than they are now.

Protection of rural populations is difficult and expensive. Village officials and police officers under threat tend to live-and-let-live with the guerrillas. Electronic and photographic surveillance inside the villages (by well-concealed long-range automatic cameras backed by good lighting) can extend the eyes and ears of the police but are only as good as the people operating them. Good human intelligence (discussed later in this chapter) provides the best hope of protection and deterrence.

Target selection

Prime targets are the people in villages at work in the fields or on the roads, and also isolated police or army posts, attacked not only for intimidation but also for acquiring weapons and ammunition.

Second only to these is the infrastructure, which becomes more interdependent as it is developed, with transformer stations, power lines, pipelines, roads, bridges and telecommunications, all vulnerable to sabotage and interdiction. Their protection draws security forces away from the ultimately more important protection of people.

Water supplies are no more and no less vulnerable than they always were to contamination or to biological agents to spread disease. Like nuclear weapons, however, the intensity of public reaction and consequently the limited credibility of the threat, are powerful deterrents to this type of attack, as was discussed in Chapter 5 (pp. 53–4).

Weapons

Weapon development was discussed in Chapters 4 and 5. Sub-machine-guns with a high volume of fire will be devastating in a road ambush. So will modern and developing shotgun systems firing buckshot or flechettes (see Chapter 4).

The development of heavy machine-guns capable of penetrating lightly armoured vehicles at long ranges across valleys is particularly applicable to rural guerrilla warfare. So are hand-held guided missiles such as MILAN (see pp. 46–7).

The weapons which have most transformed rural guerrilla conflict in recent years, however, have been the guided anti-aircraft missiles such as the Russian SAM 7 (costing less than $1,000) and the more sophisticated 'fire-and-forget' US Stinger, as provided to Afghan guerrillas (see Chapter 13). These weapons are developing fast as the superpowers, the Arabs and the Israelis, are competing for the technological lead. Unfortunately many rural terrorist movements now have rich backers (e.g. Libya and the drug barons) who will be prepared to make a big investment to counter the advantage that the security forces gain from helicopter gunships and troop carriers.

Security of premises and installations

Vulnerable premises in rural guerrilla conflicts range from isolated army or police posts to large installations, oil refineries, airfields and defended villages, with perimeters several kilometres long. Quarries, mines and other places where explosives and detonators may be stored are especially important to protect; so are transformers and pumping stations and bridges. Isolated guards to defend these are notoriously vulnerable, and long delay before help can come makes protection especially difficult.

Energy distribution and cross-country telecommunications are particularly vulnerable to interdiction. Buried pipelines and cables are less vulnerable, but usually prohibitively expensive, especially in rocky and mountainous terrain. Technological development can help in two ways: by automatic detection, cut-outs and valves to limit damage; and by extension of grid systems so that breaches can be bypassed.

Equipment available and under development for access control, identification, perimeter security, surveillance, alarms and electronic monitoring and recording of movement were discussed in Chapters 8 and their application will be further discussed in Chapters 17 and 18. Village security, enhanced by strong, well-lit perimeters, with surveillance and alarm systems, is probably the most important aspect of this.

Personal and travel security

Personal and travel security presents very difficult problems. It will be argued in Chapter 17 (p. 182–3) that it is unwise for 'amateurs' to carry firearms unless they are as well trained and psychologically prepared to use them as effectively as the terrorists are; also that an inadequate bodyguard may increase rather than decrease the risk. Facing rural guerrillas in isolation, however, may necessitate being armed, in which case any local government official or estate or works manager who has to move about may of necessity need to carry a gun and therefore to be trained to achieve the high standard of skill and reflex action needed to survive an exchange of fire. The same goes for their drivers and bodyguards, whose greatest contribution, as in an urban setting, will be to advise them on how to keep out of trouble.

Road bombs and fougasses are a favourite weapon of rural terrorists against selected assassination targets or security force patrols. They often comprise huge charges, of improvised explosives placed in culverts, or charges in roadside bushes or parked vehicles. They are most commonly fired by remote control cable or radio signal but they may also be detonated by a bullet fired from several hundred yards away to close an electric circuit between two metal plates (see p. 51). They can also be fired by the electromagnetic field from a passing metal vehicle, but this method lacks selectivity. There is, however, some scope for ingenuity in finding characteristics peculiar to the type of vehicle which the terrorist wishes to select (see p. 52).

Road mines detonated by the pressure of the wheel of a passing vehicle have been in regular use since the 1940s, with little development. They are particularly attractive for terrorists in rural areas where most of the roads are made of dirt, gravel, oil-bound sand or laterite in which it is easier to bury them than in tarmac or concrete. On rural roads, even this surface is often one way, so the mines in the verge can catch vehicles pulling over to pass. Booby traps are commonly added. Plastic and wooden mines can defeat the metal detector but a well-trained dog can sniff most explosives.

In practice, the use of probes, sharp eyes and sensitive fingers to detect where the soil or road surface has been disturbed has always been and still is the best means of finding mines, and pulling them out of the ground with a long piece of cable is the best guard against booby traps.

An efficient portable sniffer, sensitive enough to pick up the vapour from buried explosive and to give an immediate reading without the need to take it away for analysis, probably offers the best alternative to dogs in the development of mine detectors, and possibly neutron detection. As with other forms of detection, whether of persons or material, it will pay to develop multiple means rather than rely only on one.

Alarms in isolated security force posts, homes and installations, though valuable if only as a morale booster and a deterrent, are less effective in rural than in urban areas because of the response time for help to come. Transmitters and beacons can be effective but the range needs to be long so there is a limit to miniaturization. A powerful beacon concealed in the car should be able to sound the alarm when a victims are kidnapped but, to enable them to be tracked thereafter it may be necessary to conceal a beacon in something which the terrorists might allow them to keep. They might be suspicious of a radio or pocket calculator or video computer game, but less so of a heart pacemaker.

The possibility of a breakthrough in VTOL, STOL and microlite air travel for short distances is discussed in Chapter 17 (p. 182). This could have a particular application to security in rural areas.

Search techniques

Techniques for searching for bombs and guns were described in Chapter 6. Those for detecting buried mines (see pp. 145) have the greatest relevance to rural guerrilla conflict.

In areas where the processing of narcotics (coca to cocaine, opium to heroin – see Part III) is closely linked with terrorism, for example in Colombia, Pakistan and Myanmar, the use of well-trained dogs and possibly chemical sniffers with military patrols in searching villages and farms could greatly improve the detection of processing laboratories.

Intelligence

Rural guerrillas face an inherent dilemma: they cannot activate and dominate the rural population without making regular contact with them, either in the villages or at work in the fields. Such contacts are much more difficult to conceal in rural communities where visitors are noticed. This dilemma can be exploited by the security forces to acquire intelligence. Guerrillas living outside the villages may be hard to catch, but if they or their cadres live mostly inside the villages there will be people who know them and can be given incentives to tell what they know, coupled with reassurance that they and their families will be guaranteed security, if necessary in a new home, if they do.

The initial persuasion of a witness to give information usually comes when the intelligence or police officers speaking to the witness have good background intelligence and possess powerful bits of evidence with which they can surprise and confront the witness, for example that some specific person well known to the witness is involved with the guerrillas. If interrogators have immediate access to a mass of data by having with them an 'expert system' databank in their own intelligent computer or terminal, as described in Chapter 7 (pp. 72–4), they are still more likely to be able to throw the witness into confusion by exposing lies or evasions, and by appearing to know everything already.

Another source of such evidence is modern surveillance equipment, especially long-range high-resolution cameras (still or video). These can produce reliable and undeniable evidence of personal contacts in a small village community, and the sudden presentation of such a photograph or video clip can have a powerful effect on the course of an interrogation. Given judicial authority, the bugging of the home of a known cadre, or of a house where the cadre meets cell members, can produce audiotape evidence of such contacts, and of the processes of organization and intimidation, which are valuable knowledge for use in interrogation.

Another technique used with success in the past is to conceal a secret circuit in some normal piece of electrical equipment, such as a radio receiver, which is, with the aid of someone recruited as an agent, inserted in the right place in the distribution chain to be sold or delivered to a suspected guerrilla leader or cadre. This circuit will transmit signals which can enable its location to be tracked, leading the security forces to suspects' homes or headquarters and, if they are mobile, to track their movements. This was achieved even with the radios and tracking equipment available in the 1960s. It should have far greater potential, now and in the future, with the proliferation of electrical gadgets even in remote rural villages and the much greater sophistication of surveillance equipment.

Equipment under development for better identification and detection of impersonation was described in Chapter 8. Its use has equal application to both rural and urban conflicts so it will be discussed in Chapter 17.

The security forces

Rural guerrilla units can expect to have the advantage over the security forces only when they have the initiative, for example in an ambush or in a surprise hit-and-run attack on an isolated police post. In other circumstances the army or police, better armed and with better opportunities for training, will usually have the advantage if they can bring the guerrillas to battle. In the twelve-year Malayan Emergency the army and police killed or captured 5.7 guerrillas for every man they lost; even in the worst year (1950) the ratio was 2.5 to 1.

The problem is to find them or to predict their movements; this is a matter of good intelligence, and the best intelligence comes from human sources. Though these can be assisted and supplemented by hardware, no surveillance equipment has yet been invented which can equal the human eye and ear, and the human ability to differentiate between true and false.

The primary task of the security forces in rural guerrilla conflict is therefore to build up the confidence of rural communities in their own security, and in the inevitability of final defeat for the guerrillas so that they co-operate in giving information. This means, above all, enabling a permanent police presence, day and night, to be maintained and protected in every village.

A major factor in this is confidence in the rapid arrival of a reaction force if the village or the police post is attacked. The development of more reliable alarm systems and of rapid helicopter transport and gunship support should make this easier now and in the future than in the past.

The organization and accountability of the security forces – army, police and intelligence services – will be discussed in Chapter 17.

Public support

The fastest change in rural areas has been and will be in accessibility to information. The spread of the cheap transistor radio began the process in the 1960s, by opening up even the most remote villages in Latin America and Asia for the first time to the influences of the outside world. This process has continued apace and within a few years most villages will be exposed to the more compelling influence of television. Even if sentimentalists were right in thinking that remote peoples would have been better left with their subsistence agriculture and 'happy' isolation (in fact a blend of boredom, back-breaking toil and high infant mortality) that argument is now irrelevant because, as soon as the transistor radio apprised them that there were more comfortable ways of life, the demand for these became insistent. So did the demand for more information, and especially for television. While the fifty-channel flood into urban homes will not be repeated in the remote areas where rural guerrillas thrive, access for propaganda – government, dissident and foreign inspired – will be steadily increased. In this competition for the hearts and minds of the people, governments will need to seize their technological opportunities to win it.

The other field in which governments must use their advantage is intermediate technology, to enable rural peoples to raise their own standard of living. Intermediate technology is less fashionable than high technology but offers immense opportunities for inventiveness in developing cheap, simple and reliable equipment for the next step up the ladder. People walking half a mile with buckets to get stagnant water need, first, hand pumps in the village and then, when they have learned to operate and maintain engines, deep wells with motor-driven pumps. In places where the monsoons make mud tracks impassable they need all-weather roads – not a few miles of concrete or tarmac but many more miles of easily maintained roads of compacted local material – and culverts and bridges to keep the roads from flooding.

Given confidence that their standard of life, as well as the security of their villages and their families, will steadily improve if stable government is maintained, the people will be less likely to be aroused by agit-prop teams or political activists to use or support violence.

Part V

Urban terrorism

15 Urban terrorist organizations

The urban guerrilla heritage

Though there have always been assassinations and kidnaps throughout history, one of the earliest urban campaigns was that by Irgun Zvai Leumi (IZL) in Palestine in the 1940s. The term 'urban guerrilla' was not coined until 1967, after the failure of Che Guevara and his rural guerrilla *Foco* Theory in Bolivia, whereafter Latin American revolutionaries decided that, in place of the unresponsive peasants, they must redirect their efforts at the intellectuals and urban proletariat in the cities. This philosophy was expounded in Brazil in 1969 by Carlos Marighela in a series of tracts which became known as 'The Minimanual of the Urban Guerrilla'.

Urban terrorism has proved a very effective way of destabilizing democratic societies and provoking an authoritarian take-over. This was well illustrated in Uruguay in 1972 and Argentina in 1976; and in Turkey where, in 1980, urban terrorists killing twenty people a day on the streets provoked a military coup which was widely welcomed by an exasperated public. To his credit, General Evren kept his word and restored parliamentary democracy to Turkey two years later. Even if some western observers are critical of the limitations of that democracy, the urban terrorists have not so far reappeared and a large number have been reprieved and rehabilitated in society.

International terrorism in its present form is a relatively recent phenomenon; it is largely urban (though some rural guerrillas do also receive foreign support – see Part IV). It was begun more or less simultaneously in Brazil, Guatemala and Uruguay and by the Palestinians in 1968. The Palestinians, frustrated by their failure to make any impact on Israel and by the loss in 1968 of every adjacent frontier other than that with Lebanon, sought publicity for their cause by attacks on aircraft in Europe, including hijacking, a form of urban terrorism which killed relatively few people but certainly did gain enormous publicity. Latin American revolutionaries from 1968 to 1973 attempted to deter western countries from supporting their governments by kidnapping diplomats (about fifty in all). When this failed to have the desired effect they turned to seizure of embassies, which reached a peak in 1979–81, but this too failed and has been largely abandoned. Attempts to coerce governments by kidnapping their nationals in Lebanon, by Shia Muslims inspired by Iran, did have a big effect on the attitudes and policies of France and the USA.

The Palestinians

Yassir Arafat's Palestine Liberation Organization (PLO) has no permanent home unless the Israelis allow it to operate officially in an autonomous West Bank, but it is still immensely rich. John Adams in *The Financing of Terror* (1986) estimated the PLO's assets as $5 billion with an annual income of $1.25 billion. The annual income has declined since the PLO alienated Saudi Arabia and Kuwait by supporting Saddam Hussein's invasion in 1990 but Arafat still gets a certain amount of money from then and from the other Arab oil states. The PLO's main source of wealth, however, will continue to come from its investments all over the world, which would bring in an adequate operating income even if most of the oil states' contributions dried up. The PLO's chief accountant is Jawid el Gussan, a rich and successful Palestinian businessman, who runs the business like a multinational finance corporation.

The PLO's main constituent part is Arafat's own Al Fatah, which was about 9,000 strong when it was based in Lebanon in 1982. Since 1983, when it was expelled by President Assad of Syria after the Israeli invasion, it has been much dispersed and weakened.

Al Fatah is not really a guerrilla or clandestine movement. It has fought almost entirely within the Middle East, mainly fighting other Arabs in Lebanon, because the Shia community always resented the PLO's many refugee camps in South Lebanon. Al Fatah has not fought the Israelis much, nor have they carried out international terrorist operations, though some of the smaller constituent organizations of the PLO – e.g. PFLP, PFLP (GC) and PLF – certainly have. So have some militant groups within Al Fatah itself, notably Black September in the early 1970s, then Black June in the late 1970s, and the PLF in the 1980s. Black June broke away under Abu Nidal, to be based first in Iraq, then in Syria and then in Libya. The Abu Nidal group is now wholly disowned by the PLO and has devoted most of its energies in the 1980s to killing mainstream PLO representatives around the world and carrying out assassination projects for other Arab leaders who have been prepared to give them money or sanctuary.

Apart from these more militant groups, the mainstream PLO rank-and-file live as a kind of Home Guard in the refugee camps, being paid from Arafat's ample coffers and defending the camps against whoever attacks them. During their occupation, after initially rounding up several thousand of them as prisoners, the Israelis seldom attacked the camps themselves, but turned a blind eye or positively encouraged rival Arab groups to attack them.

Palestinian international terrorist activities, such as hijacks, have been carried out almost entirely by the smaller splinter groups; the number involved in this kind of activity has seldom exceeded 200 at any one time. The only achievements they can claim are the enormous publicity that they have gained from these actions (for which their techniques are discussed in Chapter 16). They have, however, gained more and better publicity from Yassir Arafat's appearances as the appointed spokesman of the exiled Palestinian people at the UN, and through his seventy recognized offices in capitals over the rest of the world. He has gained some sympathy in the Third World (where Israel is often regarded as a US puppet) and from some European countries such as Greece.

Despite the boost to the peace process by the Israeli–PLO agreement in September 1993 (see pp. 7–8), Hamas and Hezbollah will continue to initiate attacks to provoke Israeli reaction and Israeli extremists will do all they can to prevent progress. If the PLO do achieve their aim of becoming the government of a West Bank and Gaza state, there has been much scepticism about the sincerity of their renunciation of their aim of using this as a springboard to take over the whole of Israel, which is in places only nine miles wide between the hills of the West Bank and the sea. It is therefore extremely unlikely that the Israelis will ever allow a Palestinian West Bank state to become independent of their security control.

It seems, therefore, virtually certain that the present impasse will continue, with several million Palestinians, several thousand of them armed and paid as soldiers, somewhat grudgingly given house room by other Arab states. Their militant elements will keep up the spirits of the others and international terrorist acts will keep them in the limelight in the rest of the world. These individually make an impact, but collectively make it unlikely that the PLO will get the independent homeland they want in the twentieth century – if ever.

Lebanon

From 1975 to 1990 Lebanon was virtually without a central government; the different regions were run by warlords with their own private militias. There was continuous fighting, especially in Beirut, which was split between various Christian and Muslim militias. Foreign intervention was almost invariably unsuccessful and the spectre of 'another Lebanon' has been a constant restraint (like the fear of 'another Vietnam') on decisive intervention in such countries as Bosnia, Cambodia, Liberia and Somalia ever since.

Fighting began in 1975, primarily between Lebanese Christians and the PLO, whose armed presence was widely resented. The Syrians first intervened in 1975 and the Israelis in 1978 and 1982. A multinational peacekeeping force (MNF) was invited in by the Lebanese President in 1983 but was withdrawn in 1984 after suicide bomb attacks on its bases (see Chapter 16). These were perpetrated by the Islamic fundamentalist Hezbollah, sponsored by Iran, which thereafter kidnapped thirty-five western hostages (US, French, British, Italian, Irish, German, Indian and Swiss) between 1984 and 1989. Six were killed but the remainder were all eventually released between 1985 and 1991, some having been held for more than six years. Apart from some alleged concessions made by the French, German and US governments, these kidnaps appear to have achieved nothing at all for Hezbollah and Iran other than an image of barbarism.

Eventually, stability in Lebanon was restored in 1990 by the Syrian army, though they made no attempt to dislodge Hezbollah from its 'no-go areas' in south Lebanon and south Beirut. The Israelis retained a small buffer zone just north of their frontier. Lebanon was at last able to start on the road to recovery.

Iran, Iraq and Libya as sponsors of terrorism

Authoritarian governments use terrorism against their own people in every continent; many governments support and provide bases for international terrorist movements. It is, however, less common for government agents to carry out individual international terrorist attacks, presumably because these are counter-productive if they are found out. Iran, Iraq and Libya are exceptions; as well as providing facilities for Palestinian and other terrorist movements, they have also sent their own agents to carry out direct terrorist acts overseas. All three became more cautious about doing this after 1989, as they needed to improve relations with the west for economic reasons. But all of them have authoritarian governments and whether they sponsor terrorist acts in the future will depend on whether their leaders judge that these will advance or set back the achievement of their aims.

Iran used troops and police to maintain the 444-day seizure of the US Embassy in Tehran in 1979–81, holding 50 staff entitled to diplomatic protection as hostages (see Chapter 16). In 1982, 1,000 Iranian Revolutionary Guards were based with the Syrian army in the Beka'a Valley in Lebanon with the task of recruiting, training and directing the Lebanese Shia fundamentalist Army of God – Hezbollah – which killed more than 350 people in 15 bomb attacks on embassies and military bases in Lebanon and Kuwait in 1983 (see Chapter 16, p. 168). Iran also sponsored Hezbollah in holding the 35 western hostages in Lebanon in 1984–91, and it was Iran which decided that holding them was counterproductive for their national interests and ordered their release. Iran's most personal act of terrorism was the *fatwa* pronounced by the Ayatollah Khomeini himself against the British Indian author Salman Rushdie for alleged blasphemy in his book *The Satanic Verses*. This incited Muslims world-wide to murder Rushdie and offered a reward of $1 million for doing so, later raised to $2 million. This murder was prevented only by the British police establishing a 24-hour guard on Rushdie in a secret location, which entered its fifth year in 1993. The aim was clearly to deter other writers; the *fatwa* was specifically endorsed by Khomeini's successors through to 1993.

Libya in the early 1980s employed agents with diplomatic cover to murder a number of anti-Gadafi Libyans in London and elsewhere in Europe. In 1984 a member of the Libyan embassy staff in London fired a machine-gun from the Embassy window at a group of anti-Gadafi demonstrators across the street and in doing so killed a British policewoman who was protecting the embassy from the demonstrators. In December 1988 the Libyan government was alleged to have been involved in placing the bomb which blew up a US airliner over Lockerbie in Scotland, killing 270 people (see Chapter 16, p. 168). In September 1989 it was claimed that it was a similar Libyan intelligence operation which blew up a French airliner over Niger, killing 170 people. There was evidence of the fuses, as well as the perpetrators, coming from Libya. The UN demanded the extradition of the two prime Lockerbie suspects for trial and, when this was refused, the Security Council imposed sanctions and a civil aviation embargo, but shrank from imposing an embargo on oil exports, as this was opposed by France and Italy which relied heavily on Libyan oil.

Saddam Hussein of Iraq has outstripped most others in the use of terrorism against his own people, having used poison gas to exterminate thousands of Iraqi Kurds in 1988. Iraq has also provided bases for international terrorist movements. Like his Libyan counterpart in London, a man shooting from the Iraqi Embassy in Paris killed a French policeman; also, an Iraqi agent masterminded the seizure of the Iranian Embassy in London by Iranian Arabs in 1980 (see Chapter 16). Saddam Hussein would not hesitate to use the same techniques again if he thought that they would advance his aims.

Algeria and Egypt

Algeria has faced a violent reaction from Islamic fundamentalists ever since the army intervened in January 1992 to prevent the Islamic Salvation Front (FIS) from taking power in the final stages of the general election. During the election, FIS had announced that, if returned to power, they would abolish the electoral process altogether so that their rule would be permanent. The new head of state, Mohamed Boudiaf, was assassinated in June 1992. The armed forces were infiltrated by Islamic extremists and more than a hundred servicemen, including twenty officers, were charged with assisting the terrorists – four of them in a raid on an army barracks in which thirty-five terrorists killed nineteen soldiers on 22 March 1993. If the existing secular system of government seemed in danger of being overturned by the FIS, either by violence or by using the democratic process to destroy itself, there would probably be an army *coup d'état*.

Islamic fundamentalists began a terrorist campaign in Egypt in June 1992, primarily with the aim of destroying the tourist trade. A bomb was exploded in the burial chamber of one of the Pyramids, and there were attacks on tourist coaches and cafés both in Cairo and Upper Egypt. There have also been terrorist attacks on foreign business people in Cairo. The aim of the Muslim Brotherhood was clearly to bring about a collapse of Egypt's economy in the hope of establishing an Islamic fundamentalist state in the ensuing chaos.

The IRA and ETA

The IRA and ETA have a number of characteristics in common. Each has received the support, active or passive, of about 10 per cent of the population of its own province and negligible support in the country as a whole. This can be measured by the support for their associated political party, Sinn Fein and HB respectively. In the Republic of Ireland, Sinn Fein was able to attract under 2 per cent of the vote at the 1989 and 1992 general elections, even though they had declared that they would take up any seats they won in the Dáil. (In the past, their refusal to take up the seats had probably deterred many from voting for them.) On neither occasion did they win any seats, nor any in the previous election either.

Between 1969 and 1993, over 3,000 people have been killed in Northern Ireland – two-thirds of them civilians – out of a total population of 1.5 million. Nearly 900 have been killed in the Basque provinces of Spain in the same period – over 600 by ETA, half of them civilians – out of a total population of 2.25 million.

Both extort a large proportion of their funds by protection money of various kinds, mainly by threatening people with damage to themselves, their families or their property if they do not subscribe. The IRA apply this at all levels in the construction industry, from managers to labourers. One means is to coerce them into tax and social security frauds, for which building sites, with their constant flow of casual labour, are particularly suitable. They also run businesses such as taxis, first forcing the buses and normal commercial taxis off the road by intimidation (or sometimes allowing them to ply in return for a large licence fee or revolutionary tax). Their own loyal cab drivers subscribe a proportion of their earnings and the profits of the whole enterprise go into IRA funds. Racketeering – a term covering all these activities – provides the great majority of the funds for both the IRA and the Protestant paramilitaries.

The IRA are based mainly in well-defined areas of Northern Ireland, in which most of the 10 per cent who support Sinn Fein are concentrated, in West Belfast, Derry and a number of outlying areas, near the borders, such as South Armagh. In these areas they used to operate a relatively overt military structure of battalions, companies, and platoons, with commanding officers, adjutants, intelligence officers, and quartermasters. The identity of these officers was generally known to the loyal supporters, from whom they called out volunteers to act as rank-and-file, sometimes for one-off operations and sometimes continuously. The best of the volunteers in due course graduated as officers. By 1978, however, lack of discretion was resulting in the arrest of too many officers, so they reorganized into more traditional clandestine revolutionary cells or active service units (ASUs). Each of these had its hard core of officers, who picked their volunteers more carefully. An active service unit was usually about eight to twelve strong, though extras could be recruited for particular operations if needed. After about ten years' active service, by which time they might have wives and children, the hard core often move on to higher command and organization or political and propaganda work with Sinn Fein – as godfathers.

Thus the present structure comprises four levels: the godfathers; the hard core; the volunteers; and auxiliaries, who are active supporters willing to act as drivers or look-outs or, for example, to carry guns or parts of a gun to hard-core snipers so that they can go to their fire positions with nothing incriminating, and leave similarly clean, in case they are picked up in the street.

The importance of this is that most of the hard core – perhaps sixty to eighty in all – are well known to the police but cannot be convicted without evidence: they are experts in avoiding the risk of being caught with evidence. The volunteers and the auxiliaries take those risks in the knowledge that, even if convicted, their sentences will be light. Above all, the skilled and experienced hard core must be conserved.

When frustrated in Northern Ireland (e.g. by the series of public relations disasters from November 1987 into 1989, when large numbers of civilians were killed in bungled bombing operations) they send ASUs to Britain and western Europe, usually to attack either leading politicians or military personnel off duty in England, Germany, or the Netherlands. Typical examples were the bombing of the Grand Hotel in Brighton when Mrs Thatcher and her Cabinet were sleeping there in 1984. In London in the early 1990s they switched their priority to the railways and to the business centre of the City of London, giving warnings to reduce counter-productive mass slaughter. These attacks included truck bombs, each containing several thousand pounds of explosives, in the City in April 1992 and April 1993, killing four people and doing damage estimated at £600 million ($1 billion dollars).

There have seldom been more than one, occasionally two ASUs operating at any one time in England and similarly in Germany or the Netherlands. In England they sometimes recruited auxiliaries from among the local Irish communities, though they have more recently avoided this to avoid attracting police attention.

The total numbers killed in Northern Ireland itself have declined to an average of less than one-fifth of their peak of 467 in 1972. Since 1977 the average has been 85 per year, with the lowest figures of 64, 54 and 62 in 1984/5/6. After Sinn Fein's rejection by 98 per cent of the voters in the Republic of Ireland in 1986, the hard-liners who preferred the bullet to the ballot box gained an ascendancy and killings rose to 93 in 1987 and the same again in 1988, but the killing in itself had little effect other than to keep the IRA in the news. It remained six times safer (in terms of homicides per thousand) to live in Belfast than Washington, DC, and, allegedly, twenty-four times safer than in Fort Worth, Texas.

Police co-operation on the border under the Anglo-Irish agreement is good, and probably goes as far as is politically feasible. Joint patrols in a zone both sides of the border, though desirable, would arouse outrage amongst both hard-line republicans in the South and hard-line unionists in the North, and might therefore be counter-productive. Anglo-Irish relations improve every time there is an incident involving vicious or reckless slaughter of civilians, as when the IRA bombed the Remembrance Day Service in Enniskillen in November 1987, killing eleven members of Irish families mourning those who died in the First and Second World Wars. The leadership of the IRA and Sinn Fein found it politic to express regret over this incident. In March 1993, when the IRA killed two young children by placing bombs in a shopping precinct in Warrington, England, the President of the Republic of Ireland came personally to attend their memorial service to show publicly, not only her own feelings on the matter, but also those of the Irish people.

In December 1993, after a series of particularly bloody sectarian murders by the IRA and Protestant paramilitaries, the British and Irish Prime Ministers issued a joint declaration as a basis for negotiations in which Sinn Fein would be invited to take part if the IRA ceased violence and gave proof that this would be permanent. Even if there were a political settlement, however, some of the more fanatical IRA members would continue the killing – the only way of life they have known.

Among the lessons from Northern Ireland are those from the initial success and subsequent collapse of the 'supergrass' trials in 1981–3. 'Supergrass' is the slang term in the British criminal fraternity for a top-ranking police informer. A number of arrested members of both Catholic and Protestant terrorist movements were encouraged by the promise of leniency to give evidence against their former comrades. On the evidence of 10 supergrasses, 217 people were tried for terrorist offences and 120 were convicted; but 67 of these convictions were quashed on appeal on the grounds that they were based on the evidence of a single witness who had a personal interest in securing a conviction. After this, there were no more such trials.

This contrasts with the spectacular success of the similar *pentiti* trials in Italy in the same period. The reasons for this contrast are discussed on pp. 162–3.

Other west European terrorists

After the collapse of Communism in eastern Europe and the USSR in 1989–91, the west European Marxist terrorist movements also collapsed, being already on their last legs. All the leaders of the French *Action Directe* had been imprisoned in 1987; there were believed to be about forty survivors but they seem to have disbanded themselves.

There were also about twenty survivors of the German Red Army Faction and a similar number from the splinter groups of the Italian Red Brigades; both of these carried out very occasional 'symbolic' murder attempts but these may have been independent efforts by individuals. There were also occasional arson or bombing attacks on business and industrial premises.

The terrorist threat in Germany thereafter came largely from neo-Nazi extremists attacking immigrants and refugees, reacting to the flood of applicants for asylum (438,000 to Germany in 1992). Left-wing groups directed most of their efforts to attacking these neo-Nazi groups rather than to revolution.

As in Northern Ireland, the most valuable lesson from Italy was from the use of informers in the period 1980–83. There was provision in Italian law for leniency for accomplices willing to give evidence for the prosecution of others. The Italian success arose not so much from this law (which is common to most countries) as from the genius of one particular *Carabinieri* officer – General Dalla Chiesa – in applying it. On 19 February 1980 Patrizio Peci, the leader of the Turin column of the Red Brigades, was arrested and agreed to co-operate. Dalla Chiesa worked out with Peci a detailed plan for incentives and benefits to secure his participation and that of others. On Peci's evidence alone, 85 brigadists were arrested. Others were encouraged by this scheme and 389 in all offered to co-operate, from both left and right-wing terrorist movements. They were known as *pentiti* (repentants). Of these, 70 were sufficiently highly placed to give valuable information and the resulting arrests totalled 482 from left wing and 227 from right-wing groups. By 1983 terrorism of this kind had virtually collapsed in Italy. Success with the Mafia came more slowly but the murder of two popular judges, Falcone and Borsellino, led to some 300 Sicilian Mafia *pentiti* in 1992–3 and some spectacular arrests. Though the Mafia still has deep roots, this was encouraging.

Why did the *pentiti* succeed and the supergrasses fail? There were probably three main reasons. First, there was the imagination, skill and painstaking organization of General Dalla Chiesa and his team. Second, there were 389 *pentiti*, so it was usually easy to get corroborative evidence; with only 10 supergrasses, and other people afraid to speak, there was little corroborative evidence available in Northern Ireland. Third, Italian judges were prime targets for both terrorists and the Mafia; the Appeal Court judges in Northern Ireland were concerned with the processes of law rather than about keeping killers off the streets, even if they themselves believed the accused to be guilty. The Italian judges, in cases where they had no personal doubt that the accused were members of an organization which had committed many murders, may have been more ready to keep them in prison than to set them free to kill more people.

In both cases there was a moral dilemma. Peci, who was charged with personal involvement in several murders, served only a short time in prison; others, whose crimes were less grave but who had remained loyal to their comrades, received long sentences. On the other hand, if terrorism had continued in Italy at the 1978–80 rate for another five years, 400 more people – judges, trade unionists, politicians, business people, journalists and other members of the public – would be dead. How should the balance be struck between the ethics of *pentitismo* and saving 400 lives? The same question would apply to Northern Ireland; over 800 people have been killed in the ten years since the supergrass convictions (see p. 161) were quashed.

Ethnic cleansing and Bosnia

The new form of the old terrorist technique of ethnic cleansing emerged on a massive scale in Croatia and Bosnia-Herzegovina following the break-up of Yugoslavia in 1991. It also occurred in a number of the former Soviet states and on a smaller scale by neo-Nazis against Turkish guest workers in Germany; there are many other places where there is a risk of it, such as Kosovo, Macedonia and Slovakia.

Ethnic cleansing is an insidious form of terror and has probably been done in various forms since the dawn of civilization wherever majorities wished to frighten minorities into leaving their territory. In Hitler's Germany, it escalated from Stormtroopers hounding Jews out of their shops and homes in the 1930s to the massacre of 6 million Jews, gypsies and others in the concentration camps. Stalin followed suit in 1945, driving about 1 million refugees (mainly German) out of the newly liberated territories of eastern Europe. It was continued in Palestine by two Jewish terrorist movements in 1948, on a smaller scale, but permanently poisoning Arab–Israeli relations; the worst example was in the village of Deir Yassin on 9 April 1948, when 254 Arabs were massacred five weeks before Israel became independent, leading to hundreds of thousands more Arabs fleeing the country, as was the aim. (The Deir Yassin massacre was publicly denounced by David Ben Gurion, who was to become Israel's first Prime Minister, but the damage was done.)

The break-up of Yugoslavia reactivated ethnic cleansing as a calculated terrorist technique. The nation had been formed in 1919 as a union of South Slavs, and comprised six constituent republics – Serbia (the strongest), Croatia, Bosnia, Slovenia, Macedonia and Montenegro. Yugoslavia contained only about 13 per cent non-Slavs, notably Albanians and Hungarians, and nearly all of these were in the Serbian Republic. The other 87 per cent were all South Slavs, though they were divided by traditions and religions reflecting centuries of annexations of parts of the country by the three great empires of Byzantium (Orthodox Christian), Austria-Hungary (Catholic) and Turkey (Muslim). The Serbs (40 per cent of the total population) are Orthodox Christians and clung stubbornly to that through generations of occupation by the Turks. The Croats (22 per cent) and the Slovenes (8 per cent) are Catholics. The Muslims (8 per cent) are concentrated in Bosnia, but they too are South Slavs.

Under Tito (a Croat), the six republics became autonomous within the Yugoslav federation and had the right to secede, though so long as they had Communist governments this was largely theoretical. In 1991, however, Slovenia and Croatia declared their independence. Some eastern areas of Croatia contain large Serb communities which form a patchwork with Croat communities, and the Yugoslav federal army (predominantly officered by Serbs) invaded these areas, declaring the need to protect the Croatian Serbs. In addition, both the Croats and the Croatian Serb communities had their own militias. Both sides revived Hitler's technique of ethnic cleansing. They embarked on a furious campaign of threats, malicious damage, assault, kidnap and murder to induce individual families of the other community to leave their homes. This became quite easy to do as soon as their own militia had gained control of a town or village. By September 1991, both sides were exhausted and accepted UN mediation for a cease-fire and a UN force to monitor it. In effect, this froze the situation, leaving the Serbs in possession of all the areas they wanted in eastern Croatia.

Bosnia declared its independence in March 1992. Its population was a mixture of Bosnian Muslims (40 per cent), Serbs (32 per cent) and Croats (18 per cent) and others (10 per cent). Throughout the country there was a patchwork of small Muslim, Serb and Croat communities. In most districts, one or other usually had a small majority of a little over 50 per cent, but seldom much more. In the capital, Sarajevo, no community had as many as 50 per cent. There was some hostility but there was also much intermarriage and intermingling as neighbours in housing estates. For most ordinary families this was of little consequence – they had lived together for generations – until the evil genius of the political activists got to work to arouse them.

In a referendum in Bosnia in February 1992, the Muslims and Croats voted solidly for independence; the Serb minority boycotted it. The declaration of independence was a signal for all three sides to start terrorizing minority communities in their districts to drive them out. As in Croatia, they were supported by their militias and, in the case of the Bosnian Serbs, also by the Yugoslav federal army. By September 1992 the official death toll was 10,000, with another 50,000 missing and 2 million driven from their homes, throughout the former Yugoslavia. Another half a million had fled the country, mainly to Germany. Most of the refugees were families. The staunchest of Bosnian fathers, however determined to defend his home and his district, would eventually decide that the survival of his children and their mother mattered more. The Serb militia turned the knife in the wound by allowing the family to leave only if they signed a legal document making over their home to the Serbian authorities or to a Serb family.

The Bosnian Serbs had an enormous advantage in that Serbia itself provided them with heavy weapons and other supplies, whereas the embattled Muslims had no such sources of support. The UN Security Council imposed an embargo on arms and other strategic supplies.

To try to stop the killing, the UN and the EC appointed mediators, Cyrus Vance and David Owen, who proposed in January 1993 a federal solution for Bosnia, with three predominantly Serb provinces, three predominantly Croat and three predominantly Muslim, with a tenth mixed province around Sarajevo. Sadly, this solution might simply be an invitation for further ethnic cleansing by the dominant community in each province to drive the minorities out of it. The UN asked NATO to be ready, in the event of the federal solution being accepted by all sides, to send a 75,000 strong peacekeeping force to Bosnia, but it was hard to see how any such force could cover every house in every street and village to prevent this ethnic cleansing continuing.

In April 1993 the leaders of all three Bosnian communities signed their agreement to the Vance-Owen plan – the Bosnian Serb leader only under intense pressure from President Milosevic of Serbia, who was becoming alarmed at the impact of the UN sanctions on Serbia. The self-appointed 'Bosnian Serb Parliament', however, overturned this agreement and the UN abandoned the dispatch of its 75,000 strong peace-keeping force. Instead, it was agreed that the UN would protect six small 'safe areas' for the Muslims, including Sarajevo, leaving the 32 per cent Bosnian Serb minority in possession of 70 per cent of the country – a triumph for their campaign of ethnic cleansing.

This failure by the United Nations undid much of the good which had been done in 1990–1 by its firm and united stance against Saddam Hussein's aggression in Kuwait. As *The Economist* commented on 19 May 1993:

The reassessment of western willpower is not confined to ethnic expansionists. There are others who need to work out how dangerous it would be to do something that America and Europe do not want them to do. North Korea's Kim Il Sung must soon decide whether to make a nuclear bomb. Saddam Hussein is wondering whether he can get away with an assault on the Kurds of northern Iraq. To all such people, the Gulf war made a quarrel with the West look hazardous. The Bosnian decision, the culmination of 23 months of dithering, does not.

In terms of creating human misery, ethnic cleansing is one of the most loathsome of all the forms of terrorism which has developed in this bloodstained twentieth century. Though the Serbs were the greatest offenders, all three communities in Bosnia were seen to be guilty of it, with proven cases of savagery to unarmed civilians including women and children. The soldiers on the ground witnessed the misery and were appalled, whichever community the victims belonged to; they were creditably ready to risk their lives to try to alleviate it, however frustrating this might be. The reluctance lay with the politicians, in the UN and in governments, and with the public opinion they had both to guide and to satisfy. They asked why, for example, British and French soldiers should die in Bosnia, or Pakistanis in Somalia, if the local communities and their leaders or warlords preferred to kill each other than to live together. Even more decisive, probably, was the politicians' assessment of whether the forces they could afford to send would be drawn into an insoluble commitment from which there was no exit. This may explain why the US government was willing to send 28,000 US troops to Somalia (see pp. 139–40), but not to commit any at all to Bosnia.

The problems of peacekeeping and peacemaking are further discussed in Chapter 19.

16 Urban terrorist techniques

Damage to property

A number of contemporary groups using political violence prefer to avoid inflicting human casualties for fear of alienating public sympathy. These include some of the more militant environmental and animal rights groups. They set their bombs and incendiary devices to go off during the night and sometimes warn the authorities or firms that, unless they concede to their demands, the next bombs will be set off in hours of peak activity, with maximum casualties, though this threat is seldom carried out.

The devices for precisely timed delay or remotely controlled firing are adequate for their needs. The likeliest changes are in their selection of targets. Maximum disruption can already be caused by putting a major computer system out of action, but the greater interdependence of business and industry and the growing mass and complexity of computerized records will make high technology industries, finance and insurance companies increasingly vulnerable. Hardware, software and communications will all be vulnerable and disruption by hacking or feeding in fake programs may be more effective than bombing or burning. The development of more reliable technology and procedures for computer security will provide the best answer.

Bombs to kill

The worst recorded single terrorist bomb outrage was on 23 June 1985, when Sikh extremists planted a bag containing a bomb in the hold of an Air India jumbo jet flying from Montreal to India via London, which exploded in mid-Atlantic, killing 329 people. It was almost certainly fired by a delay fuse (possibly set in motion by an altitude fuse) because it went off near the end of the Atlantic flight. On the same day, a bag being unloaded from an Air Canada aircraft exploded (killing two baggage handlers) in Tokyo Airport where it had touched down en route for India. There was evidence in this case too of Sikh involvement in Canada, and the bag was presumably labelled to Tokyo rather than India to divert suspicion, and intended to explode over the Pacific. The subsequent investigation suggested that in both cases, a Sikh 'passenger' appears to have checked in with hold baggage but not to have boarded the aircraft, a serious lapse in routine airport and airline security which cost – from two bombs – 331 lives. These lives might also have been saved if hold baggage had been subjected to vapour detection before checking in, as described for Singapore Airport (see Chapter 18).

The Lockerbie air disaster on 21 December 1988 further underlined the need for tighter control of all cargo and passenger hold baggage, when Pan American Flight 103 was blown up at 31,000 feet by a terrorist bomb in the forward cargo hold. All 259 passengers and crew were killed, and the centre part of the aircraft with its fuel tanks hit the Scottish town of Lockerbie, killing 11 of its inhabitants, bringing the death toll to 270. The bomb was in a suitcase alleged to have been packed and loaded in Malta by two Libyan intelligence officers working as airline ground staff, and thus able to use their airport access to label the suitcase as unaccompanied baggage through to New York via Frankfurt and London. The bomb probably had a delay fuse intended to fire over the Atlantic but, due to late take-off from London, it fired over Scotland, enabling the story to be pieced together from the debris. The measures needed to reduce the risk of disasters like these are discussed in Chapter 18.

The bloodiest series of bomb attacks was perpetrated in 1983, when Hezbollah terrorists in Lebanon bombed the French and US embassies in Beirut on 18 April 1983, killing 50 people, and then the US and French bases of the multinational peacekeeping force (MNF) invited in by President Gemayal, when 240 US Marines and 60 French para-chutists were killed on 23 October 1983. A further 11 bombs were exploded in December 1983 on targets in Kuwait, including the French and US embassies – a total of over 350 killed in 15 attacks. In the two biggest, the attacks on the French and US MNF bases, suicide drivers were employed to drive huge truck bombs into the heart of the target, and were then blown up with their trucks by another Arab with a remote-control device.

The most serious aspect of these bombings was that they led to the withdrawal of the MNF, an indisputable surrender to terrorism which encouraged further terrorist acts, not only by bombing but also by kidnapping US and other western hostages.

Bombing is also the main technique used by the IRA in attacking police and military targets (including off-duty police officers and part-time locally recruited soldiers). Bombing involves very little risk to the bomber. The tilt fuse (see pp. 52–3) in a bomb fitted with magnets can be slipped underneath the body of a car or in the wheel arch, and the safety device removed, in a few seconds, putting not only the intended victim but also an indiscriminate number of passers-by at risk, with the murderer safely out of the way. It does not need a brave or adventurous person to kill in this way, so it is likely to grow in popularity among terrorists.

The same could be said of the remote-controlled bomb planted in a small boat used by Lord Mountbatten on vacation to fish in an estuary in County Sligo in the Republic of Ireland. This was an attractively safe way to kill an old man out with his family and a young Southern Irish boatman, but in this case it did prove counter-productive. Admiral Mountbatten had been a Commander-in-Chief in the Second World War, much respected both in Europe and the USA and, at the age of 79, was unlikely to harm the IRA in the future. The public anger in the Republic of Ireland was such that the murderer was eventually caught. Contributions from the USA to the IRA also fell and have not staged any lasting recovery.

The precise delay fuse (see pp. 50–1) made a spectacular début in the bombing of the Grand Hotel in Brighton in an unsuccessful attempt to murder Mrs Thatcher and her Cabinet (though five other people were killed). As for most terrorist operations against major defended targets, planning for this one began long in advance – in 1981 with a two-year target date for the Conservative Party conference in October 1983 – but the hotel in that year proved unsuitable so it was postponed until the 1984 conference. Again, world-wide public disgust created a climate in which the murderer was eventually caught and convicted. Since then, more meticulous and efficient searching (primarily by explosive-sniffing dogs) combined with good background intelligence has thus far prevented any repetition of this type of attack by the IRA.

Perhaps the most cold-blooded bombing technique on record was that attempted by the Syrian-sponsored Nezar Hindawi at London's Heath-row Airport in April 1986. He first made a Southern Irish chambermaid pregnant in a London hotel, and returned to the Middle East. He later returned, promised to marry her in Israel, and said he would arrange flights. He came into the UK disguised as a member of a Syrian airline crew, carrying a Syrian passport and papers, which the Syrian govern-ment admitted issuing. He lodged in the official Syrian aircrew accommodation in London. He told the girl he had booked her on an El

Al flight but that he, as an Arab, would have to fly by an Arab airline and would join her there.

In the taxi on the way to the airport he gave her a holdall, asking her to take it with her. It contained a bomb, which was not detected by the normal Heathrow X-ray baggage check. An Israeli guard employed by El Al at the boarding gate, however, was suspicious and searched it. There was a flat plastic explosive charge in a false bottom and an ordinary calculating machine, in working order, which proved to contain an additional electric circuit to fire the bomb, which would have exploded at high altitude killing all the passengers, including Hindawi's unsuspecting girlfriend and his unborn child.

When the operation was prevented by the El Al guard, the Syrian Embassy helped Hindawi to hide, but he was arrested and convicted. Britain cut off diplomatic relations and expelled the Syrian Ambassador.

The continuing miniaturization and growing reliability of electronics will provide the likeliest development of bombs in coming years. It will become easier to conceal minute and sophisticated precise delay or remotely controlled firing mechanisms within the increasing number of pocket computers, etc., which people will carry. The development of more precisely guided vehicles may obviate the requirement for suicide drivers. But the use of nuclear, chemical and biological weapons will be neither more nor less likely than in the past (see pp. 53–4), as the restraints on their use are social and psychological rather than technological.

Guns and missiles

Murder by shooting is the favoured method used by terrorists to pick out individual targets when they want to avoid the counter-productive indiscriminate casualties which may be caused by bombs. Developments most likely to affect this technique are the use of laser sights, which enable terrorists to hit their target at short ranges without either aiming or even showing the gun (see p. 37). Further development of silencers so that the silenced gun is short enough to fit into a smaller bag may facilitate this; so could the application of the three-round burst with light caseless ammunition (pp. 37–40) to sub-machine-guns.

For longer ranges, sniper rifles with night vision aids (image intensification and thermal imagery) will become more effective, possibly with a lock-on facility which, given accurate night range-finding, will aim the weapon for the correct trajectory. This could be effective for a night sniper hoping to hit a target in a predetermined spot (e.g. the entrance to a building or a footbridge) from a window some distance away.

For longer range still (in daylight) the heavy machine-gun with armour-piercing ammunition may be further developed for use against lightly armoured vehicles (e.g. VIP limousines or armoured Land Rovers).

Recent years have seen increasing use of expensive and sophisticated surface-to-surface and surface-to-air missiles (SSM and SAM) by terrorists, generally of Soviet or east European origin and redirected by Arab governments, notably Colonel Gadafi's. Continuing development of these weapons for use by regular armies will ensure that new and more efficient versions will become available for terrorists. Lighter hand-held missiles with more accurate and foolproof guidance systems and heat- or metal-seeking weapons can reduce the advantages of armoured vehicles enjoyed by security forces. The elimination of smoke and flash will increase the chances of a getaway by ambush teams or terrorists firing from windows.

The helicopter will become increasingly vulnerable to improving SAMs of the Javelin and Stinger types (see pp. 47–9).

Intimidation and racketeering

'Necklacing' was a particularly vicious form of terror used primarily against elected or appointed local officials in 'black-on-black' violence in the townships in South Africa. A rubber tyre is filled with petrol and ignited round the neck of a victim who is bound so that he cannot shake it off. The screams and the writhing agony have an especially daunting effect on the community and exercises terror in its most literal form. Whether or not the cause is justified, this kind of cruelty must be unreservedly condemned, and is probably likely to repel rather than attract support.

Intimidation is not always as extreme as necklacing. It can start, as Hitler's Brownshirts showed in the 1930s, around the homes and shops of Jews, first warning them to get out and then harassing them until they did so, the first stage of ethnic cleansing. This is the technique used by some animal rights activists against laboratory workers testing new pharmaceutical products or hospital supplies on animals – following the Nazi technique, with 'animal torturer' instead of 'Jew' in the slogan. They carry it further by putting paint-stripper on cars and sometimes starting fires with petrol bombs. On four occasions in 1982 they posted letter bombs to leading politicians and in 1986 they attached magnetic bombs under research scientists' cars. The leader of the Animal Liberation Front (ALF) encouraged his members by writing that it was a perfectly feasible aim to drive the great majority of laboratory staffs to abandon their jobs by this kind of intimidation.

The ALF also, in November 1984, attempted to punish a large confectionery manufacturer, Mars, for financing dental research at Guy's Hospital. They delivered two poisoned chocolate bars to the BBC and a Sunday newspaper asking them to warn the public not to eat Mars Bars. No one was poisoned because, apart from these two, the other forty or fifty bars smuggled on to the shelves of retail outlets contained only a leaflet claiming that they were poisoned when they were not, but a number of children were terrified when they saw the leaflets after they had eaten one of the bars. This did not endear the ALF to the public but the incident did cost Mars (who, for safety, withdrew and destroyed 3,000 tons of bars) about £3-million.

Product contamination or the threat of it are, however, much more often used to intimidate companies into paying a ransom than for political coercion.

More lethal forms of intimidation have been used by political terrorists in Spain and Northern Ireland. ETA have extorted large sums in revolutionary taxes from business people in the Basque country by threatening death or damage to property if they do not pay.

In the Republic of Ireland the IRA is alleged to have extorted money from a corporation by threatening to kidnap executives or staff if they refused to pay. (The Irish government located the bank into which the money was paid and seized it.)

Guerrillas in Angola and southern Sudan have also attempted to disrupt government development projects by abducting expatriate workers and holding them for several months, in order to deter people from working on the projects and to coerce the contractors into abandoning them.

There are numerous means of intimidating corporations and individuals to convince them it is not worthwhile to continue what they are doing, or to extort money to finance further terrorism, both by rural and urban terrorists. Much of it probably goes unreported so it is a technique which must be expected to continue.

Future techniques are likely to centre increasingly around electronic data processing (EDP), computer, hardware, software and communications, (described in Chapter 7). The potential cost can be so enormous that corporations may well be intimidated into changing their policies (e.g. by ceasing to trade with Israel) or paying ransoms in response to the threat of such disruption without it ever actually taking place.

Kidnapping

More conventional forms of kidnapping of individuals to secret hide-outs, usually in urban areas, have been widely used for extorting money (for either criminal gain or funding further political activity and terrorism) or political concessions, including changes in governments' policies and release of prisoners. It is, in fact, one of the most ancient and most international of coercive techniques, and was very prevalent in medieval times. The abduction of sons and daughters as victims (whether as mature heirs or infants) has long been found to be the most effective form of coercing the most robust of leaders and business executives. The Anglo-Saxon origins of the word 'kidnap' were to seize (nab) a child (kid). It has been especially applied in recent years by criminals in Italy and Colombia.

The techniques used for abduction and incarceration of a hostage vary greatly with the environment. In Lebanon, between 1975 and 1991 there was no effective government or law enforcement (see Chapter 15); it was very easy for militia groups to seize victims in the streets and conceal them in the honeycomb of apartments in the areas of Beirut which they controlled. In a more orderly environment, a complicated plan with many months of preparation may be needed.

The most lucrative political kidnapping on record fell into this latter category. In 1974 a Marxist-Peronist movement, the Montoneros, kidnapped Jorge and Juan Born, the two sons of an ageing father who had built up the biggest firm in Argentina, Bunge Born, which he was looking forward to handing on to them. The brothers were in early middle age with children at school, and lived as neighbours. The terrorists placed them under discreet surveillance and observed that, though heavily guarded, they usually left home at the same time in order to escort all their children together to school in the suburbs of Buenos Aires. They took three cars, one dropping the children and the other two proceeding on into the city, the two brothers in the back of one car followed by another escort car with more bodyguards.

The Montoneros employed about fifty terrorists in all. Nineteen did the actual kidnap, working in five teams. They selected a site on a broad tree-covered boulevard with narrow parallel service roads on each side. On a signal that the convoy had left home, they set up diversion signs blocking the main boulevard for tree-lopping and diverted all traffic into the service roads, where two trucks were used to collide with the two cars. Terrorists, dressed as policemen, shot dead the chauffeur and escort in the brothers' car, 'arrested' and beat the other bodyguards, handcuffed them under their car, and drove the brothers away. The bystanders, not surprisingly, preferred to look the other way. Another twenty to thirty terrorists were involved in guarding the hideouts and in logistic duties. A command cell conducted the negotiations and extorted $60 million from the old man before releasing his sons seven months later.

A group of similar size kidnapped the British Ambassador to Uruguay, Sir Geoffrey Jackson, in 1971. In this case he was able to detect at least three of the surveillance teams: one posing as a young couple with a baby picnicking in a park opposite his home; a couple on a motor scooter who regularly tailed his car on its various routes to the embassy, sometimes cutting in to test the chauffeur's reactions; and a 'courting couple' in a doorway opposite the embassy gate. For the abduction they staged an 'accident' with his car in a narrow one-way street and employed four or five more teams to block all the access roads leading on to the getaway route to give them a clear run. He estimated that about thirty others took part in the roster of guards during his eight months in captivity.

There may therefore be from five to ten different cells operating, each from three to eight strong: a reconnaissance cell, perhaps doubling with one or more surveillance cells; a snatch squad, usually about five strong; a number of diversionary teams as in the cases described; possibly a shuttle team with a van to which the victim is quickly transferred so that the snatch squad does not actually take the victim to the hideout; this team may also serve as the logistic team to supply the hideout; there may be several cells sharing the task of guarding; and there will be a command cell to plan and control the operation and to negotiate and distribute any ransom obtained; there may well be a separate cell with the necessary criminal and banking contacts to launder the money. In a well-ordered clandestine political movement, these cells will be isolated from each other as much as possible, with only the cell leaders (or perhaps even the leader of a group of cells) having contact with one particular member of the command cell. Each cell will know only who and what it needs to know.

This all refers to kidnaps by political movements containing an ample supply of volunteers who do not expect to be paid more than their keep and are unlikely to give way to offers of rewards to betray the movement.

Criminal gangs are much more economical with personnel. For a well-guarded target, they may still spend six months in reconnaissance, surveillance and planning, but they may employ only five or ten people at most, since each one will expect a large slice of the ransom if he or she is going to resist police rewards to give information.

The longest recorded political kidnaps were those of the western hostages in Lebanon in 1984–91, some lasting more than six years (see p. 156). Apart from these, William Niehous, an American businessman, was held for 1,219 days in Venezuela in 1976–9. He survived the ordeal, both physically and mentally, and was sustained, as

Sir Geoffrey Jackson was, by a strong religious faith. He did his best to develop a human relationship with his captors in the correct belief that this would make them less likely to kill him. He was eventually rescued when a patrol came across the hideout accidentally.

Another model of survival was Leon Don Richardson, kidnapped by political terrorists in Guatemala in 1981. He is founder and chairman of a multinational metal group based in Australia and Hong Kong, and was kidnapped by eight armed terrorists while visiting a subsidiary in Guatemala. He was held for about a hundred days and most of the negotiation, both with him and a colleague in Australia (Tom Dundon), was done by a woman who spoke fluent English with a Canadian accent. She referred to him contemptuously as a 'piece of merchandise' and from this and other indications he deduced that he was of more value to them alive than dead. He thereafter took the initiative, alternately aggressive and agreeable to his guards, and gained psychological dominance over them. This, coupled with superb negotiating techniques used by Tom Dundon and his advisers, and good police co-operation, resulted in the kidnappers' cutting their losses and releasing him without taking the risk of collecting a ransom. (This and about sixty other case studies are discussed in more detail in Clutterbuck, *Kidnap, Hijack and Extortion,* 1987.)

One case that demonstrated a new and grisly technique was the kidnap of Gerard Jan Heijn, vice-chairman of a retail chain in the Netherlands, in September 1987. The kidnappers killed him on the first day but they cut off his finger either just before or just after he died and put it in a freezer. Several weeks later, they sent it to his family and the doctors judged that it was 80 per cent certain that he was alive when it was cut off. On the strength of this, despite no other proof of life, the family paid a ransom, in full co-operation with the Dutch police. Though it was too late to save Mr Heijn, this did enable the police to arrest the principal kidnapper, who confessed to the crime; a number of suspected accomplices were also arrested.

Both criminal and political kidnapping have proved effective enough in achieving their aims to make it likely that this form of crime will continue. Huge ransoms have been paid, prisoners have been released, and there is at least a suspicion that the Hezbollah in Lebanon, as creatures of Iranian fundamentalism, have successfully induced the French, German and US authorities to modify or change their policies in various ways in order to get hostages released.

The technological developments likeliest to help kidnappers are in the fields of tapping communications (Chapter 3), and possibly in as yet unknown development of drugs with which to make hostages more ready to talk. Most developments (including the latter) are, however, more likely to assist in countering kidnapping and some of these are discussed in Chapter 17.

Hostage seizure

The term 'hostage seizure' is used to differentiate the holding of hostages in a known location (e.g. in an embassy) from kidnapping to a secret hideout. Most hostage seizures are domestic, to apply pressure on families, acquaintances or colleagues. They are sometimes used by criminals on the run in a desperate attempt to evade capture.

Political hostage seizures are done to attract publicity, though hostage-takers have occasionally been given safe custody to a chosen location, sometimes even with a ransom, in order to spare the lives of hostages (e.g. at the Dominican Embassy in Bogotá in 1980). On one occasion (in Iran in 1979–81 – see below) the government actually co-operated with the hostage-takers and this, of course, added a unique new dimension. Normally, however, the police will surround the premises in overwhelming force, and thereafter have the initiative. It quickly becomes clear that the hostage-takers (and the hostages) are totally dependent on the police for their food, their survival and their eventual destiny, so the only thing left for them to gain is publicity. They probably knew this all the time, so that is usually their primary aim.

The seizure of the Iranian Embassy in London in 1980 was a typical example. In April 1980 six anti-Khomeini Iranians of ethnic Arab origin seized Khomeini's embassy in London, together with twenty-six hostages. The police surrounded the embassy within a few minutes. The terrorists made some extravagant political demands (e.g. the release by Khomeini of ninety-two prisoners in their province) but neither they nor anyone else expected these to be granted. After five days of constructive negotiation (during which five sick or pregnant hostages were released) the terrorists shot one of the embassy staff and threatened to shoot others at forty-minute intervals until they were granted safe custody out of the country. The British Army SAS Regiment therefore raided the embassy and rescued the remaining hostages (except one whom the terrorists shot during the rescue) and killed five of the terrorists – all except one, who succeeded initially in masquerading as a hostage. The real aim, however, was publicity. Literally hundreds of press and television cameras and reporters converged into Hyde Park, which was across the road from the embassy. When one of the hostages (a British BBC technician) obtained the time of transmission of a BBC World Service broadcast and ensured that the terrorists heard it, their delight was unrestrained, and most of the tension was lifted. Though all but one of the terrorists chose to die rather than surrender, they did so in the knowledge that their case had been brought forcibly and dramatically to the attention of the world.

The seizure of the US Embassy in Tehran by Islamic fundamentalists on 4 November 1979, with over 50 staff who were entitled to diplomatic protection, was not specifically ordered by Khomeini but, as he condoned it within a few days and thereafter deployed large police and military forces to prevent the lifting of the siege, the Iranian government must be condemned as responsible for the 444 day detention of the hostages and thus for the most flagrant breach of the Vienna Convention and of civilized international behaviour in history. After a bungled rescue attempt, the US government negotiated the release of the hostages by releasing some of the Iranian assets frozen when Khomeini had deposed the Shah earlier that year. Unfortunately, now that the precedent has been created and Iran appears to have lost nothing from the episode, it must be assumed that, when they judge that their vital national interest justifies it, other unscrupulous leaders may emulate his example.

The only technological developments likely to assist hostage-takers in selecting targets and planning their seizures are improved techniques for bugging, eavesdropping and hacking. Technological developments should generally strengthen the hand of those responsible for security of premises and access control; this will be discussed in Chapter 17.

Hijacking

Hijacking an aircraft, train or ship is another form of hostage seizure; the premises seized happen to be mobile, but it is generally known where they are. Moreover, wherever it occurs, the environment is 'urban' rather than 'rural' in its nature; the aircraft, train or ship is a miniature extension of urban life. The types of pressures exerted on the hostages and on those negotiating for their release are similar to those in urban rather than rural situations; so are the techniques used by the terrorists.

The primary aim of most hijacks, as of other hostage seizures, is to gain publicity for a political cause. Occasionally individuals have used hijacks to escape from or get to some specific place. Sometimes they have achieved political blackmail or ransom.

The heyday of hijacking was the period 1969–72, when the average was eighty per year (a peak of ninety-one in 1969 – mainly to Cuba). In January 1973 the introduction of the 100 per cent search at the airport boarding gates reduced this to an average of thirty from 1973 to 1981. Since 1982 the annual average has been reduced to fewer than twenty –

less than a quarter of the peak. The chances of an aircraft's being hijacked are now one in half a million (twenty in 10 million take-offs).

Hijacks do, however, have a political effect greater than almost any other terrorist act because of the dramatic treatment they receive from the media, and especially on television. The most notorious example was the hijack of a TWA Boeing 727 (Flight 147) from Athens to Beirut in June 1985. Most of the 145 passengers, plus the crew, were Americans; after a number of women, children and other nationals were released, there were 108 hostages. One young American had been murdered during the flight. The hijackers were Shia fundamentalists demanding the release of over 700 Shia prisoners captured during and since the Israeli invasion of south Lebanon in 1982. The US television channels surpassed themselves in arousing and exploiting American emotions in order to attract viewers, which enormously strengthened the hijackers' hand and made negotiation almost impossible. Eventually President Reagan shrewdly sensed that there were only two people who had any possible influence over the hijackers and were themselves anxious lest a terrorist triumph would increase the disruptive power which the fundamentalists were already able to exert: these two were Nabih Berri, leader of the moderate Shia Militia, and President Assad of Syria. Faced with the passion and publicity generated by the media, Reagan made the best deal that he could, saving the lives of the remaining hostages, but the hijackers went free.

A similar publicity bonanza dogged the handling of the hijack of a Kuwaiti airliner in April 1988, again by Shia fundamentalists, first to Iran, thence to Cyprus, and finally to Algiers. Again, many of the world's television stations behaved appallingly, with conjecture or leakage of possible negotiating ploys or rescue preparations, giving the terrorists the initiative and the publicity they wanted. The hostages were saved (except for two, murdered and contemptuously thrown out on to the tarmac in front of the cameras) but, once again, the murderers were given safe custody back to an ecstatic welcome in Lebanon.

This kind of media irresponsibility is an immense encouragement to terrorism and the growing multiplicity of competing television channels may make this worse. Even if reckless use of the media so as to put lives at risk were made a criminal offence, this would have little effect on hijacking since both the crime and television transcend national frontiers and jurisdiction.

After the hijack of the Kuwaiti airliner and the bombings of Pan Am Flight 103 over Lockerbie in 1988 and of the French airliner over Niger in 1989, Islamic terrorists attempted no more hijacks or bombings of aircraft in flight for the next four years. This was presumably because they had found that these did their cause more harm than good; also because their previous sponsors, notably Iran, Libya and Syria, had become more concerned with improving their image with the west for economic reasons.

Meanwhile, technological developments are likely to make it possible to improve aviation security; and these are discussed in Chapters 17 and 18.

17 Developments in countering terrorism

Security of premises and installations

Travel and personal security are of little value unless the individuals under threat can work, live and sleep in a secure environment. The current and developing technology for the protection of premises was discussed in Chapter 8.

Access control through authorized entrances for staff, visitors and vehicles depends not only on technical aids but more still on training and the alertness of security staff in applying them. Would-be intruders, hoping to reconnoitre or carry out a terrorist attack, will use every possible trick to deceive the guards.

No barrier is impregnable and the principle of concentric rings, procedural and physical, to give warning and impose delay, was set out in Chapter 8; the importance of developing alarms with a higher detection probability (DP) and a lower false alarm rate (FAR) was particularly stressed. This is a field in which there will almost certainly be progress in coming years.

In some countries, more sophisticated bullet-proofing of office buildings is becoming necessary, and flexible armour such as Kevlar will be useful. In one multinational company office in a Latin American city, for example, as well as bullet-proofing of all windows on lower floors, the executive suite and conference room on the top floor have flexible Kevlar curtains which can be drawn across all windows at the touch of a switch, in the event of suspicion that terrorists have occupied rooms in other high buildings within firing range.

Security of computer centres and of computer hardware, software and communications, will become increasingly important as the degree of interdependence and reliance on EDP increases year by year. Bugging, hacking, computer fraud and the detection and countering of all these is a developing science in itself, with a continuing battle of both inventiveness and wits comparable to the historic leapfrog between armour and the weapons to penetrate it.

Search techniques and research

The prospect of detecting explosives would be greatly enhanced if the majority of countries of the world, including all the main industrial countries, agreed to a comprehensive system of tagging explosives, especially detonators (see pp. 57–8).

Detection of electronic devices is developing fast, because of growing concern about bugging, hacking, industrial espionage and computer fraud. It should be possible to apply some of this technology to detection of electrical firing devices, notably the precise delay fuse (like a video timer) of the type used in the bomb attack on the Grand Hotel in Brighton in 1984 (see pp. 50–1).

Supplementing all of these, there is still much scope for developing aids to the normal senses (sight, smell, hearing and touch) of human searchers. A typical example of this is the use of fibre optics to enable an operator to insert the 'eye of a camera' through narrow and tortuous gaps to see round corners or under or behind objects before they can be safely removed (see p. 57).

The watchword for search techniques must be multiplicity. Reliability will lie in placing many hurdles of different kinds across the path. Priorities for research are further discussed in Chapter 20.

Personal and travel security

Individual victims of terrorists – politicians, officials, business people, or targets for intimidation – are most at risk when they are travelling, especially by car, and to a lesser extent by air. The essence of travel security is unpredictability, particularly regarding time and route. The majority of kidnaps occur on the road between home and work. A kidnap or assassination requires more organization than is generally realized (e.g. see pp. 172–6) and the kidnappers need to know that their target will pass a selected spot suitable for a kidnap and getaway within a definite time bracket. If strict discretion is maintained over the movements of potential targets and they vary their time, route, type of car, and so on, the chances are that the kidnappers will turn away and look for an easier target.

Similar discretion is advisable over air or sea travel, and especially regarding the date and time of arrival at the seaport or airport, since this will clearly reveal the time and place of the start of a car journey. The

IRA twice attempted to ambush (with huge roadside car bombs) the cars of judges who had failed to conceal the fact that they were returning from holiday to Northern Ireland via Dublin at a stated time; in one case (in 1987) the IRA killed the judge and his wife; in the other case (1988) they confused the judge's car with that of another man travelling on the same ferry and killed him instead, with his wife and child.

Though not comparable in importance with the value of unpredictability, various equipment can be installed to improve security for car travel. Light armour is widely used by VIPs, but is not proof against heavy machine-guns or missiles. Internal locking, two-way radio, alarms and tracking systems are other valuable aids, but the use of multiple aerials (and armour) may reveal to a sophisticated observer that the car is a special one. Unless the VIP is publicly recognizable (e.g. a president or senior minister) greater safety may be achieved by travelling in an unostentatious car and changing it frequently (e.g. using a series of company fleet cars of the type normally used by junior executives).

Security against aircraft hijacking is in the hands of airports and airlines (see Chapter 18). All that individuals who are potential targets can do is to avoid airports or airlines with a bad security record, report lapses if they notice any, and ensure that neither they nor their staff reveal which flight they are using. Potential targets should also be as inconspicuous as possible during check-in and boarding, and especially so if the aircraft they are in is actually hijacked.

The most intriguing possibility for safer VIP travel will be opened if there is a revolutionary breakthrough in the power-to-weight ratio of engines – similar to the breakthrough of the steam engine in the late eighteenth and the internal combustion engine in the late nineteenth centuries. There is no scientific reason why some similar discovery, either in design or in fuel, should not occur, with reduction in size and weight comparable to the miniaturization of computers achieved successively by transistors, printed circuits and microchips. Given a very small engine capable of generating a jet with a powerful enough thrust, the personal microlite or vertical take-off aircraft could become both practical and cheap. With the air at low altitudes filled with such traffic, it would be almost impossible for terrorists to pick out their targets or to predict when and where they are likely to be.

Weapons

It is generally unwise for potential victims of terrorists to carry guns unless they are not only fully trained to use them but also psychologically prepared to shoot to kill without hesitation. The terrorist certainly will be trained and 'psyched up' to shoot; he or she will hold the initiative whereas the victim will be surprised and shocked; the terrorist will also be covered by other terrorists similarly prepared. The likely effect of the victim's drawing a gun will be to get himself shot before he can use it. If it is decided that an armed response to possible terrorist attack may be necessary, this should be provided by fully trained bodyguards. Even the most dedicated bodyguards, however, may be a liability if they are hopelessly outnumbered and outgunned (terrorists are usually armed with sub-machine-guns and are seldom single-handed). In fact, the most valuable contribution of trained bodyguards is that their advice may keep their principal from ever getting into a dangerous situation.

As was pointed out in Chapters 4 and 16, developments in personal weapons are likely to help the terrorist rather than the counter-terrorist, because they may be easier to conceal, and because higher rates of fire and laser sights will favour the aggressor with the initiative rather than the defender restrained by the principle of minimum force and firing only in response.

Nevertheless, the first weapons designed to be concealed in a brief-case were to help bodyguards to avoid drawing attention to themselves (to be fired by 'aiming' the briefcase, not with a laser sight). Sophisticated night vision equipment may assist the security forces and help both in pre-empting a night attack and in preventing the escape of terrorists after it.

Development of heavier weapons such as HMGs, mortars and hand-held guided missiles, while necessary for conventional armies, will be wholly to the advantage of terrorists. So will that of indiscriminate weapons such as grenades, bombs and mines.

Aids to training in the use of weapons, such as simulators and 'pop-up' target ranges, are unlikely to be available to terrorists as they are not compatible with a clandestine lifestyle, so security forces should be better trained individually in quick response and accurate fire. Indeed, for the same reason, terrorists will generally have practised less often with live ammunition than soldiers or armed police officers, and this will to some extent mitigate the surprise factor mentioned above.

Non-lethal incapacitating weapons, which temporarily disable friend and foe alike, are one of the dreams of security forces for dealing with hijack, hold-up or hostage situations but at present the problem of achieving an instantaneous knock-out effect, to prevent the terrorist from shooting or throwing a grenade, has not yet been solved. One conceivable line of research was mentioned in Chapter 5 (p. 54).

The security forces

Many police services have specialist riot and anti-terrorist squads. Personnel in these squads should regularly be rotated back to normal police duties: otherwise the squads may take on a character of their own, and are likely to lose contact and sympathy with the public.

Specialist anti-terrorist squads ('commandos' or 'rescue squads') are sometimes found by the police or by the army or by a 'third force' (as in Germany). In France the 'Intervention Group' (GIGN) is provided by the National Gendarmerie, and handles both criminal and political terrorist interventions. This gives it the advantage of having taken part in several hundred rescue and other operations with live ammunition, whereas the German (GSG9) and British (SAS) forces deal only with political terrorists. This advantage is offset by the fact that the resolution of a criminal case (e.g. the holding of a hostage in a house) demands great restraint and the minimum use of force, for which police firearms officers are trained, whereas intervention against heavily armed terrorists who have shown their readiness to shoot freely and to kill without mercy demands a military attack, with fire and movement, to capture or kill them before they kill any more victims. The training of a person's reflex actions for these two roles is very different, and it may be difficult for the same person to perform with confidence in one role on one day and the other role next day. The GIGN, however, have been successful in both.

GIGN again demonstrated their coolness and skills along with two heroic French women on 14–15 May 1993. A masked and mentally deranged gunman, Eric Schmitt, took twenty-one children aged two and three as hostages in a nursery school in a suburb of Paris with their teacher, Laurence Dreyfus. Schmitt had a pistol and wired 2 kg of explosive in packets around the room, keeping the electric detonating switch in his hand; he threatened to blow up the school (and himself) unless paid 100 million francs (£12 million) ransom. He released some of the children but kept others overnight and into the next day. Mme Dreyfus insisted on staying with them and behaved with great courage, continuing normal routines to keep psychological damage to the children to a minimum. She explained the masked man and his gun initially as 'repairing the heating' and later as 'a wolf hunter'. She arranged delivery of sleeping bags and pyjamas and put the children to bed at the normal time. The gunman allowed the fire brigade doctor, Evelyne Lambert, to come in to attend the children and she also stayed with them. The GIGN surrounded the building and were visible on the rooftops with their guns; they also installed pinhead cameras. They managed to brief Dr Lambert on their rescue plan and, when Schmitt was exhausted and asleep in the early hours of the morning, she silently dressed the children and moved them to the far corner of the room. Two GIGN marksmen came in and shot him as he awoke, throwing mattresses over the children in case he managed to detonate the explosives as he had said he would. This also prevented them from seeing too much. Mme Dreyfus and Dr Lambert both became Chevaliers de la Legion d'Honneur.

This incident was in marked contrast to the attempt to break into the premises of a religious cult in Waco Texas on 19 April 1993. The leader of the Davidian Branch sect, who claimed to be the Messiah, David Koresh, exercised hypnotic control over the members of his cult, ninety-five of whom lived in a fortress-like compound, heavily armed. The ninety-five included seventeen children and there were allegations of 'free love' including child abuse. On 28 February, agents of the Federal Bureau of Alcohol, Tobacco and Firearms attempted to raid the compound. The cult had been tipped off and opened fire with automatic weapons. Four agents and six cult members were killed and sixteen agents wounded. The next fifty-one days were spent in negotiation and Koresh periodically offered to surrender if given opportunities to broadcast, which he was, but he invariably broke his word. Eventually it was decided to mount an FBI raid to rescue the children and disarm Koresh and his followers. On 19 April the FBI, after giving an ultimatum, smashed down the walls with military engineering tanks and released tear gas. The cult members fired on the tanks and set fire to the buildings at a number of points simultaneously; within thirty minutes the entire compound was ablaze. It was forty-five minutes before fire engines arrived and by this time eighty-six of the ninety-five cult members were dead, including seventeen children; only nine people managed to escape. There were reports that Koresh had shot some of the cult members rather than allow them to surrender but the state of the bodies was such that it was hard to be sure how far this was so. Significantly, none of the children escaped. The FBI were widely criticized for the conduct of the rescue; also for failing to appreciate how fanatically Koresh would resist and that he might persuade or coerce his followers to commit mass suicide. There was a precedent for this when 913 members of another American religious cult, the People's Temple, committed mass suicide in Guyana in November 1978. It was certainly surprising that the FBI had no fire-fighting equipment on the site when they broke in.

The tactical handling of rescue forces does require skilled judgement and timing, as was illustrated by the contrasting stories of two rescue attempts, in Malta in 1985 and in Karachi in 1986.

On 23 November 1985 three Palestinian terrorists hijacked an Egyptian Boeing 737 en route from Athens to Cairo and forced it to land at Luqa Airport in Malta. After their ultimatum had been rejected, the hijackers shot ten passengers (two dead and eight wounded) and clearly intended to carry out their threat to shoot more. An Egyptian commando force landed and as soon as it was dark, eleven hours later, attempted a rescue, but, under the pressure of the threat to kill more passengers, their preparations had been inadequate. They entered through the belly door into the cargo hold, where they placed a charge to blow an entrance through the floor of the cabin above. This was intended as a diversion from the main attack over the wings. There was confusion and the aircraft caught fire. There is some doubt as to whether the fire was caused by the commandos' explosive or by a terrorist grenade, but fifty-seven more passengers died, most of them from inhaling smoke fumes. Only one hijacker survived and he was later sentenced to twenty-five years' imprisonment for murder of the two passengers before the rescue attempt.

At 6 a.m. on 5 September 1986 a Pan American 747 was seized on the ground while refuelling and embarking transit passengers at Karachi Airport. Despite intelligence warnings, four Arab hijackers dressed in the uniform of airport security guards, waving fake passes, were allowed to drive their van on to the ramp (an inexcusable lapse in security) and stormed up the gangway through the embarking passengers, one of whom they shot (presumably to terrorize the rest). The aircrew, acting on Pan Am standing orders, escaped by ropes from the flight deck, making it impossible for the aircraft to take off. The Pakistani commando force arrived and were told to be ready to mount a rescue operation in the early hours of the following morning – about twenty-four hours after the hijack. Presumably with the story of the Egyptians in Malta in mind, they were ordered to make detailed preparations and rehearse on an aircraft set aside for that purpose on the other side of the airport. The aircraft captain (now in the Control Tower) warned that the aircraft's generators would run out of fuel at about 9 p.m., but nothing was done to prevent or make allowance for this. At 9 p.m. the aircraft lights dimmed and went out. The hijackers, thinking that this indicated an impending attack, panicked and starting shooting the passengers in the dark. They killed another 16 (making 17 in all) and wounded 127 more. The rescue force took fifteen minutes to reach the scene and it was twenty-five minutes before they had collected ladders to enter the aircraft.

It is easy to criticize the Egyptians for going in too hastily and the Pakistanis for taking so long to respond to the crisis. The best answer is for a rescue force to get two separate teams to the site as quickly as possible. One team should make an immediate plan to go in if it becomes necessary, say if the terrorists start killing hostages. That team should remain at instant readiness for this, using every hour they have thereafter to improve their plan, find better means of access and assemble equipment. Meanwhile, the second team should study the site, make a model or mock-up if possible, and develop and rehearse it until it is time to relieve the first team. The first team, after a rest, then use the time available to improve the plan further with the mock-up. But there is always one team ready for instant response.

This is the approach used by the British SAS, who have earned a very high reputation and are in immense demand to train other national forces all over the world, especially in Commonwealth countries. There are SAS units trained in the same way (and with common origins in 1941) in Australia and New Zealand. The main reason for the excellence of the SAS is their system of selection. Unlike GSG9, they do not recruit directly. They get their men from other regiments of the British Army in which they have served for at least two years and have gained outstanding appraisal reports. The SAS get so many applicants that they need consider only the outstanding ones. These are then invited for intensive tests – physical, mental and psychological – in Hereford where, on average, only one in ten is selected, the other nine being returned to their regiments. Those who get into the SAS are therefore the *crème de la crème* of the army, and this is the foundation of their morale.

Within the SAS, one squadron provides the anti-terrorist force for six months at a time, and has a year or more on other duties in between (e.g. in Northern Ireland) so that it does not get stale. That squadron finds three rescue teams, each of a troop (about twenty-three men). At any time of the day or night, one of these teams is at instant readiness, with a helicopter standing by. A second team is training in barracks, ready to follow up. The third team is stood down or on leave. They are kept at 100 per cent fitness, physically and psychologically, and at concert pitch in their reflexes and weapon handling. This is maintained by regular exercises in their ricochet-proof 'killing house', where they practise rescues with live ammunition, with one of their number in turn acting as a 'hostage' surrounded by figure targets representing terrorists. This breeds mutual confidence. Their morale is comparable to that of some national football squads, in which every man has got there by giving every ounce of his body in every match in every team during his progress to selection, and goes on doing so in his determination not to be dropped.

Intelligence

Protection of the population from guerrilla warfare and terrorism depends above all on good intelligence. Intelligence organizations vary between countries: the commonest weakness is lack of co-ordination between rival political, police and military intelligence services. In Britain in the intelligence community comprises the Secret Intelligence Service (MI 6), the Security Service (MI 5) and the Police Special Branch, co-ordinated by various committees and supplemented by other intelligence agencies (e.g. military, industrial, economic, topographical and scientific).

An intelligence service must operate secretly. If the sources from whom it gets its information suspect that their identities may be widely accessible, the information will at once dry up. There have been numerous examples of this, especially in Italy in 1976–8. The dilemma for governments lies in the need for intelligence services to be accountable to the public. This is best done by making the directors of the service accessible to a supervisory committee (normally from the legislature or the judiciary). These directors should also, within reason, be accessible to politicians and to journalists who are prepared to honour 'off-the-record' or 'non-attributable' information. The front-line intelligence officers must, however, be accessible to no one who does not need to know them, for if their faces are known it is an easy matter to follow them to their informants whose confidentiality may be literally a matter of life and death. The directors must be answerable for the actions of their subordinates but not required to reveal their identities unless they are charged with an offence.

Working from all this information (including that of their own Special Branch) the police are the primary arm of law enforcement and guardians of public safety. In dealing with guerrilla warfare and terrorism, the army may be called in to support them but only very rarely (e.g. in Northern Ireland from 1970 to 1976) has the army in the UK taken over prime responsibility for security from the police. In many countries, especially the less developed ones, the army more often dominates.

Intelligence and personal surveillance are the most promising fields for development of effective counter-terrorist aids, provided that they are regarded as supplements to human intelligence and not as substitutes for it and that there are effective safeguards for civil liberties.

Computerized databanks of personal information and information about personal possessions (e.g. cars, weapons, homes, clothing) and personal habits (e.g. the *modus operandi* of known criminals and terrorists) are already of great value to police forces in quickly identifying links between apparently unconnected pieces of data. These computer systems are increasingly linked internationally between police forces; their potential was discussed in some detail in Chapter 7. Thus far, however, they have been used only for data about known or highly suspected criminals or terrorists; there is a strong political and public reluctance to allow their use to be extended to data on people about whom there are no grounds for suspicion. This concern is healthy and justified, because it is at present almost impossible to guarantee that an individual police or intelligence officer who has memorized such information cannot communicate it undetected by word of mouth to someone not authorized to receive it. So long as this is the case, there will always be people (e.g. criminals or members of unscrupulous credit companies) who will be prepared to offer attractive bribes for such information.

It is therefore especially urgent to develop parallel means of preventing or, should prevention fail, of detecting abuse. Otherwise, the community will continue to be denied the full use of one of the most effective weapons in protecting it against violence. These safeguards will be all the more necessary if there is a major upsurge in crime and terrorism, because public opinion will then demand and accept much wider recording of personal data, as has already happened in Northern Ireland, and the opportunities for abuse of it would be likely to cause both an erosion of civil liberties and, in due course, a backlash against it.

An upsurge in violence would also necessitate the recording of a wider range of information, the issue of identity cards (discussed, in the next section) and registration of where people live, including notifying the police of overnight tenants, which is already done in a number of European countries. A great deal of this information is, ironically, already recorded by private companies for people holding cheque cards and credit cards, but this is not perceived to carry the same risk of abuse as if it were held on a national computer.

Tight safeguards are also necessary for other aids to police detection, such as tapping and taping of telephone calls and bugging, also of electronic monitoring and tagging.

The devastating influence on terrorism of the whole process of drug trafficking, from the rural cultivation areas to the streets of prosperous countries, was assessed in Part III. It was concluded that it must primarily be fought on the streets of the USA and western Europe. Further development of means of detecting drugs and possibly also of detecting drug addicts must be given high priority, and the traffickers and addicts must be identified and taken off the streets.

Identification and prevention of impersonation

The years 1991–3 saw a widespread crumbling of the prejudice against the use of electronic information technology to enable police and immigration authorities to check the identity of citizens of democratic societies. The crumble has been gradual. In 1968, the first outburst of international terrorism prompted ICAO to propose the use of machine readable passports (MRP), but it was not until 1990 that a number of states, led by Australia, Canada and the USA, began to issue them. By 1993, fifteen states had introduced them (including those three plus Germany, the UK and others) with another fifteen about to do so. The method was optical character reading (OCR), in which all the data could also be read by eye by the holder and there was no means of recording any other (i.e. secret) data on the MRP (see Chapter 8).

Germany had by 1993 issued machine-readable ID cards (MRI) to all German citizens and machine-readable visas (MRV) to visitors from countries for which visas were required. The Dutch planned to follow suit by 1995. Of the twelve EC countries only Denmark, Ireland and the UK had announced no plans to issue ID cards at all, MR or otherwise.

None of these cards – MRP, MRI or MRV – carried any biometric data (digital fingerprints, etc.) whereby to check whether the cardholder was an imposter. Two initiatives in this direction were, however, taken by the Dutch (in 1991) and the Germans (in 1993), whereby regular travellers through Amsterdam and Frankfurt airports were invited to volunteer for prior screening and recording of finger or hand biometric data to enable them to pass through a fast stream for embarkation and disembarkation. This had great advantages both for the traveller and for airport security. These initiatives were mentioned briefly in Chapter 8 and will be described more fully in Chapter 18.

Eventually, the use of MRP, MRI and MRV with biometric data must spread to cope with the growth of crime, domestic and international, including fraud, drug trafficking and terrorism. Opening the EC internal frontiers in 1993 has made this even more urgent.

A useful start would be to invite holders of bankers' cards to have fingerprint data recorded both on their cards and on the bank's computer. A fingerprint scanner in the 'hole in the wall' would then ensure that no one who stole the card could get money with it. There would be plenty of volunteers to enjoy this safeguard. This could be extended to checking credit cards at the larger outlets which have a line to the bank or credit company on which they can check that the cardholder has the funds to honour the transaction. The scanner would add very little to the cost and would pay for itself many times over in reducing losses from card fraud.

This procedure should soon convince the non-criminal members of the community (i.e. the great majority) that the advantages of being able to prove their identity far outweigh any anxieties they might have. For example, the fear that the OCR data on a stolen ID card might give unauthorized access to criminal records would be wholly removed if it were invalid without the fingerprint on the scanner. The key to success, as in the Amsterdam and Frankfurt experiments, will lie in starting each of these schemes by calling for volunteers. When others see what is to be gained from it, they will all want to join.

In the future, the use of MR travel documents supported by biometric data will, after its voluntary start, spread quickly. The 100 per cent issue of MRP, MRV and MRI in Germany should also be followed throughout the EC and be enhanced by biometric data to prevent abuse of the system, especially at the police spot checks which will be necessary to catch the criminals who try to dodge from country to country once they are within EC external frontiers.

Eventually, this combination (MR documents with biometric data) should prove to be the most effective single weapon in combating terrorism, drug trafficking and other international crimes.

The balance between security and civil liberties will be assessed in Chapter 20.

Interrogation and justice

Conviction both prevents and deters terrorism and crime; it depends upon hard evidence such as will leave a judge and jury in no reasonable doubt of guilt.

Once enough evidence has been obtained for the police to arrest a suspect for questioning, the suspect is the most important witness; the suspect's demeanour and reaction to questions are, or should be, material evidence. The suspect has an absolute right of silence, but the community – as later to be represented by a judge and jury – should also have an equal right to place whatever interpretation they judge fit on any refusal to answer questions. This is as valid a part of their judgement of guilt as the answers or demeanour of a witness under cross-examination in court. For this reason, every interrogation should be recorded on audiotape or, if the police consider the case to be a serious one, on videotape. These tapes also provide a safeguard against improper interrogation. They are already used by police, and sealed copies are given at once to the suspect. These must be shown to be identical to any tape later presented in evidence, and it is now technologically possible to ensure that neither the police copy nor the suspect's copy can be tampered with undetected. These procedures will now make it possible to change the terms of the standard caution without any danger to a person who is innocent. Currently in the UK, accused people are told that they are not obliged to say anything but that anything they do say may be taken down and used in evidence. The caution should now be:

> You are not obliged to answer my questions and you have the right of silence. My questions and your answers or silences will be recorded on this video/audio tape. One copy of the tape will be given to you and another copy to the prosecution. You and the prosecution will be free to present any parts of this tape as evidence at your trial, and the jury will draw what conclusions they think fit.

The basis for successful interrogation and for subsequently presenting convincing evidence is the interplay of proven facts with statements and answers given by the suspect and other witnesses, both during interrogation and in court. This structure is built up both from prior background intelligence and subsequent investigation, both of facts and of witnesses. It is the spotting of discrepancies that detects a liar and convinces a jury. Confronting people who are lying with facts at variance with what they have said will disconcert them and lead them to tell further lies which can also be detected. For this purpose the maximum possible use must be made of fact-gathering resources now available, including long-range high-resolution cameras (both still and video), identification, and detection of impersonation. Where appropriate, evidence of movement produced by electronic monitoring can be valuable in detecting discrepancies. All of these techniques have been described above, and must be used to best advantage if society is to curtail the alarming growth of crime in recent years, and to control the threat to life and denial of liberty created by terrorism.

One more reserve power must be held in readiness. Trial by jury has over the centuries been a guardian of freedom and justice; it can, however, be made unworkable by intimidation of both juries and witnesses. This has already necessitated the suspension of trial by jury for terrorist offences in the Republic of Ireland (since 1962) and in Northern Ireland (since 1973). In recent years in England, 'jury-nobbling' has become rife, and so has the intimidation of witnesses. There have also been a number of notorious cases in which juries have returned perverse acquittals out of pure terror of the consequences of a guilty verdict. It is, of course, the richest criminal and terrorist organizations which can afford to apply either bribes or threats for this purpose – especially those financed by massive fraud or drug trafficking.

To counter this, Parliament should legislate to empower judges, if they think that there is a serious risk of perversion of the course of justice by such pressure or intimidation to direct that neither the witnesses nor juries should be seen in court by anyone except the judge and (in the case of witnesses) by the jury. (Sadly, the proof of connivance of some lawyers with crime and terrorism, especially in Germany and to some extent in the UK, precludes the otherwise desirable right of the lawyers also to see the faces of the jury and witnesses.) CCTV technology now makes this procedure feasible. The jury would sit and the witnesses would give evidence in rooms which were quite separate from the court (they need not be in the same building) with a system of cameras and screens to be controlled by a court official so that the appropriate people can or cannot see the faces of the others. Everyone would see the judge and the accused. No one at all would see the jury. They, however, would see the faces of the witnesses. Everyone, including the public, would hear the voices, but the public would see only the judge, the court officials, the lawyers and the accused. The identity of the jurors would be disclosed to no one. Their selection and their deliberations would be monitored by an 'Ombudsman' organization appointed by Parliament on the recommendation of the Judiciary.

No one *needs* to see the jury's faces though, to judge whether they are lying, the jury do need to see the faces of witnesses and of the accused. This is precisely the position of, say, politicians being interviewed on television. They can be seen by the viewing public, who can make up their own minds, by judging their words and their demeanour, whether the politicians are telling the truth. In fact, with faces close up on camera, the viewers can probably make a more informed judgement than if they were looking across a large room. Politicians, however, cannot see their viewers, nor do they know who or where they are, nor do they need to. But the public are the 'jury' the politicians have to convince.

18 Airport and airline security

Access to aircraft

The technological aids available or under development for aviation security were discussed in Chapters 6 and 8. The importance of tightening security against both hijacking and aircraft sabotage was highlighted by the massive mid-air bombs in the Air India and Pan American aircraft in 1985 and 1988 (killing 329 and 270 respectively) and the TWA and Kuwaiti Airlines hijacks in those same two years (Chapter 16). There are other less spectacular incidents every year; there was in particular a spate of hijacking in Russia from 1990 to 1993. Such incidents also have political and social effects out of proportion to the numbers killed; after the 1985 TWA hijack to Beirut, in which one passenger was killed, it was reported that 6 million Americans cancelled their flights to Europe and the Middle East during the subsequent year.

There are essentially three avenues for getting a bomb into the hold or cabin of an airliner: first, via the ramp, smuggled aboard by airport staff in the course of refuelling, maintenance, loading cargo and kitchen supplies, cleaning, and so on; second, in hold baggage checked in by embarking passengers or transferred from connecting flights; third, smuggled into the cabin by passengers with hand baggage. Hijackers are, of course, passengers, so the embarkation processes should detect any weapons they are carrying on their persons or in their cabin baggage, and should also direct particular attention to passengers whose profile is most likely to fit that of a hijacker.

The problem is to devise a security system which is commercially realistic, and which is to be acceptable both to operators and passengers, because otherwise some will find ways to evade it; also to lay down common international standards and find ways enforcing and financing them.

Ramp security

Ramp security should be the easiest to enforce, since the ramp is wholly under the control of the airport authorities and of staff employed by them. The first essential is watertight control of every means of access to the ramp, land-side to air-side; through maintenance areas, cargo sheds, kitchens, and so on; from the terminal buildings; and from outside the airport. Second, every one of the people issued with staff passes giving such access – engineers, cleaners, kitchen, fuel and cargo handlers – should be security vetted; their passes should contain digital biometric data (see Chapter 8) to prevent impersonation. Third, all air-side activities should be monitored by airport security staff checking passes, using metal and explosive detectors and, where necessary, hand search. All cargo and kitchen supplies should be similarly monitored. Vapour sniffing should detect drugs and other contraband as well as explosives. Finally, particular care should be taken to confirm identification and to control visiting aircrew, since some airlines have connived in enabling terrorists to gain access disguised as aircrew (see the Nezar Hindawi case, pp. 169–70).

Hold baggage

Ideally, all hold baggage should be subject to a 100 per cent security check by at least three different tests, each testing different characteristics, for example enhanced X-ray, vapour and neutron. In the immediate future, however, this is impracticable, not only on grounds of cost, including the internal reconstruction of air terminals, but chiefly because the extra delay in throughput at busy airports would be unacceptable both to operators and the travelling public – except in the wake of a major air disaster. The interim solution should therefore include

1 maximum security for flights likeliest to be targeted
2 focus on passengers and bags posing the highest threat
3 multiple checks of bags arousing any doubt
4 strict reconciliation of passengers and baggage.

Many airports (e.g. Gatwick and Singapore) have special boarding and loading procedures for high-risk flights, and any flight or any group of passengers can be diverted through this procedure if reasons to do so arise. At Gatwick, the hold baggage for high-risk flights is put through an enhanced X-ray machine (VIVID) which gives the operator a range of tests (described in Chapter 6). This – the first machine in the flow – is calibrated to give the highest possible detection probability (DP) while accepting a relatively high false alarm rate (FAR). Any bag which does not wholly satisfy the operator is passed on to an EGIS vapour detection machine which should detect any known explosive, but it is not 'real time', that is the sampling and analysis takes a minimum of 30 seconds.

Also under test at Gatwick is the Thermal Neutron Analysis (TNA) machine, again reinforced by enhanced X-ray and/or vapour detectors. This is used to check a percentage of the baggage of certain flights, mainly of US carriers. The selection of the bags to go through TNA is made by profiling – questioning and checking documents – of people waiting to check-in, as will be described for El Al – by staff acting on specific criteria reinforced by their own hunches. A similar system of profiling operates at many other airports, though not all use such an expensive range of equipment.

A hypothetical plan has been assessed for one of the busiest dedicated airline terminals at JFK Airport, New York. This has a peak load in a 3-hour period of 19 international flights, carrying 6,000 passengers, with 12,000 bags, that is 4,000 bags per hour, or 70 bags per minute. These bags go down seven conveyor lines, each handling ten bags per minute. The hypothetical search system involves four stages. First, every bag would go through an enhanced X-ray machine (such as VIVID as described for Gatwick) – one on each of the seven conveyors – set for the highest DP (i.e. a statistically negligible chance of missing a bomb) but accepting a 10 per cent FAR. On average, therefore, these seven machines would accept 3,600 of the 4,000 bags but reject 400 (probably all false alarms). These 400 then go through a second machine (perhaps TNA, CPNX or EDEN) which again accepts on average 360 but rejects 40. A third machine, perhaps a sensitive vapour detector, is set for the highest possible DP, but at an even higher FAR; it may therefore reject 20 of the 40, and these 20 are then hand searched. The second and third machines can cope with the load of all seven conveyor lines, so there are nine machines with a total cost of $3 million. The financing of the installation and operation of such a system is discussed later in this chapter. It may well provide the best practical pattern for future development.

Baggage reconciliation

Just as important as profiling and searching is baggage reconciliation. A simple means of reconciliation at smaller airports is to lay out all the baggage on the tarmac beside the boarding steps. No bag is loaded until a boarding passenger indicates it, and both then board. Although there have been suicide bombers on the ground, there is no substantiated case of a bomber blowing himself up in the air with his own baggage.

In larger airports there are automated systems which should be 100 per cent reliable, such as Videcom now being used by British Airways. Each baggage label carries a bar-code, which is repeated on the passenger's boarding card. Both are tagged as they are boarded or loaded. A bag label for which no matching passenger boarding card has been issued activates a red light and it is not loaded. Provided that a matching passenger boarding card has been issued, the bag is loaded, but if no passenger is checked aboard with that boarding card the computer flashes an alarm indicating the discrepancy and the bag will be unloaded. The computer will also indicate precisely where it is located in the hold.

Transfer baggage presents its own problems. Ideally, every bag transferred to a connecting flight should go through an enhanced X-ray and/or vapour test, but this can in practice usually be done only for selected flights. The best alternative is for all international flights to use the same computerized baggage reconciliation system. In that case, as at initial loading, the bag can be found and removed if the passenger fails to board the connecting flight. The adoption of a common reconciliation system is, fortunately, spreading rapidly, not only because an airline whose security fails to inspire confidence will lose passengers, but also because the system probably pays for itself by reducing the day-to-day misdirection and loss of baggage which costs airlines a lot in compensation.

In February 1993 the British government announced a plan for compulsory baggage reconciliation for all international flights from British airports to be implemented by the end of 1993, dependent on supplies of equipment. While smaller airports might use manual means, the bar-code method would be used on larger airports. And *all* unaccompanied baggage would be searched. At the same time, the British government announced a target of 100 per cent search of all hold baggage on international flights by April 1996.

Passengers and cabin baggage

Passenger and cabin baggage security is often kept separate from hold baggage security because, in most airports, hold baggage is handled and loaded by the airline from the moment of check-in, while passengers themselves, with their cabin baggage, are handled by the airport. The first essential for passenger security is lacking in many airports – segregated 'pipelines' for arriving and departing passengers. These exist at many modern terminals, such as Heathrow Terminal 4, Gatwick North and Geneva, where the pipelines are on separate floors, with no possibility of mingling anywhere between the 'passengers only' barrier to the aircraft door. In others, the passengers pass in corridors in which any incoming passenger can exchange hand baggage with a departing passenger whose baggage has already been searched. This means that the would-be hijacker has only to arrange for an accomplice to arrive at about the same time from a low security airport (and there are sadly many of these) and pass across a bag containing a gun or a bomb in the corridor. Brussels Airport was typical, up to 1993. After check-in and search, embarking passengers shared the huge shopping centre with disembarking passengers – both for as long as they liked. This was no doubt good for airport finances, but bad for security.

The two Singapore-Changi terminals have a different system which gets the best of both. As in Brussels, each terminal has a common shopping centre, but embarking passengers are searched *after* that, at the entrance to the boarding lounge for their particular flight, which is insulated from all other passengers. This does, however, cost a lot in personnel and (if enhanced X-ray and magnetometer are used at every gate) in equipment, because each piece of equipment will be used at well below its capacity.

Another common weakness lies in transit passengers' cabin baggage. At most long-haul refuelling stops, both transit passengers and disembarking passengers leave the aircraft (for cabin cleaning, etc.) but the transit passengers are allowed to leave their cabin baggage on board. There is no way of telling whether a bag in the overhead locker belonged to a transit or to a disembarking passenger, so a terrorist has only to book to the refuelling stop and disembark, leaving a bag, with the bomb, in the cabin. The simple solution is for all passengers, disembarking or in transit, to take all their cabin baggage off the aircraft, so that the cabin can quickly be checked (using dogs, hand-held sniffers and gamma-ray detectors) during refuelling. If, as is often the case, the airport makes its money by exposing transit passengers to its shopping centre, then the Singapore system must be used – a search at the boarding gate after shopping. This is done at Dubai Airport (the great majority of whose passengers are in transit) but is of little use if the bomb bag has already been left aboard by a passenger who has disembarked.

Detecting potential terrorists

The highest security is that achieved by Israeli Airlines (El Al). For a variety of reasons it would be impracticable to apply this generally, but certain lessons from the El Al experience could well be applied. Although El Al flights have been the prime target for hundreds of Arab terrorists since 1968, few attacks have been driven home and fewer still have succeeded. This has been achieved at the cost of an average check-in time of three hours. Passengers are profiled from their ticket applications and by informal interrogation during the check-in process. This profiling and interrogation is aimed to detect not only potential terrorists, but also 'naive carriers' carrying something (e.g. a gift for delivery) for someone else (such as in the Hindawi case described on pp. 169–70); there is also another menace, the 'casual courier', usually a student, who accepts a free or partly paid ticket in exchange for agreeing to deliver a package (which may blow him or her up). All El Al baggage may be hand searched, and that of every passenger not established as totally safe by the profiling certainly will be. El Al can do this because they fly only about 20 aircraft, all based on a single hub (Tel Aviv). They fly to 33 destinations, in almost every one of which they run a dedicated sub-terminal, with boarding procedures totally insulated from other passengers and, in most cases, from non-El Al staff. They have only 170 take-offs per week (about 70 from Tel Aviv), and employ 3,500 staff. The security of their flights is vital both to their national survival and to their prestige, so it is heavily subsidized. No other airline could afford the personnel required without such a subsidy, and the world's airports would seize up if every airline required a three-hour check-in.

David Webb, whose research was mentioned in Chapter 7, has suggested another approach to detecting potential hijackers by using knowledge-based computers to detect links between apparently un-connected passengers. It may be assumed that a team to hijack a wide-bodied aircraft would comprise at least four or five people. They would have bought their tickets separately, possibly in different countries. They would check in separately, and keep well clear of each other in the departure lounge. All passengers (other than those profiled in advance – see next section) could be required to give certain information, e.g. in purchasing an air ticket, applying for a visa or, most probably, in answering a number of standard questions in the check-in or emigration process. All of this information could be fed into a computer system programmed to take note of certain aspects, such as personal, be-havioural, ethnic or national characteristics, possessions carried, entry to the county, stated purpose of visit or journey, source and procedure used for buying air tickets, where they spent the last few nights, and how they got to the airport. These individually would mean nothing, but collectively might narrow down the very small number of passengers who could conceivably be hijackers and, more importantly, link the four or five together. Given an expert system using the new Risc technology (see Chapter 7), these indicators and links would be revealed almost instantaneously, in time for these four or five people to be quietly picked out in the boarding lounge and taken for further questioning. Separate professional interrogations of this type often indicate suspicious discrepancies, and the passengers' reaction to the additional questions might well add to the suspicion.

A fast stream for passengers posing no threat

The Schiphol Travel Pass (STP) system was briefly mentioned in Chapter 8. This was a trial, initially restricted to Dutch business people who used the airport regularly and travelled without hold baggage. They enrolled voluntarily to take advantage of an automated fast stream through immigration. For an enrolment charge of Fl 50 ($30) and an annual fee of Fl 175 ($100), the volunteer received a smartcard with a microchip carrying a coded number and digital fingerprint data. The volunteer passed through two automated gates. The first gate checked the validity of the card. At the second gate the volunteer placed a finger on a scanner and the card in the slot; the gate opened if they matched. The whole process took 15 seconds. The cardholder was also asked to carry a valid Dutch passport, but this was checked only if there was some doubt. After a three-month test with 200 volunteers, the system was thrown open in April 1991; by early 1993 more than 1,000 people had enrolled.

The German equivalent was initiated in January 1994 at Frankfurt Airport. If successful, the aim was to introduce it at every major seaport and airport in Germany and later to extend it internationally. The initial motivation arose from the opening of EC frontiers in January 1993, necessitating tighter immigration control at external frontiers and points of entry to the EC. This required a more thorough check of non-EC nationals including an identity check from passports or other documents. One purpose was therefore to release staff to concentrate on these checks by automating border processing for travellers who presented no risk and had enrolled in the scheme.

Enrolment was voluntary. During the trial period it was free but, once it is fully established, there will be a one-off enrolment charge of DM10 ($4). It will be open only to people possessing a machine-readable passport or ID card, which can activate the German national police computer (NPC).

Volunteers will be able to apply for enrolment in writing to enrolment officers of the Federal Border Guard *(Bundesgrenzschutz – BGS)*, presenting their machine-readable passports or ID cards, with which the BGS can activate the NPC for an immediate security check: BGS also have the right to do a background check if needed, and to revoke the enrolment if new factors arise.

Later, when the scheme is fully established, there will be BGS enrolment offices at every major German seaport and airport giving international access. On enrolment, the traveller's biometric data (initially left and right thumbprint and left and right-hand geometry, to decide during the trial period which is best) was recorded on the computer. Hand geometry was the system selected.

Unlike the Dutch, the Germans had no additional smart-card; the machine-readable passport or ID card was the only document needed. The biometric data were recorded only on the computer and was directly matched to the traveller's hand. There were two turnstiles: the first opened automatically when the machine-readable passport or ID card was validated by the computer, indicating that the lawful holder of that card had already been security checked. The second gate established that the person presenting it was the lawful holder: it opened when the person's hand was placed on the screen and again the computer matched it. (The actual hand, of course, is better than having biometric data on a card as it cannot be forged.)

As noted in Chapter 8, the biometric data stored on the computer were limited purely to what was needed for matching and could not be used to construct the hand geometry, or to connect with any fingerprints held on police files.

If the scheme is successful, the Germans will encourage all the EC countries to join the scheme, and other countries later. The only condition will be that the user carries a machine-readable document which can be used to do the initial security check, and to be validated at the first turnstile. The British at present have no ID cards, but they are now issuing machine-readable passports (MRPs) which carry the same standardized data as German passports do (see Chapter 8). These data (name, date of birth, passport number, date of expiry, and so on) are in optical character reading (OCR) letters, which the holder can read as well as the machine; there are no other data on the card. These OCR data could be read by the German machine, which could at the same time record that the holder had been security checked by the British authorities (i.e. that the holder was enrolled in the scheme). With the massive interlocking memory capacity of Risc systems, the computer could also bring forward hand geometry data for matching at the second barrier. There would thus be no procedural problem in accepting voluntary enrolment of both German and British travellers to move freely through automated gates at any German or British airport.

A total of thirty countries have, or will shortly have, these same standard MRPs with the same OCR data, including Australia, Canada, Finland, Germany, Ireland, Japan, Singapore, the UK and the USA. All of these are stable democracies with computerized police records, so any of them could also join the scheme when they wish. So – when they too get standardized MRPs – could other EC and EFTA (European Free Trade Association) countries. International travellers from all of these countries would then be able to have shorter check-in times and automated fast-stream processing on entering or leaving their own or any of the other countries. This can remain voluntary; once its advantages are apparent, there will be no shortage of volunteers. Applied internationally, the scheme would enormously improve security and save money, by enabling staff to avoid wasting time on passengers who do not present any risk, and to concentrate their attention on those who do; it will be a highly efficient form of profiling.

Enforcing and financing common standards

There is a crying need to lay down and enforce other common international standards of aviation security. The main international carriers most often pick up their bombs or hijackers, not at big international airports, but at Third World or holiday airports, which could not conceivably afford the million or half million dollar explosive detectors being tested at JFK and Gatwick. It is therefore in the own interest of the big countries (especially the G7 countries and Russia, who between them operate 80 per cent of the world's commercial air traffic) to subsidize security at smaller airports, by helping to pay for equipment and personnel, or possibly by providing and operating dedicated international sub-terminals in the same way as El Al do (though not quite so meticulously as to require a three-hour check-in).

The common standards should be laid down by the International Civil Aviation Organization (ICAO), an agency of the UN. ICAO already does lay down standards in general terms in its Annex 17, but it has no teeth to enforce them. With 164 members ICAO (like its parent UN) is too cumbersome for executive action, but it does have a Council of 33 which includes 11 ex-officio members (rather like the permanent members of the UN Security Council), comprising the big carrier countries, including the G7 countries and Russia. Those 11 could be authorized to monitor and enforce the common security standards on behalf of ICAO. This would involve discreet monitoring of all airports licensed for international traffic and, in the event of the monitors finding unsatisfactory standards, enforcement would be in three stages: first, there would be a discreet warning to an offending airport that it must rectify the shortcomings by a certain date; second, if it failed to do so, there would be a public warning to all member airlines that security at that airport was unsatisfactory and that they should superimpose their own supplementary security measures; and third, if it still failed to rectify the faults, there would be a boycott of that airport by all 11 ex-officio members (with over 80 per cent of the world's traffic) and by any of the other 153 members who chose to join it. (The procedure for such a boycott was set out in the Bonn Convention at the G7 Summit in 1978.)

The third stage should never be necessary. Even a partial equivalent to the second stage – a public warning in 1986 by the FAA to US carriers only – is said to have cost Athens Airport $300 million, and this galvanized them into improving their security.

Financing, including the subsidizing of security in small airports, should again be organized by ICAO, in the form of a levy on every international air ticket. This must be payable as a 'tax' by the airline direct to a fund operated by the ICAO security enforcement agency (run by the 11), not simply absorbed into the airline's own security budget. ICAO would then allocate the fund as they judged best to raise the standard for all travellers.

A $5 levy on each international ticket should be enough. At a big airport, the hypothetical system described earlier in this chapter for 1,200 bags in a 3-hour peak load at a JFK airline terminal required equipment costing $3 million. Another $2 million for structural work and for extra staff for one year would bring the first year's cost to $5 million. Out of the $5 levy, $1 per bag would bring $1,200 × 365 = $4.38 million for the 3-hour peak and, with the other 21 hours of lesser peaks and off-peak flights, the income should be well over $5 million, nearing $10 million. Since each passenger was assumed to have two bags (600 passengers, 1,200 bags), between $1 and $2 per passenger would be more than enough to pay all the installation costs and a full year's operation. The balance of the total $5 levy ($3–4) would therefore be available for other improvements to finance ongoing research for improved equipment and – above all – for subsidizing better security at smaller airports as described. Few passengers or airlines would object to a $5 levy for security, provided that it was universally applied to every airline.

Part VI

Conclusions

19 Stopping people killing each other

Likeliest areas of instability

New kinds of terrorism have been thrown up by the end of the Cold War, mainly the revival of ethnic cleansing. A few extreme Marxist and terrorist movements survive, increasingly subsidized by drug trafficking; some other generators of terrorism persist, notably the Arab–Israeli conflict and Islamic fundamentalism. In response, more positive attitudes for peacemaking are developing, and protecting people against terrorism is assisted by technological developments, especially in the detection of explosives, surveillance, access control, biometric identification and intelligence. To meet the challenge of intimidation, modification of legal process may be needed. But, in developing these things, it will be essential to develop effective means of preventing their abuse and safeguarding civil liberties.

For convenience, the likeliest areas of conflict and instability are summarized in Table 5. They have been discussed more fully in earlier chapters.

Peacekeeping and peacemaking

The world cannot yet dispense with its armed forces because, as exemplified by Saddam Hussein, there will always be ambitious leaders who will try to grab territory or resources if they judge they are likely to succeed. Modern armed forces should, however, be so designed that they can adapt to a peacekeeping or peacemaking role. In this context, peace*keeping* refers to maintaining peace once it has been agreed by the warring parties and peace*making* to the use of forces to compel one or both parties to stop fighting. The massive growth in the demand for peacekeeping forces in 1992–3, under UN command or under the command of governments acting on behalf of the UN, gradually led

Table 5 Likeliest areas of conflict

Area	Types of conflict	Others affected
WEST EUROPE		
All EC and EFTA countries	Refugees and backlash, drug traffic, Mafia and other crime	
Spain, UK	Ethnic terrorism and backlash	France, USA
EAST EUROPE		
Bosnia, Croatia	Serb aggression, ethnic conflict	UN, NATO, CIS
Macedonia, Kosovo	Serb aggression and repression	Islamic states
Albania, Bulgaria, Romania	Minority tensions. Involvement in neighbouring conflicts	Turkey, Greece, Balkan states
CIS		
Armenia, Azerbaijan, Georgia, Moldova, Tajikistan	Ethnic, religious and border conflicts and civil wars	Russia, CIS, Turkey, Iran, UN
Russian Federation	Old guard resistance to reform	CIS
Autonomous areas in Russia	Demanding independence	Russia, CIS
MEDITERRANEAN		
Arab–Israeli	Deep-rooted ongoing conflict	UN, USA, Iraq
Cyprus	Deep-rooted ongoing conflict	Turkey, Greece
Greece, Turkey	Internal unrest may recur	
Jordan	Palestinian or Iraqi take-over	Egypt, Saudi, UN
Egypt, Algeria	Islamic fundamentalist threat	France, USA
Libya	Interference in Egypt, Chad, etc.	UN, OAU, USA
Tunisia, Morocco	Internal rebellion	France, USA, UN
AFRICA		
Sudan	Islamic clash with black south	Egypt, Libya
Burundi, Rwanda	Tutsi–Hutu conflict	Neighbours, UN
East Africa	Warlord anarchy (e.g. Somalia)	UN, OAU, USA
West Africa	Warlord anarchy (e.g. Liberia)	UN, ECOWAS
Angola, Mozambique	Civil war and aftermath	Neighbours
South Africa	Racial conflict	Neighbours

Table 5 (continued)

Area	Types of conflict	Others affected
GULF STATES		
Iran	Aid subversion (eg Hezbollah)	Arab Gulf, USA
Iraq	Pursue control of all Gulf oil	Arabs, Iran, USA
Monarchies	Vulnerable to internal revolt	Iraq, Egypt, USA
CENTRAL ASIA		
Ex-Soviet Asian republics, Afghanistan	Ethnic, Islamic, drug related; competition for influence by Turkey, Iran and Pakistan	Russia, CIS, Turkey, Iran and Pakistan
SOUTH ASIA		
India	Sikh–Hindu–Muslim	Kashmir, Pakistan
Pakistan	Army–Islamic rivalry	Kashmir, India
Sri Lanka	Tamil–Singhalese–Muslim	India
EAST ASIA		
Cambodia	Pol Pot terror; ethnic cleansing	Vietnam, China
Myanmar	Hated regime; minorities; opium	Neighbours
Thailand, Laos	Drug traffic; link with Pol Pot	Neighbours
Hong Kong	Heroin traffic; Triads	UK, China
Indonesia	Corruption; separatism	Neighbours, UN
Philippines	Communist and Muslim terrorism	USA, Indonesia
Japan	Attacks on world-wide activities	USA, UN
North Korea	Sponsors terrorism. Nuclear?	USA, UN
LATIN AMERICA		
Venezuela, Brazil	Drug traffic; internal strains	Colombia, USA
Colombia, Peru	Drug Mafias, terrorism, crime, risk of coup	USA and Europe
Central America	Still underlying instability	UN, USA, Cuba
NORTH AMERICA		
USA	Internal Islamic terrorism? Attacks on world-wide activities	
Canada	Quebec separatism	France, USA

Table 6 UN peacekeeping and peacemaking, April 1993

Country	Troops	Annual cost ($m)
Somalia	16,700	1,500
Ex-Yugoslavia	24,363	602
Cambodia	19,253	1,411
Lebanon	5,251	146
Western Sahara	1,603	29
Cyprus	1,539	19
Golan Heights	1,119	36
El Salvador	377	39
Iraq and Kuwait	320	40
Israeli borders	248	31
Angola	105	39
India and Pakistan	38	7
Mozambique	3,620	206

Source: UN figures published in *The Economist* 1 May and 12 June 1993

them increasingly into a peacemaking role in 1993–4. Table 6 gives an estimate of the number and annual cost of UN peacekeeping and peacemaking operations in April 1993.

At the end of 1991, there were less than 15,000 UN troops deployed world-wide in a peacekeeping role. During 1992 over 75,000 more were dispatched to Bosnia, Cambodia, Croatia and (initially under US command) to Somalia. In the past, most UN peacekeeping was done by contingents from smaller countries, not from the permanent members of the Security Council, nor from members of NATO or the Warsaw Pact. In 1992 the majority of the 75,000 came from the USA (in Somalia), Canada, the UK and France. Peacemaking (and to a lesser extent peacekeeping) involves casualties, and there was a groundswell of public questioning 'Why should we send our troops to risk their lives for Serbs, Croats, Muslims, Cambodians and Somalis, who insist on shooting each other? Why don't we leave them to sort out their own mess?' There was also argument about who should pay the bill.

Wherever possible, it is best for neighbours to provide troops on a regional basis, since it is they who have most to gain from containing the conflict. The West African soldiers sent to Liberia and the Russians sent to Georgia, Moldova and Tajikistan were not included in the 75,000, and there were 15,000 West African troops in Liberia alone.

But where a regional solution is not possible, it is in the world's interest to stop such conflicts spreading and, some would say, the world's duty to provide humanitarian aid. It is rare for the majority of ordinary families to want the wars, and it is they who suffer the most. Ethnic cleansing and murder in the name of God (Muslim, Hindu, Sikh or Christian) are now the most vicious forms of terrorism.

The first essential is to maintain the unity of the permanent members of the UN Security Council, first manifested in the Gulf Crisis of 1990. Since then, neither Russia nor China has vetoed anything important, though this has required much prior discussion behind the scenes. There is a very strong case for Germany and Japan becoming permanent members, provided that they revise their constitutions so that they can pull their full weight in providing armed forces. With seven permanent members, it would be sensible to revise the power of veto so that two of the seven would need to apply the veto to block a resolution. It would be necessary, however, to permit any who voted against a resolution which was passed to opt out of participation in active military action, though all should be obliged to co-operate with passive sanctions such as observing a mandatory boycott or blockade. For the time being, Russia and China probably have enough interest in retaining the economic co-operation of their fellow permanent members not to make unnecessary difficulties, but their attitudes may change as they gain strength and confidence, especially the Chinese.

NATO as an executive arm for the UN

The UN has repeatedly proved that it is too ponderous to operate an executive headquarters to command a day-to-day military operation. It is now becoming generally accepted that a member government (such as the USA in Korea in 1950, Kuwait in 1991 and Somalia in 1992) acting on behalf of the UN may be better: or, better still, NATO, which now has fifty years' experience of operational command of international armed forces, having been formed under General Eisenhower as a continuation of the Allied Command, forged by him in the fire of liberating West Europe in the last two years of the Second World War.

NATO has already held a number of meetings of a wider body, the North Atlantic Co-operation Council (NACC), at which NATO's sixteen countries were joined by nineteen others in March 1992, including eleven former Soviet republics and some of the east European states. It would be a mistake to make NATO too cumbersome so, when required to command an international peacemaking force on behalf of the UN, its staff should be reinforced by representatives of only those countries contributing to the force, which could of course include countries like India, Japan or Australia, far removed from the North Atlantic.

For this peacemaking role, NATO should be prepared to form an advanced headquarters, to take command in the area of operations and, where the possibility of such operations is contemplated, a planning cell should be dispatched in advance.

Funding

The funding of UN peacekeeping forces has thus far been unsatisfactory. Many governments have been late with their contributions and others have failed to contribute at all. The UN should agree that basic costs should be paid by each country for its own contingents, and that extra costs should be paid from a central UN fund, to which all UN members would subscribe pro rata (based on their GNP). Basic costs are defined as those which the country would pay in any case if the unit, ship or aircraft were at home, that is daily pay, food, accommodation, equipment, maintenance and so on. Extra costs would cover transport to the area of operations, extra fuel, accommodation, ammunition, etc. Since this kind of activity has clearly come to stay, subscriptions high enough to build up this fund, with a substantial reserve, should be initiated at once as a condition of UN membership.

20 Civil liberties and the rule of law

The rule of law in face of intimidation

One of the primary aims of terrorists is to make the liberal system of law unworkable by intimidating witnesses and juries. They hope thereby to have credible grounds for accusing the government of repression. It was in the face of this that trial without jury for terrorist offences was introduced in Northern Ireland in 1973 (as it already had been since 1962 in the Republic of Ireland). In Northern Ireland, however, the trial is conducted by a single judge, subject to full rights of appeal to a court of three judges. Justice would better be seen to be done if there were three judges at the trial itself, of whom two could be junior judges, stipendiary magistrates or Queens Counsel temporarily seconded from the UK, though this would necessitate prolonged personal protection thereafter. An alternative would be the CCTV technique for safeguarding the identity of jurors and witnesses (described on pp. 192–3). This is now technologically quite practical.

There should certainly be a reinterpretation of the 'right to silence' (proposed on pp. 191–2), whereby the court can put its own interpretation on refusal to answer questions (presented as a tape recording at the trial), just as it interprets a failure by a person to provide a convincing explanation in court for something he or she is shown to have done. Again, only the guilty have anything to fear from this. It is already applied in certain cases in the Republic of Ireland and in Northern Ireland.

In dealings with terrorists who calculatedly try to make the law unworkable, it is all the more justifiable to offer incentives for evidence from informers and to give them whatever protection is needed. This provided the greatest single breakthrough in fighting the Red Brigades in Italy and thereby saved hundreds of lives. In Northern Ireland, absence of corroborative evidence led the Appeal Court to quash a number of convictions, though in some cases the Appeal judges gave the impression that they themselves had no doubt of the guilt of the person convicted. A court in which the witness could feel confident of not being identified and, better still, a jury able to hear and see but not to be seen, would probably have overcome this problem.

As well as granting immunity or leniency for Queen's evidence, it is essential that any witnesses or informers likely to be at risk should be given protection and, if they desire it, provision of generous funds to enable them and their families to start a new life in a new place. This was certainly done in the first and most successful experiment in this field in Malaya in 1958–60 (pp. 125–6). Both there and in Italy few of the informers or other witnesses giving 'dangerous' evidence have suffered retribution. The cost of rewards and protection is negligible compared with the cost of damage done by terrorism. Alison Jamieson, in her Conflict Study on *Collaboration* (1993 – see p. 226) has recorded that over the peak of the 'supergrass' period of incentives to informers in Northern Ireland and its aftermath (1978–85), the total cost of protecting those who had given evidence against former accomplices amounted to £1.3 million. A single IRA bomb in the City of London in April 1992 did damage costing £300 million, and a similar bomb in April 1993 at least as much again. Rewards for information are probably the most cost-effective weapon in the anti-terrorist armoury.

Other forms of intimidation, such as demands for protection money and racketeering (see pp. 159, 172) must also be firmly dealt with: first, by extending the same guarantees and protection to informers as above; second, by freezing all the assets of people accused of these crimes and those of their families and colleagues, during investigation; and third, by confiscating these assets if they are found guilty. The onus would be on the family to provide proof of legitimate sources of any money or property in their possession. This, again, has been done in Northern Ireland.

Now that their internal frontiers are open, it is time to link up the EC's judicial systems. All EC countries should accept the obligation to extradite any accused person for trial in the country where the offence was allegedly committed, according to that country's laws and judicial procedures. There must be no exception made for offences claimed to be 'political'. Any court in the EC should have power to subpoena any witness from any EC country to give evidence in that court.

Laws to help fight terrorism

Legislation is needed for stricter control of the possession and movement of arms, ammunition and explosives. This could be greatly improved by an agreement by civilized nations to tag all explosives with a colour code system which would identify their source and enable their progress to be recorded (see pp. 57–8).

Registration of private security companies is inadequate in most countries, especially in Britain. The 100 largest British security companies, which handle 90 per cent of the trade, are voluntary members of the British Security Industry Association (BSIA) which does enforce professional standards of both managers and guards. There are, however, at least another 600 small security companies which undercut costs by employing poorly trained guards at low wages which many of them are prepared to accept because they have criminal records, and perhaps also because they hope to supplement these wages by dubious use of the opportunities available in this business. Control could be exercised in one of two ways. Either all security companies should be required by law to register with the BSIA, accepting its monitoring of their recruitment and professional standards as a condition of being allowed to practise (like doctors being required to register with the British Medical Association). Alternatively, this compulsory registration could be with a government body, which would serve the same purpose. The first is probably the better alternative, and would be welcomed by the hundred or so large and responsible security firms which are currently undercut by 'cowboys' to the benefit of criminals and terrorists.

Reckless use of the media in such a way as to put lives at risk should be treated like reckless driving. If an editor, reporter or producer recklessly or wilfully reports a terrorist incident, or reveals measures to pre-empt it or to catch the terrorists, in such a way as to increase the risk to life, a court should convict him or her whether anyone was killed or not.

In November 1974, after IRA bombs killed twenty-one people in Birmingham, the Prevention of Terrorism Act became law within a week and, with only minor adjustments, has been renewed by Parliament every year since then. This would clearly not have been possible unless legislation had been held ready in draft for such a contingency. Other powers may be kept in force but not used, such as the power of detention without trial, introduced in Northern Ireland in 1971 but not used since 1976. If there were a major crisis, for example a series of massacres such as to create a risk that the population might take the law into their own hands, virtually the entire top line of the IRA's godfathers and hard core (sixty to eighty people – see p. 160) could be detained.

Legislation which should be held ready in draft might include Tenants' Registration, whereby every householder and innkeeper would be required to register the names and National Insurance numbers (or ID card numbers) of everyone resident in the house overnight. In some European countries this is already required by laws which specify periods within which arrivals and departures (permanent or temporary) must be recorded. This is very valuable, not only for keeping track of criminal suspects or supporters, but also for detecting houses being used for sheltering them or for other unlawful purposes. Though this would be counter-productive in normal times, it might be justified and necessary in certain specified areas (e.g. Northern Ireland) if both the circumstances and public opinion demanded it.

If it were decided that the issue of ID cards was not at present justified, then at least the necessary legislation, machinery and materials for immediate implementation should be held in readiness, as they clearly were (along with ration cards, etc.) as part of the mobilization plans for the Second World War; such legislation would take account of the experience of other countries which have had to take such action. In France, for example, legislation was passed in 1986 to prevent people leaving the scene of a crime, enabling the police to demand proof of identification and to detain them if their identification was in doubt. If anyone declined to co-operate in providing such proof, the police could refer to a magistrate who had the power to order photographs and fingerprints to be taken.

Power to increase the permitted duration of detention for questioning should be held in reserve in case a concerted attempt to circumvent existing procedures, coupled with an upsurge of crime, were to make it necessary. In Italy in 1978 for example, calculated disruption by intimidation of the processes of investigation by magistrates led the government to extend the time and postpone hearing of the case for an indefinite period. They also permitted 'informal interrogation' (i.e. it was not admissible as evidence) without the right to have a lawyer present. Spain, after a spate of ETA murders in 1985, authorized detention of suspects incommunicado for up to ten days (reduced in 1987 to three days extendable to five).

Abuse of rights by lawyers may also need to be covered. In Germany in the 1970s, leading figures in the middle-class Red Army Faction included a number of lawyers who had not given sufficient proof of involvement to justify arrest. These lawyers, representing leading terrorist comrades under arrest or undergoing trial, skilfully disrupted the processes of investigation and court proceedings and, in the course of privileged prison visits to the clients, acted as couriers and channels for orders and communications; some also smuggled weapons and radios into the prison. The German government therefore legislated to bar from the courts any lawyer who had supported terrorist activities or disrupted legal proceedings, and applied stricter control to prison visits.

Laws to suspend jury trial or to safeguard the identity of jurors and witnesses (see pp. 192–3) could also be held in readiness, in case intimidation or corruption (by criminals as well as terrorists) made this necessary to prevent interference with the course of justice. The 1986 package of laws in France enacted non-jury trial for terrorist offences by a *Cour d'Assises* comprising a president and six assessors (all judges – the French separation of the Judiciary and Advocacy allowing quite young 'examining magistrates' to act in this capacity).

France also tightened migration and extradition procedures on the Spanish frontier in 1983–4 at Spain's request. Again, the complexity of such legislation justifies holding it in draft.

Drugs and illegal money

Chapters 9, 10 and 11 identified the $300 billion narcotics profit as one of the biggest generators of terrorism and criminal violence in the world. Its evil effect spreads from the Third World countries in which the narcotics are cultivated and processed, to the affluent countries in which most of them are consumed, especially Europe and the USA, but spreading increasingly as affluence grows in the producing countries themselves.

While the USA and Europe (including the CIS) should give every possible co-operation to those producing countries willing to tackle the problems of drug cultivation, and the countries through which narcotics are transported, the only real cure will be in cutting off the money paid by addicts on the streets of the consuming countries themselves.

The cure proposed in Chapter 11 is to impose perpetual imprisonment (life-meaning-life sentences) for drug traffickers, both to keep them out of circulation and to deter others, and to commit addicts to compulsory treatment until they are passed as cured, thereafter to be subject to regular blood tests and immediate return to compulsory treatment at the first sign of re-addiction.

Coupled with drug trafficking is the illegal money it generates, hand in hand with the illegal money created by fraud, counterfeiting and extortion. In some countries the amount of illegal money in circulation is already having a dangerously destabilizing effect on the economy.

As well as tackling narcotics consumption, it will therefore be necessary to tackle the laundering of money from all these sources. Laundering is done primarily through electronic transfers between banks. While most western banks are legally obliged and willing to give access to customers' accounts if the police can produce evidence that they may contain money illegally obtained (see Chapter 3), it may be difficult to produce such evidence without first examining the account – a Catch-22 situation. A full right of access, subject to safeguards and monitoring by the Judiciary, must be extended internationally if this problem is to be solved. A further problem is that banks are willing to take any money without asking questions and to transfer it instantly by electronic means to another bank, after which the police trail will grow cold. To overcome this, western governments will need to legislate to ban their banks from any transactions with foreign banks which do not maintain proper records and make them available for scrutiny, subject to reasonable judicial safeguards.

Technological research

Chapters 3–8 highlighted three areas in which technological research is most urgently needed: detection of explosives; identification including prevention of impersonation; and aids to intelligence.

Explosive detection is of particular importance to aviation security, and it was proposed in Chapter 18 that this should be funded out of a \$5 security levy on every international air ticket to be collected and disbursed by ICAO. About half of this levy would be needed to install detection equipment at airports and to pay extra staff to achieve and maintain agreed ICAO standards, especially including subsidies to small airports carrying international traffic without the economies of scale. Much of the remainder, running into hundreds of millions of dollars each year, should be dispensed in grants to aid research projects specifically approved by ICAO. Since an element of commercial competition will produce the best research, such grants should pay only part of the cost of the projects. The developer of an equipment which won adoption by airports would be contracted to refund a small percentage of its sale price until its total grant was repaid.

Research into identification and anti-impersonation systems also has an application to aviation security, as described in Chapters 8 and 18. This research should also qualify for grants from the ICAO air ticket levy, but it also has a much wider application (for fighting drug smuggling and crime, for police spot checks to pick up illegal immigrants and wanted persons, and for a variety of commercial purposes, including validation of bank or credit cards). It should therefore also be funded by governments, banks, and so on, which should, like ICAO, be able to recover a share of their grants from manufacturers whose resulting sales justify this. The G7 countries, and others of similar outlook (such as the Scandinavian and Benelux countries, Austria, Switzerland, Australia and New Zealand) would gain from forming a pool, to make the best use of funds by avoiding wasteful duplication, and to gain the best advantages from the results. Though it is tempting to suggest pooling of research itself, this would be unwise as it would prejudice the element of commercial competition which is vital for revolutionary innovation.

Aids to intelligence were discussed in Chapters 2, 7 and 17. These are particularly important in dealing with terrorism, drug trafficking and international crime. The two main areas in which research is needed are in surveillance equipment and computerized data processing, especially with international links. The same basis should be applied: grants by governments, preferably co-ordinated by G7 or an enlarged international body as described for identification systems, to support and encourage the pursuit of research by competing commercial firms.

Other important areas of research include: prevention and detection of computer crimes, including viruses and hacking and of legal international transfer and other means of laundering money; aids to personnel selection and screening; identification and anti-impersonation (of which more later); explosives detection; and the development of personal VTOL and STOL aircraft, including the possible quantum leap to a dramatically lighter engine. All of these things were discussed in appropriate chapters.

Public safety and civil liberties

Sir Robert Mark, probably the wisest and most successful British policeman in the twentieth century, summed up the dilemma: 'Total freedom is anarchy; total order is tyranny.' The law has to inhibit the freedom of criminals and thoughtless idiots in order to protect the freedom of law-abiding people. Every law, therefore, exacts a price in civil liberties; also, any law can be abused.

Most people accept the interference with their freedom when they are searched at airports, as preferable to being blown up or hijacked. Most people would welcome digital fingerprint data on their bank cards to ensure that no criminal could steal their money through a hole in the wall. Most regular travellers would welcome the prior profiling and biometric identification needed to join the fast stream for arrival and departure at airports as described in Chapters 8 and 18.

Some people, however, would resent having to carry machine-readable ID cards. This objection can no longer be sustained. Eight of the twelve EC member governments now issue ID cards, all but the British, Danes, Dutch and Irish: the Dutch will have theirs by 1995. Most EC citizens already carry more than one card – bank, credit, rail, etc. – which contains electronic or magnetic data (usually on a black strip). The rising level of sophisticated crime, the opportunities for fraud, and the price paid for terrorism and drug trafficking are such that no civilized society should any longer accept the right to conceal identity when identification is lawfully and reasonably required, as it already is every time a person draws money from a bank or enters or leaves a country. The liberty of individuals to lead a double life without risk of their family finding out is not worth the price of denying the police the means of detecting an IRA bomber, a car thief or a drug pusher.

Machine readability of ID cards, passports or visas presents neither technical nor ethical problems, as was explained in Chapters 8 and 18. These chapters also described the pioneering experiments of the Dutch and Germans to develop the use of biometric data to prevent impersonation, which it does far more effectively than a photograph or signature. Again, only the guilty have anything to fear.

It will be essential, however, to ensure that these safeguards for the majority are not abused by unscrupulous officials or police officers to harass other members of the public by, for example, repeated and unnecessary checks of the same person, or worse, by selling information about individuals to commercial companies. Modern computer systems provide their own built-in answer to this. Machine-reading of data (be it simply of name and date of birth, or of biometric identification) by definition involves the data on the card passing through a computer system. This system could also automatically record the date and time and the code number of the police officer or official making the check. Computers now have ample memory capacity, and 99 per cent of this information would never need to be called up – any more than the police need to examine the millions of fingerprints left every day on doors, tables, chairs and glasses, unless a crime is committed. In both cases, the data can be wiped off after a period if not used. By these means, the system will be able to deter or prevent or, if these fail and there is a complaint, to detect any abuse at police spot checks or by officious bureaucrats.

Terrorism is the recourse of a tiny minority who know that they could never get democratic acceptance of their views. Dissent is healthy and constructive, but it can never justify bombing, killing, wounding or intimidation. Crime is an arrogant assault on other people's liberty. The civilized majority has always, throughout history, accepted a rule of law placing limits on the freedom to harm others. There is no valid claim of liberty to conceal identity, and certainly no right to impersonate someone else. The claim of a right to kill must never override the ultimate civil right to live.

Sources and bibliography

Main sources of facts

The Economist, filed 1972–93, with *The Economist Index*
The Times, filed 1974–93
Control Risks *Briefing Book*, a monthly analysis of events in countries subject
to security and political risks world-wide. Published in London and available
on subscription. Filed 1982–93. Prior to that, *The Annual of Power and
Conflict*, filed 1971–82
Encyclopaedia Britannica

Other useful reference books regularly consulted were *The Economist
Yearbook* (1992 and 1993), *Whitaker's Almanack* (1993) and *The Encyclopaedia
of Dates and Events* (1991) London: Hodder & Stoughton
The most useful journals for technological updating were *Security Industry*,
International Security Review and *Intersec*. Personal correspondence with
manufacturers often led to demonstrations of their equipment, in which the
security manager of Gatwick was also very helpful.

Part I Introduction

1 Conflict in the post-Communist world
2 A new kind of peacekeeping

Cannings, D. (1990) *Policing in Europe towards 1992*, London: Home Office
Clutterbuck, R. (1990) *Terrorism and Guerrilla Warfare*, London and New
    York: Routledge
Clutterbuck, R. (1990) *Terrorism, Drugs and Crime in Europe after 1992*,
    London and New York: Routledge
Dobson, C. and Payne, R. (1986) *War without End*, London: Harrap
Kitson, F. (1979) *Bunch of Five*, London: Faber
Laqueur, W. (1977) *Guerrilla*, London: Weidenfeld & Nicolson
Laqueur, W. (1987) *The Age of Terrorism*, London: Weidenfeld & Nicolson
Wardlaw, G. (1982) *Political Terrorism*, Cambridge University Press
Wilkinson, P. (1986) *Terrorism and the Liberal State*, London: Macmillan

Part II Technological development

3 A vulnerable society

Alexander, Y. and Kilmarx, R. A. (Eds) (1979) *Political Terrorism and Business*, New York: Praeger
Clutterbuck, R. (1987) 'The future of political violence and terrorism', *Journal of the Royal Society of Arts* April: 376–86
Clutterbuck, R. (1990) *Terrorism and Guerrilla Warfare*, London and New York: Routledge
Clutterbuck, R. (1990) *Terrorism, Drugs and Crime in Europe after 1992*, London and New York: Routledge
Ellen, E. (1986) *Violence at Sea*, Paris: ICC Publishing SA.
Jenkins, B. (1985) *Terrorism and Personal Protection*, Boston, Mass: Butterworth
Richardson, L. (1986) 'The urgency of detergency (or how money laundering is carried out)', *TVI Report* 6 (3): 12–22 and 6 (4): 43–50 (in two parts)

4 Personal weapons
5 Missiles, longer range weapons and bombs

Brasseys (1982–6) *Battlefield Weapons Systems and Technology Series*, London: Brasseys
Dobson, C. and Payne, R. (1979) *The Weapons of Terror*, London: Macmillan
De Leon, P. and Hoffman, B. (1988) *The Threat of Nuclear Terrorism*, Santa Monica, Calif: Rand
Hogg, I. (ed.) (1986) *Jane's Infantry Weapons*, London: Jane's Publishing; also personal interview and correspondence
Macksey, K. (1986) *Technology in War: The Impact of Science on Weapon Development and Modern Battle*, London: Arms and Armour Press
Pengelly, R. (1982) 'G11: Worth waiting for?', *Defence Attaché* 1: 22–5
Raschen, Col. D. G., OBE, Royal Military College of Science, Shrivenham, personal interviews and correspondence

6 Detecting explosives, bombs and guns

Bozorgmanesh, H. (1987) 'Bomb and weapon detection' *Terrorism: An International Journal* 10 (3): 285–7
Kindel, S. (1987) 'Off-the-shelf technology', *Terrorism: An International Journal* 10 (3): 281–4
Knowles, G. (1976) *Bomb Security Guide*, Los Angeles, Calif: Security World
Morris, D. (1986) *Dogwatching*, London: Jonathan Cape
US Congress OTA (1991) *Technology against Terrorism: The Federal Effort*, Washington, DC: US Government
US Congress OTA (1991) *Technology against Terrorism: Structuring Security*, Washington, DC: US Government
Yallop, H. J. (1980) *Explosion Investigation*, Edinburgh: Forensic Science Society
Yallop, H. J. (1980) *Protection Against Terrorism*, London: Barry Rose

Also interviews and correspondence with Lt Col. A. J. Wright, RE, and Major
J. R. Wyatt, MBE, RE, at the Royal School of Military Engineering, Chatham

7 Intelligence and the microelectronics revolution

This chapter is based mainly on visits and interviews with

Professor Richard Gregory, of Bristol University, who has combined his
medical and computer expertise to become the leading thinker in Britain on
artificial intelligence;

Dr John Hulbert, who, as Chief Superintendent of Police, developed some
highly original computer systems for police intelligence and now runs his
own computer research and development company, Cogitaire;

Dr David Webb, who worked with John Hulbert in this development;

Dr Masoud Yazdani, Lecturer in Computer Science at the University of Exeter

Writings by two of these, easily understandable to the non-professional, were
consulted throughout:

Webb, D. (1987) 'Artificial Intelligence: Its potential to create an impact in the
fight against terrorism', Paper presented to a symposium at the Office of
International Criminal Justice, University of Illinois at Chicago, August

Yazdani, M. and Narayanan, A. (eds) (1984) *Artificial Intelligence: Human
Effects*, Chichester: Ellis Horwood.

8 Physical security

Clutterbuck, R. (1987) *Kidnap, Hijack and Extortion*, London: Macmillan; New
York: St Martin's Press

Clutterbuck, R. (1990) *Terrorism and Guerrilla Warfare*, London and New
York: Routledge

Clutterbuck, R. (1990) *Terrorism, Drugs and Crime in Europe after 1992*,
London and New York: Routledge

Davidson Smith, G. (1990) *Combating Terrorism*, London and New York:
Routledge

Federal Bureau of Investigation (1982) *Crisis Reaction Seminar*, held at the
International University for Presidents, Maui, Hawai, 1982; Washington, DC:
FBI

Jenkins, B. (ed.) (1985) *Terrorism and Personal Protection*, Boston, Mass:
Butterworth

MacKenzie, G., McLoughlin, A. A. and Twiss, G. (1983) *The Security
Handbook*, Cape Town: Flesch

Moore, K. C. (1976) *Airport, Aircraft and Airline Security*, Los Angeles, Calif:
Security World

Part III Drugs, political violence, and crime

9 *Cocaine*
10 *Heroin and hashish*
11 *The consumers*

Adams, J. (1986) *The Financing of Terror*, Sevenoaks: New English Library, ch. 9, 'The Narc-Farc connection'
Andean Commission of Jurists (1991–93) *Andean Newsletter* and *Drug Trafficking Update*, each published monthly in Lima
Browne, D. (1988) 'Crack', *Observer*, 24 July
Control Risks, *Briefing Book:* monthly 1982–93
'Drugs: Prevention begins in Peru', *The Economist*, 16 July 1988
Goldsmith, C. (1987–8) 'Drugs: The threat to society', *Sitrep International* 1: 2–4, 2: 3–11, 3: 4–10 and 4: 4–11, September 1987 to July 1988 (in four parts)
Posner, G. (1989) *Warlords of Crime: The New Mafia*, London: Macdonald Queen Anne Press
Simpson, J. (1993) *In the Forests of the Night*, London: Hutchinson.

Part IV Rural guerrilla warfare

12 *Rural guerrillas – Latin America*
13 *Rural guerrillas – Asia and Africa*
14 *Development of rural guerrilla warfare*

Andean Commission of Jurists (1991–3) *Andean Newsletter* and *Drug Trafficking Update*, each published monthly in Lima
Asprey, R. (1976) *War in the Shadows*, London: Macdonald
Clutterbuck, R. (1984) *Conflict and Violence in Singapore and Malaysia*, Boulder, Col: Westview; (1985) Singapore: Brash
Clutterbuck, R. (1987) *Kidnap, Hijack and Extortion*, London: Macmillan; New York: St Martin's Press, ch. 16, 'Anti-development abductions'
Clutterbuck, R. (1990) *Terrorism and Guerrilla Warfare*, London and New York: Routledge
Clutterbuck, R. (1990) *Terrorism, Drugs and Crime in Europe after 1992*, London and New York: Routledge
Control Risks, *Briefing Book:* monthly 1982–93
Control Risks (1987) *South Asia: Political Forecast 1987–89*, London: Control Risks
Corbett, R. (1986) *Guerrilla Warfare from 1939 to the Present Day*, London: Orbis
De Soto, H. (1989) *The Other Path*, London: Taurus
Goldsmith, C. (1987–8) 'Drugs: The threat to society', *Sitrep International*, 1, 2, 3 and 4, September 1987 to July 1988 (in four parts)
Kitson, F. (1979) *Bunch of Five*, London: Faber
MacKenzie, G., McLoughlin, A. A. and Twiss, G. (1983) *The Security Handbook*, Cape Town: Flesch.
Mao Tse-tung (1992 ed. S. Griffiths) *Guerrilla Warfare*, Baltimore, Md: Nautical & Aviation Publishers

Mockaitis, R. (1990) *British Counterinsurgency, 1919–60*, London: Macmillan
Sarkesian, S. (1993) *Unconventional Conflicts in a New Security Era: Letters from Malaya and Vietnam*, Westport CT: Greenwood Press
Scott Palmer, D. (ed.) (1992) *Shining Path of Peru*, London: Hurst
Simpson, J. (1993) *In the Forests of the Night*, London: Hutchinson
Strong, S. (1992) *Shining Path*, London: Harper Collins
Strong, S. (1993) *Shining Path: A Case Study in Ideological Terrorism*, Conflict Studies no. 260 London: RISCT

Part V Urban terrorism

15 Urban terrorist organizations
16 Urban terrorist techniques
17 Developments in countering terrorism
18 Airport and airline security

Adams, J. (1986) *The Financing of Terror*, Sevenoaks: New English Library
Alexander, Y. and Kilmarx, R. A. (eds) (1979) *Political Terrorism and Business*, New York: Praeger
Bishop, P. and Mallie, E. (1987) *The Provisional IRA*, London: Corgi
Cannings, D. (1990) *Policing in Europe towards 1992*, London: Home Office
Clutterbuck, R. (1987) 'The future of political violence and terrorism', *Journal of the Royal Society of Arts* April: 376–86
Clutterbuck, R. (1987) *Kidnap, Hijack and Extortion*, London: Macmillan; New York: St Martin's Press
Clutterbuck, R. (1990) *Terrorism and Guerrilla Warfare*, London and New York: Routledge
Clutterbuck, R. (1990) *Terrorism, Drugs and Crime in Europe after 1992*, London and New York: Routledge
Control Risks, *Briefing Book*, monthly 1982–93
Davidson Smith, G. (1990) *Combating Terrorism*, London and New York: Routledge
Dobson, C. and Payne, R. (1982) *Terror: The West Fights Back*, London: Macmillan
Dobson, C. and Payne, R. (1986) *War Without End*, London: Harrap
Hertz, M. (ed.) (1982) *Diplomats and Terrorists: What Works, What Doesn't*, Washington, DC: Georgetown University
Hill, R. (1990) *Problems of International Cooperation to Improve Standards of Aviation Security with Reference to the Passenger*, St Andrew's University, unpublished PhD Thesis
Jamieson, A. (1993) *Collaboration: New Legal and Judicial Procedures for Countering Terrorism*, Conflict Studies no. 257, London: RISCT
Jenkins, B. (1982) *Terrorism and Beyond*, Santa Monica, Calif: Rand
Jenkins, B. (ed.) (1985) *Terrorism and Personal Protection*, Boston, Mass: Butterworth
Lodge, J. (ed.) (1981) *Terrorism: A Challenge to the State*, Oxford: Martin Robertson
Lodge, J. (ed.) (1987) *The Threat of Terrorism*, Brighton: Wheatsheaf
MacWillson, A. (1992) *Hostage-Taking Terrorism*, London: Macmillan

O'Brien, B. (1993) *The Long War: the IRA and Sinn Fein 1985 to Today*, Dublin: O'Brien Press

Selth, A. (1988) *Against Every Human Law*, Sydney: Pergamon Press

Steer, S. (1988) 'Maltese trial ends with 25 year sentence', in *International Law Enforcement Reporter*, Washington, DC, 412–14, Dec.

Stewart, G. (1992) *Migrants, Minorities and Security in Europe*, Conflict Studies no. 252, London: RISCT

US Congress OTA (1991) *Technology against Terrorism: The Federal Effort*, Washington, DC: US Government

US Congress OTA (1991) *Technology against Terrorism: Structuring Security*, Washington, DC: US Government

Wardlaw, G. (1982) *Political Terrorism*, Cambridge University Press

Part VI Conclusions

19　*Stopping people killing each other*
20　*Civil liberties and the rule of law*

Kitson, F. (1979) *Bunch of Five*, London: Faber

Lodge, J. (ed.)(1987) *The Threat of Terrorism*, Brighton: Wheatsheaf

Richardson, L. D. (1986) 'The urgency of detergency (or how money laundering is carried out)', *TVI Report* 6 (3): 12–22 and 6 (4): 43–50 (in two parts)

Turner, S. (1986) *Secrecy and Democracy: The CIA in Transition*, London: Sidgwick & Jackson

Wardlaw, G. (1982) *Political Terrorism*, Cambridge University Press

Wilkinson, P. (1986) *Terrorism and the Liberal State*, London: Macmillan

Index